How to Maximize Your Child's Learning Ability

*A Complete Guide to Choosing and Using
the Best Games, Toys, Activities,
Learning Aids and Tactics for Your Child*

Dr. Lauren Bradway
Barbara Albers Hill

Authors Choice Press
San Jose New York Lincoln Shanghai

How to Maximize Your Child's Learning Ability
A complete guide to choosing and using the best games, toys,
activities, learning aids and tactics for your child

Authors Choice Press
an imprint of iUniverse.com, Inc.

For information address:
iUniverse.com, Inc.
5220 S 16th, Ste. 200
Lincoln, NE 68512
www.iuniverse.com

Originally published by Avery

ISBN: 0-595-18248-8

Printed in the United States of America

Contents

Acknowledgments

I am grateful to my coauthor, Barbara Hill, for her enduring enthusiasm for our project, and to Joanne Abrams, our editor at Avery, who continually challenged us to clarify our thoughts and our words.

Thanks to friends who freely shared their expertise with me: Laurna Champ, Ph.D., parenting specialist; Larry Engelmann, audiologist; and Darleene Harris, psychometrist. And thanks to the following teachers I interviewed: LeAnn Butin, Mary Ann Seefeldt, Trudy White, and Jerri Wilson, who make it a practice to teach to all styles of learners—whether by making banana splits to teach the "b" sound or by taking a trip to a planetarium to experience a night sky. These fine teachers equate life experiences with learning.

My special thanks goes to Dr. Jerry White, director of the counseling center here at Oklahoma City University where I work, for his continuing support of my writing, and to my daughter, Isabel, for her willingness to share me with the computer that so often claimed my weekend time at home.

And finally, I am indebted to the hundreds of children who, over the years, have granted me access to their personal perspectives, frustrations, and insights about their particular learning styles.

Preface

This book is the result of twenty years of hand-picking materials and fine-tuning techniques that have helped the children who come to me for speech, language, and reading remediation become better learners and, as a result, more confident human beings. My training and clinical experiences were what led me to select the best toys, learning aids, tactics, and activities to use with my young clients. How to Maximize Your Child's Learning Ability will help you do the same for your child at home.

Within this book, I will explain the discovery that has helped me to help my clients: that pinpointing a child's personal style of learning and then tailoring the interactions, playthings, and activities that are part of his ordinary home life to fit that style will help him become a happier, better rounded, more academically successful individual.

You'll find this book the perfect tool for identifying your own learning style and that of your child, and for putting this newfound information to use during your regular play times to head off potential classroom struggles and to lessen or eliminate any that already exist. Your child will gain self-confidence and needed skills from your gentle guidance of his play and, if your child is of school age, of his homework. You—particularly if your time with him is limited by the demands of job, home, and other children—will gain the peace of mind that comes from knowing that your everyday interactions are exactly what he needs to reach his full potential. Here's how it all began . . .

During the 1970s, two gentlemen by the names of Richard Bandler and John Grinder developed something called Neuro Linguistic Programming (NLP) from studies about peoples' "preferred modalities"—that is, their favorite ways of absorbing information. At about the same time, I was also noting the existence and effects of distinct learning styles among the much-younger people who constituted my practice in communication disorders. Bandler and Grinder went on to organize NLP seminars, designed to make participants aware of communication patterns and to change unwanted habits or behaviors. I put *my* recognition of learning style's impact to work for my young clients.

You see, in my office at Oklahoma City University's counseling center, every day of the week, I encounter children who are wrestling with a learning problem or two. I talk with them, test them, confer with their parents, and then set up therapy programs when needed. The nature of my work dictates that I see many of these children over a span ranging from several months to—in the most severe cases—as long as ten years. So I've had the luxury of observing the development of different types of learners, and what I've witnessed from the earliest days of my career has supported my conviction that the way a child learns during his first years has a very predictable effect on his later ability to socialize, to perform athletically, and to function in the classroom. In fact, I've been able to anticipate the label of "Learning Disabled" in my clients and to predict their grades with incredible accuracy, simply by determining their inborn learning style.

It was also apparent from the start that the conclusions I'd reach about learning style after evaluating a particular child—did he prefer to use his eyes, his ears, or his sense of touch to absorb the information around him?—rarely came as a surprise to Mom and Dad. Most of these parental "suspicions," I found, had begun way back in the child's infancy, because the methods he used even then to explore his surroundings, combined with the kinds of toys he most enjoyed, made his preference for looking, listening, or moving pretty obvious. But it was just as obvious that no one was putting this valuable knowledge to work for the child! I was quickly convinced that if a child's learning style could be identified in infancy, before family experience had a chance to exert any influence, it must surely be inborn. And—much more important—awareness of this style could be a most useful piece of information to parents eager to plan the experiences and play the games from which their child would derive the most benefit—and the most fun!

To test my theory, I asked some parenting-class members at the Infant Center in Oklahoma City to complete a checklist of behaviors typical of infancy, marking those items that seemed to describe their babies. (A copy of this checklist appears on page 39.) I used educated guesswork to list the infant behaviors. It seemed likely that a baby "Looker" would explore with his eyes and hands, enjoy toys he could manipulate, and delight in the sight of familiar faces and objects. A "Listener," I reasoned, would babble early and often, prefer toys that made noise, and respond quickly to familiar voices and to music. To wear the label of "Mover," a baby would have to be physically active, achieve motor milestones somewhat ahead of schedule, and love to be held and rocked. Naturally, many babies would have characteristics from two or even three of the categories. Nevertheless, I felt that a strong preference would be evident.

When the parents had finished their task, I observed the babies myself and completed a second checklist on each one. When I compared my more-objective observations with those of the parents, I found our conclusions to be identical in almost every case. So, learning style *could* be determined in infancy. This simple fact revealed two exciting possibilities. First, armed with knowledge of their baby's learning style and with carefully chosen toys and activities, parents could use their child's everyday play times to develop his weaker skills while reinforcing his natural strengths. Second, parents' early recognition of their child's learning style would give them plenty of time to gear their play and interactions with him towards building the skills that he would need as a student.

And, sure enough, in the years since my discovery of the major role played by learning style in a young child's development, I've been able to minimize my clients' classroom problems and help them become happier children. Language delays, poor eye-hand coordination, lagging reading-readiness skills, distractibility, weaknesses in the visual and conceptual skills needed for art and arithmetic—all have been improved simply by employing the teaching methods, the playthings, and the learning materials best suited to a child's age and preferred learning style.

Why is it important for a child to achieve learning-style balance? Certainly, a child absorbs quite a bit of information on his own, by way of his preferred sense. But, because school work and socializing rely on so many different skills—phonics on Listener skills, for example, and number formation on Looker skills—a child left to learn through a single style usually has less success than a child who can put all of his senses to work.

Fortunately, it's simple to encourage new ways of perceiving and learning. By making it a practice to sing, chant, and hum to a seemingly unappreciative Mover infant, you'll gradually sharpen his ability to listen. And, while a baby Looker may initially be less than thrilled by long periods of holding and rocking, persisting with these actions will slowly increase his sensitivity to touch. In fact, once you begin to think in terms of your child's learning style, you'll automatically change the tone and style of your daily interactions with him—and this new approach is what will help you help him to maximize his learning ability.

Bill and Judy Lynner, for example, used some of the infant techniques discussed in Chapter Two to encourage their eight-month-old Mover to meet their gaze when they spoke or sang to him and to sit still long enough to enjoy a picture book. The Friedlanders employed several of the techniques for toddlers (see Chapter Three) to improve their Looker daughter's vocabulary from less than ten words to a level appropriate for two-and-a-half-year-olds—and within only six months! The DeVitos needed even less time, and a handful of activities geared for preschoolers (see Chapter Four), to help their Listener son overcome his confusion over letters and numbers and his anxiety about attending kindergarten.

But, what of the older child, the school-aged Looker, Listener, or Mover, who gets top grades in language arts and social studies but struggles endlessly with penmanship and such hands-on projects as map making and artwork? Or the after-school soccer star who is in constant demand when teams are chosen in gym class but holds a seemingly permanent spot in his grade's lowest reading group? Can anything be done to help a child whose particular style of learning is already affecting his happiness by slowing his progress in math or science, reading or language?

The answer is *yes!* Whether your child is two-and-a-half or twelve, in preschool or in junior high, the tools, toys, methods, and activities outlined in this book can be used to help him reach his potential. *How to Maximize Your Child's Learning Ability* will show you that though your child's learning style is an inborn and permanent feature, you can help him develop other ways of learning and, in doing so, round out his overall development.

Sprinkled throughout this book, you'll find a series of Learning Style QuickChecks, similar in design to the one I originally compiled for my Oklahoma City parenting class, but tailored to various age groups from babyhood through adulthood. These QuickChecks will help you to identify both your child's style of learning and your own.

In Chapter One, you'll discover how these learning preferences affect you, your child, and all of your daily dealings with your child. Additionally, Chapter One contains a list of child-development warning signals—indications that your child may need assistance from a developmental optometrist, pediatric neurologist, or other professional.

Beginning with Chapter Two, you'll be taken step by step through infancy, toddlerhood, the preschool years, kindergarten, and grades one, four, and eight—key points in a child's development. In each chapter, you'll see the world through the eyes of three same-aged but different-style learners. It's important to note that although your child may show preferences in two categories—for instance, he may be a Looker-Listener or a Listener-Mover—these case studies profile children who each have only one learning style. This has been done to better highlight the characteristics of each type of learner.

After presenting the case studies, every chapter discusses a topic that is of relevance to the age group being examined. For example, in Chapter Two, "Learning Styles in Infancy," we look at simple ways in which you can improve a baby's receptiveness whenever you tend to or play with him, while Chapter Three, "Learning Styles in Toddlerhood," explains how you can choose the type of day-care program that would best suit your child.

Each of the chapters dealing with younger children lists dozens of specific toys, games, and techniques that are appropriate for that age group. These activity suggestions have been grouped according to the skill that you wish to build—looking, listening, or moving. First, you'll learn how to enhance an existing skill through activities and toys that draw upon that skill. Then, you'll learn how to encourage the development of a lagging skill through activities and toys that are multisensory in nature—that involve both the sense to be developed and another sense. Those multisensory playthings and games that employ a child's preferred sense are, of course, the ones that will work best for him.

Beginning in first grade, children are expected to master certain prescribed subject matter, and the ability to cope with class work and homework assignments becomes a priority. Chapter Six through Chapter Eight take subject-by-subject looks at the relationship of learning style to a child's school performance. Tips are also provided for working with your child's teacher, choosing appropriate extracurricular activities, and selecting homework strategies that best suit the learning style of your child. In Chapters Seven and Eight—which discuss fourth graders and eighth graders, respectively—techniques are presented for improving your child's academic performance in specific subjects, such as science, social studies, and language arts.

Because each chapter focuses on one age or grade, you'll find it easy to locate the information you're looking for. For instance, if your little learner is five years old, by turning to Chapter Five, "Learning Styles in Kindergarten," you'll be able to read about other children—Lookers, Listeners, and Movers—who are the same age as your child. These case studies, coupled with a QuickCheck specifically designed for a five- to six-year-old, will allow you to easily determine your child's learning style. Chapter Five also contains a wealth of suggestions designed to enhance and develop the learning skills of the kindergartener, as well as a section on picking the best kindergarten class for each type of learner.

A special chapter, Chapter Nine, "Learning Problems and Possibilities," is designed to provide guidance for the parent whose child may require assistance beyond learning-style-based techniques. This chapter examines learning problems that can become learning disabilities, as well as learning disabilities of other origins. Information is provided about standard educational and diagnostic testing, and definitions of common diagnostic terms are included. Finally, treatments and therapies are examined, and suggestions are provided for parents who wish to offer their child maximum at-home support.

The concluding chapter of the book summarizes the role of learning style in everyday activities and examines how the three different styles eventually affect education and career choices. A recommended reading list is included for those parents who wish further information about learning patterns in children and adults, and a resource list guides the reader to distributors of those recommended toys, games, and educational materials that may not be available in stores.

As you browse through the lists of toys, techniques, and learning strategies, please bear several things in mind. First, be aware that my suggestions for the enhancement and development of your child's learning skills are just that—suggestions! I don't for a moment intend that they serve as ironclad rules around which parents should restructure their home lives, nor do I feel that it's important to try each and every one in a determined quest for academic perfection. What's important, however, is that you consider your child's and your own personalities when making toy and activity selections. Each of us is unique, after all, and an idea that you find quite appealing or that you feel would be just perfect for your little learner may be discarded just as quickly by the next parent!

Second, I urge you not to restrict yourselves to the recommended toys and educational materials if your search of store shelves turns up something even better. Nor should you limit your activity choices to a single list within a chapter if you spot an idea listed elsewhere that sounds like something your child would really enjoy. For example, you may feel that your young Looker would be enthralled by a particular toy from a list aimed at non-Lookers. Go ahead and try it; no doubt, you'll be right!

Finally, please remember that in presenting the learning-style modification techniques that follow, my goal is not that your child become class president, valedictorian, or world-class athlete, but simply that he move through his childhood and teen years as a happy, well-adjusted individual. Positive results may well occur immediately, but often take much longer. If your child is of school age, you can certainly look for improvement from one report card to the next. If he is younger, and so has little incentive to focus his energy on any sort of self-improvement, winning him over to a particular toy or activity may take several tries spanning several months. But, whether your child is fourteen months or fourteen years of age, you're sure to get the best results when your times together are unhurried, undertaken when you're both relaxed and rested, and kept short enough to end on a high note.

It's been hammered home by my clinical experiences that what a child is like in the crib foreshadows what he'll be like in the classroom, on the playing field, at club meetings, and at home. It stands to reason, then, that the earlier parents understand their child's style of learning, the better their chance to help him improve and broaden that style by gently shaping his home experiences. We know that early learning preferences hold firm over time. Though one learning style will continue to take the lead throughout your child's life, *How to Maximize Your Child's Learning Ability* will enable you to reinforce those skills and traits with which your child was blessed at birth while also encouraging those skills that do not come as naturally. And it's a tossup as to which of you will be more delighted with the results!

Lauren Bradway
Oklahoma City, OK

A Word About Gender

Your child is certainly as likely to be a boy as a girl; however, our language does not provide us with a genderless pronoun. To avoid using the awkward "he/she" or the impersonal "it" when referring to your child while still giving equal time to both sexes, the feminine pronouns "she," "her," and "hers" have been used in odd-numbered chapters, while the male "he," "him," and "his" appear in all the rest. This decision was made in the interest of simplicity and clarity.

Introduction

I first met Joey Billings late in his kindergarten year. This bright six-and-a-half-year-old had started school as an inquisitive, outgoing chatterbox, but an ensuing eight-month struggle with printing, drawing, and letter recognition had left his self-esteem badly battered. Joey had taken to calling himself "dumb-head" and "crazy," and lately had begun inventing reasons to stay home from school.

Because of his classroom difficulties, a special education setting had been recommended for Joey for first grade. His mother, distraught over the effect this confirmation of his feelings of inadequacy would have on her son, wanted to know what she could do at home to help him avoid the transfer and regain his self-confidence.

To determine Joey's learning style, his mother and I took a close look at his interests and preferred ways of learning. Next, we compiled a list of activities that would draw on Joey's well-developed vocabulary and excellent verbal skills—his inborn *Listener* skills—while improving his visual memory, printing, and eye-hand coordination—the lagging *Looker* skills that were causing him so much distress. Throughout these consultations, I called upon my background in educational diagnosis and remediation, my familiarity with the Listener style of learning, and my experiences with similarly troubled schoolchildren. For her part, Mrs. Billings needed only her knowledge of her son.

Three things were resolved at the start. First, Joey's home "therapy" must be fun. Simple mazes and snap-together blocks soon replaced the puzzles that Joey found so frustrating, and projects and outings were planned with the boy's interests in mind. For example, an ant farm and trips to the planetarium and video arcade were all used as fun ways to focus visual attention. Moreover, game-like strategies were employed to incorporate Joey's strong verbal skills with beginning reading and writing. For instance, the letter *T* was printed in green and called a "tree," and when writing, Joey pretended that each letter sat on the grass, some with parts that reached underground, others with parts that touched the sky.

Second, Joey's mother and I decided that all activities and techniques would be presented to Joey as *play*, rather than as a prescription for academic success. Thus, Joey would not feel pressured to "succeed" at what appeared to be a task.

Third, it was important that everything could be implemented in a minimum of time and as part of Joey's and Mrs. Billings' ordinary routines. Joey's mother, like so many parents with jobs and other children, simply couldn't squeeze any extra one-to-one time into her day.

Just four months later, and in plenty of time for first grade, Joey's readiness skills tested on grade level. Mrs. Billings continued tailoring her son's home experiences to his Listener learning style throughout the year, and, to her delight, Joey's June report card praised both his strong reading skills and his positive attitude toward school!

I've met many Joeys over the years. Of course, they didn't all share the strong language skills that are part of the Listener learning style. Some have been Lookers, with excellent visual skills but difficulty hearing the distinction between sounds, and trouble following directions. Others have been Movers, with great coordination but problems recalling and using what they'd seen and heard. But, no matter what the child's age or gender, and no matter what the lagging skill that led his parents to consult me, a communication disorders specialist, in the first place, an understanding of that child's learning style has enabled his parents to help him in the same way Mrs. Billings helped Joey.

You see, even so-called "remedial" activities can be approached at home through a child's strong suit, allowing him to have fun and do what interests him while actually bolstering a weak skill. Multisensory teaching devices, which are based on the same practice of simultaneously appealing to two or more senses, have long been a staple of extra-help programs. These materials have become equally popular in the classroom, where they take such forms as science kits, hands-on math apparatus, and books on tape. And, for a child too young to have displayed specific weaknesses, shaping his interactions and play according to the way he learns best will ensure a pleasingly balanced development. With his toys, his outings, and even his physical care approached with his learning style in mind, the child will be happy at home, happy at play—and happier still for having been able to circumvent potential learning problems! And his parents? What greater thrill could Mom or Dad have than watching their child bypass frustration and classroom problems on his way to becoming a well-rounded, sociable, confident individual? What greater benefit could there be than to watch their relationship with their child blossom as they gain a new understanding of his needs?

Joey was a client, so I was able to guide his mother's home-therapy efforts in person during our office sessions. But, since this book contains all that I shared with Mrs. Billings—the same background information, the same Learning Style QuickChecks, and the same explanations of the toys and tasks best suited for each of the three types of learners in each age group—*How to Maximize Your Child's Learning Ability* will perform exactly the same function for you.

Just what should you do once you've identified the learning style of your own child? Is it really possible to help your child become a balanced learner? Can you, for example, introduce wind instruments to encourage the love of music in your budding pianist, yet still provide opportunities for his social and physical growth? Can you further channel the energy of your preschool gymnast by enrolling her in dancing school, but also make time in her busy schedule for activities that will boost her language and art skills? In the long run, can you encourage the areas in which she naturally shines and still give support to her less-favored skills—even if you're apart for many hours of the day?

The upcoming chapters will demonstrate that the answer is a reassuring "Yes," because the tactics and toys that have worked for me don't have to be added to an already hectic day. Your understanding of your child's learning style will enable you to incorporate recommended techniques into existing family work and play times.

Read this book, and you'll discover why there's a link between certain skills, balanced learning, and a child's happiness. Fill out the QuickChecks, and you'll gain a new understanding of your child's learning style and of that style's effects on his everyday life. Use the activities and techniques recommended for your child's age and orientation, and you'll do wonders for his development and self-esteem and for your interactions with him. And, most important, have fun!

Chapter One

Learning Styles and Lifestyles

When you step out the door on a spring morning, what is it about your surroundings that seems to command your attention? Is it the violets blooming on the windowsill across the street and the fact that everyone suddenly seems to be wearing pastel colors? Do you first sense the sun's warmth and the way the stiff breeze feels as it ruffles your hair and clothing? Or do you find yourself glancing at the street sweeper hissing its way around the corner while you idly wonder whether your neighbor is ever going to replace that missing muffler?

It's more than coincidence that you find yourself drawn to the sights, the sensations, or the sounds around you above all else. Throughout our lives, we use all of our senses to learn, but tend to consistently favor one sense over the others. This natural preference dictates how we learn best—by looking, listening, or moving—as well as what we learn and how quickly we learn it. Quite often, this preference also helps shape our attitude toward the whole learning process.

This chapter contains information that will familiarize you with the Lookers, Listeners, and Movers in your life. A Learning Style Quick-Check for Parents (see page 16) will enable you to identify your own learning style, and you'll discover how this style colors your daily dealings with your child, and how your child's style can either complement or clash with yours. Then, you'll be given a look at some common child-development stumbling blocks, as well as the professionals who can help your child overcome these problems.

UNDERSTANDING THE THREE LEARNING STYLES

A substantial capacity for achievement is programmed into every one of us at birth. As adults, we'd certainly like to be able to say we've fulfilled our potential; but many of us, thinking back to past learning problems or a disinterest in school, have good reason to suspect otherwise! Consider the brilliant student who later finds himself limited to a series of low-profile jobs because of problems relating to clients and coworkers. Or the dynamic public speaker who gives up his dream of college teaching because of his poor writing skills. Or the gifted high school athlete who is wooed to a prestigious university on scholarship, only to buckle under academic pressures during his freshman year. Fortunately, it's possible for today's parents to rescue their children from a similar fate.

Throughout our lives, we learn by absorbing and using different bits of information from the world around us. Researchers and educators often make reference to "visual," "auditory," and "kinesthetic" or "tactile" learners, depending on whether the subjects in question most often rely on their eyes, their ears, or their sense of touch. However, I've found it simpler to use the terms "Lookers," "Listeners," and "Movers" to describe the way the children in my practice learn best.

While there's certainly no right or wrong way to learn, nor is there a way to hand-pick one's learning style, my years of working with youngsters have convinced me of the tie between well-developed Looker and Listener skills—those skills that allow us to follow directions, visualize, pronounce, remember, and reproduce material—and a child's classroom and social well-being. Without fail, stronger skills have meant happier, better-rounded children. So this matter surely warrants close attention from parents!

Is there a connection between gender and learning style? Might girls have an easier time than boys fitting into the school picture? It depends. You see, many girls favor the Listener style of learning, being sensitive to sounds and very attentive to such social cues as facial expression, speech pattern, and tone of voice. They also tend to have larger vocabularies and speak earlier than boys. It's been shown that many boys, on the other hand, have sharper visual skills, better coordination and muscle control, and a more accurate sense of space than their female counterparts. So boys are most often Lookers, who possess some of the skills that will benefit them as schoolchildren, or Movers, who won't find the going as easy.

There are certainly as many exceptions to this rule as there are female athletes and artists, or male lecturers and composers. It's also important to remember that learning patterns aren't always clearly defined and may be found in combination with other styles, as in Looker-Movers or Looker-Listeners. But, you're bound to recognize a number of people you know in the following descriptions, indicating that many people clearly exhibit one particular style.

What Are the Characteristics of a Looker?

Lookers are visual learners who rely on the sense of sight when absorbing information. They are naturally drawn to sights of familiar objects, and quickly pick up on and remember visual cues like motion, color, shape, and size. Most Lookers have excellent eye-hand coordination, with an inborn tendency to look at something and then quickly put their hands to work to show what they've learned about it. In fact, most Lookers excel at all fine motor activities—activities that involve both the eyes and the small muscles, such as those in the fingers.

Baby Lookers, for example, prefer gazing at the pictures and turning the pages of a book to actually listening to the story. Lookers in preschool and kindergarten are attracted to puzzles, blocks, cutting and pasting, and other activities that involve their eyes and hands. Drawing and printing come easily, as does the memorizing of words as "pictures"—hat, boy, dog, and so on—by the beginning reader. It comes as no surprise that Lookers go on to enjoy board games, art projects, crafts and models, calculators and computers, video games, and TV sports.

Lookers meet fine motor milestones—those aided by their superior eye-hand coordination—with ease. Because Lookers tend to ignore other types of stimulation in favor of the sights around them, however, they must work at developing their language ability, their social skills, and their full-body coordination.

What Are the Characteristics of a Listener?

Listeners are auditory learners, with a preference for sounds and words over information taken in by either sight or touch. Since stimulation to the ears translates into spoken language, Listeners tend to be early talkers and possess very elaborate vocabularies.

As babies, Listeners are easily soothed by music and familiar voices, and they delight in imitating sounds. Listener toddlers and preschoolers love to sing and recite songs and rhymes, ask a seemingly endless stream of questions, and have clear, precise speech. They show an early interest in reading, and, in the primary grades, love to read aloud and are able to follow directions with ease. As you can imagine, older Listeners enjoy listening to tapes and the radio, are quick to memorize, and favor games that involve speaking aloud, like "Mother, May I?" and *Password*. They like to read for pleasure, and often involve their friends in making up and acting out stories.

Because Listeners concentrate so much of their energy on language, it's not unusual for them to lag behind their age mates in areas commonly associated with the senses of sight and touch: namely, visual and motor skills.

What Are the Characteristics of a Mover?

Movers are tactile (or kinesthetic) learners, preferring hands-on learning through both touch and movement. The information that Movers take in through the sense of touch translates into gross motor movement—large-muscle activity involving the arms, hands, legs, and feet.

Movers are usually restless, wiggly infants who are soothed most easily by rocking and cuddling. They are early crawlers and walkers, and during the preschool years are drawn to climbing, jumping, block building, and riding wheeled toys. Their natural coordination and excellent sense of space result in their taking more physical risks than other children.

By kindergarten, most Movers' problems with sitting still and paying attention have come into play. Full-body activities in wide-open spaces are more their style! By first grade, fidgeting and distractibility have caused most Movers to begin to fall behind in academic areas, while their seeming fearlessness and commanding physical presence have made them leaders outside the school. At the same time, the frantic pace typical of most Movers makes them impatient and easily frustrated. Their needs are immediate, and their willingness to pursue difficult tasks almost nil. Movers are also an emotional lot—as quick to anger as they are to display glee.

Older Movers delight and excel in sports and outdoor activities, from soccer, swimming, and martial arts to camping, hiking, and animal care. But their continued focus on the physical, often to the exclusion of sight and sound stimulation, typically leads to language delays and classroom difficulties.

HOW YOUR LEARNING STYLE AFFECTS YOUR CHILD

What type of learner are *you*, the parent? The answer, you'll soon see, can have tremendous implications for both your child's school and social success and your own ability to encourage her along the way. To determine your personal learning style, take the Learning Style Quick-Check for Parents on page 16. You're likely to find your responses either divided somewhat equally between two of the learning styles or heavily weighted to just one style. In either case, you'll have a clear picture of the method or methods you prefer to use to absorb information from the world around you.

The learning-style label you've just assumed will prove to be a very useful tool as you continue through the chapters ahead, for when adapting the described methods and materials to your own child in your own home, you're bound to find that understanding yourself will help you understand *her*! In my work, you see, I've found that until parents recognize their own learning style, most assume that their children take in information from their surroundings just as they, the parents, do. (It's natural, I suppose, to view children as extensions of ourselves.) This assumption is fine when parent and child happen to share the same learning style, because Mom or Dad, calling on her or his own past experiences, can react to the child's efforts to socialize and learn with understanding and realistic expectations. But, to encourage the well-roundedness that will pay the child such big dividends later, *all* of her senses must be exercised. To do this, both parents and child sometimes have to venture into sensory territory that's unfamiliar to them.

And, what of the parent and child with *different* learning styles? Not surprisingly, they face more of a challenge, with the path of their interaction frequently made rocky by the simple fact that one's inborn gifts may quite naturally be the other's weakest areas. But, when this happens, a bit more patience and a dose of self-discipline are really all that's necessary for the two to work and play together successfully.

Picture the different experiences of a Mover mother—an avid cross-country skier—and her Listener husband—a free-lance writer—as they relate to their somewhat clumsy, very sociable four-year-old son, who's a Listener like his father. Mom loves to encourage the boy's physical side with riding toys and sandbox play, but finds herself depending on reminders from the child himself to read him his nightly story. Dad and son, on the other hand, prefer playing with board games or a magnetic alphabet to their equally necessary batting practices and playground trips. In their efforts to help their son become a balanced learner, you see, both parents must sometimes put aside their personal preferences. But, to their delight, Mom and Dad each get just as many opportunities to share with their son the activities they find most exciting.

From the very start, it's natural for parents to typically (though unconsciously) offer their children the types of stimulation they enjoy themselves. For instance, the insurance-broker mother, a Listener, fills her baby's room with rattles, music boxes, and even a radio. Meanwhile, Dad, a carpenter, acts on the well-developed sense of touch he shares with other Movers as he launders the baby's sheets twice for softness, diligently fills the humidifier every night, and moves the crib away from a drafty window. And this practice doesn't end with babyhood. Parents, in fact, unconsciously approach all child-care tasks from the vantage point of their personal learning style, with Mover Dad turning the child's nightly bath into an opportunity for a rubdown and powder massage, while Listener Mom seizes the moment to talk about soap bubbles or the strange workings of a bath sponge.

And the child's reaction? She either encourages or discourages more of the same stimulation by her instinctive reactions, which stem just as naturally from her own learning style as her parents' actions do from theirs. Your infant may turn toward the sound of your voice, widen her eyes at the sight of something special you're showing her, or ignore you in favor of her own body movements. Your preschooler may leap at the chance to play with you and really stick with the activity, or allow her attention to drift elsewhere. And your older child may respond to your words and overtures with eagerness, smiles, and questions, or give you the unmistakable feeling that you've been "tuned out"! Depending on your learning style and on hers, you see, the playthings and activities you've been offering your child may be either what she naturally craves or what she instinctively ignores. But even when your attempts at interacting seem unappreciated because they don't happen to reinforce your child's inborn learning style, persistence on your part will encourage her to "stretch" in areas vital to her overall development.

Your own learning style has significance beyond the kinds of stimulation you offer your child. An awareness of it can actually help you or your spouse understand your youngster's frustrations. It's quite common for my clients' parents to admit to having faltered in the same areas as their child. "Math was always my hardest subject, too," one father, a disc jockey, told me. "I just couldn't remember math facts. I'm embarrassed to say it, but I was still using my fingers to count when I was in high school."

A mother of a struggling reader confided, "I never could figure out how to 'sound out' words either, so I know what my daughter is going through. Unfortunately, I'm not much help to her, because I still don't know how!"

I meet parents of preverbal two-and-a-half-year-olds who were late talkers themselves, parents of overly aggressive kindergarteners who shudder at memories of their own childhood tantrums, parents of socially reluctant preschoolers who are themselves quite timid—and the list goes on and on. Exactly how intelligence and learning styles are inherited is not yet understood, but there is strong evidence that children often take after a parent or a parent's family in both of these areas.

Dr. Rita Dunn, Director of the Center for Study of Learning and Teaching Styles at St. John's University in New York, and Dr. Kenneth Dunn, of City University of New York's Queens College, have spent sixteen years researching learning patterns. In their work with clients, they've observed time and again that a familial connection exists between the learning style of grandparents, parents, and children. The Dunns frequently refer to Richard Restak's *The Brain: The Last Frontier*, published by Doubleday (New York, 1979). This book supports the idea of inherited learning style, concluding that the presence of pronounced styles in earliest infancy makes it possible to rule out environmental influence in favor of heredity as a cause of learning patterns.

In dozens of cases, sets of twins reared separately have "found" each other years later. Their astounding similarities in personality, career choice, and a host of such likes and dislikes as hair style and mode of dress make another strong case for the inheritance of sensory preference. During the course of my own practice, I've found that in over 80 percent of my cases, a child's learning style is either identical to that of one parent, or a blend of both the parents' styles. Another 10 percent of parents are quick to liken their child to a close relative. Particularly when learning disabilities are present—as can happen when learning-style preference exists in an extreme form—family patterns are so strong that genetic counseling is often recommended to prepare a learning-disabled parent for the likelihood of producing a child with a similar disability.

You can see evidence of this heredity factor every time you catch yourself thinking, "Gosh, she's exactly like her mother (or grandfather or aunt)!" following anything from a child's disastrous attempt at ice skating, to her delight in long afternoons curled up with a book, to her furious keyboard banging because those piano-playing fingers won't do her bidding. And, actually, these wry observations of similarity to a family member are a lot more than casual comments. They're proof of how obvious children's styles of learning can be!

So, in the long run, it's possible that you and your child will interlock like puzzle pieces because you share a learning style; but, it's just as likely that she'll favor the style of your spouse (or your brother or your mother), making her a very different type of learner from you. And, of course, learning styles are even more likely to differ in adoptive, step, and foster families, where the match isn't genetically programmed at all, but is dictated by chance.

Whether your child's sensory preferences are like yours or not, there's no question that they will affect every aspect of her life, from social behavior, to leisure activities, to tolerance for adversity. Even family relationships may be shaped by these preferences, as child and parent or child and sibling approach each other according to their own styles. You'll be sure of both your child's style and your own once you've completed the QuickChecks in this and other chapters. More important, you'll soon learn the steps you can take to help your child maximize her learning ability by further developing *all* her learning skills.

WHEN ADDITIONAL HELP IS NEEDED

Occasionally, social and learning difficulties may persist despite a parent's best efforts to rectify them, because these particular problems stem not from a child's learning style, but from factors such as hearing loss, hyperactivity, or poor vision. If you suspect that there's a reason other than learning style for your child's difficulty with reading or math, her problems relating to others, or her struggles with speech or coordination, or if you sense that her problems—regardless of cause—are too severe for you to remedy, it may pay to err on the side of caution by seeking advice from medical and educational professionals trained to work with these types of developmental delays. For details on what to look for and when to take this important step, please see the inset on page 13. For further information on learning problems, see Chapter Nine, "Learning Problems and Possibilities."

WHY MODIFY A CHILD'S LEARNING STYLE?

What of children whose development is somewhat uneven, but well within "normal" limits? Couldn't we just leave them alone? There's certainly nothing *wrong* with a Looker child who, left to her own devices,

Red Flags in a Child's Development

There are certain conditions and behaviors that, when they appear during the course of infancy and childhood, may signal a problem that requires professional assistance. This inset outlines what you should look for and where you should turn for help. A child may show several of the red flags listed in a particular category—language, for instance—or she may show only one. In either case, it's a good idea to consult the appropriate expert listed below. The inset on page 252 explains the focus and qualifications of both those professionals mentioned here and those to whom you may be referred.

Language

In the area of language, a child should be seen by a family physician, pediatrician, or audiologist if she shows the following behavior:

- *In the first year of life, she does not turn to the source of sound.*

- *At age one, she does not respond when her name is called.*

A child should be seen by a speech-language pathologist if she shows the following behavior:

- *At age two, she has not yet said her first word.*

- *At age three, she has not combined words into short sentences.*

- *From the time she begins to talk, she has consistently unintelligible speech.*

- *At age three, she frequently repeats words and phrases, and she seems to struggle—blinking and stammering, for example—to get the words out.*

- *In the first grade (or later), she regularly mispronounces certain sounds.*

- *In the first grade (or later), she has trouble with phonics and cannot blend letter sounds or sound out printed words.*

Gross Motor Skills

In the gross motor area, a child should be seen by a pediatrician or family physician if she shows the following behavior:

- *In infancy, she appears "floppy," and has unusually weak muscle tone.*

- *At age one, she cannot sit without support or cannot crawl with alternating arms and legs.*

- *She never seemed to stabilize from the time she learned to walk, and still falls often and appears excessively awkward or clumsy.*

- *She has great difficulty learning to ride a bike, skate, hit a ball, or perform other activities typical of her age group.*

- *She is overly active and seems unable to control movement and attentiveness.*

Fine Motor Skills

In the fine motor area, a child should be seen by a pediatrician or family physician if she shows the following behavior:

- *During the first year of life, she cannot follow moving objects with her eyes.*

- *During the first year, she fails to make eye contact with family members.*

- *In the preschool years, she is slow to develop such self-help skills as feeding, dressing, or hand washing.*

A child should be seen by a developmental optometrist or ophthalmologist if she has the following difficulty:

- *During the school years, she has difficulty copying from the blackboard, loses her place while reading, or tires quickly from reading.*

grows up to be a rather reticent computer whiz. Nor is it the end of the world when a high school Listener, her weaker skills similarly unchallenged, opts out of science and math courses as soon as she can because those grades are playing havoc with her cumulative average. And it's a rare classroom that doesn't contain a few Movers, marking time as they wait for the dismissal bell that signals freedom from classroom frustrations.

But life can hold so much more for these children that it doesn't seem fair to relegate them to a humdrum existence when parents can, with so little effort, round out those young lives with a special activity here and a new approach there—all for the purpose of opening every possible door!

Some information, a bit of organization, and access to tried-and-true toys and techniques are all you need to first understand how your child learns and then maximize her ability to do so. To find out exactly how to extend your child's options for the future by adding a healthy—and mutually enjoyable—balance to her learning skills, read on!

Learning Style QuickCheck for Parents

Directions: Check all statements that best describe you. Then, total the checks in each column and compare column totals. You will probably find that most of your answers have fallen into one, or perhaps two, of the three categories, indicating which of the learning styles you favor.

Looker	Listener	Mover

1. Communication: When talking with others . . .

☐ I watch the speaker carefully.	☐ I consider myself a good listener.	☐ I often touch the person I'm speaking to.
☐ I prefer to observe rather than talk, and I tend to be quiet.	☐ I love to talk and am very verbal.	☐ I tend to express myself nonverbally, using gestures.
☐ I speak in simple, clear language.	☐ I excel in verbal expression, and I have a large vocabulary.	☐ I have difficulty finding the right words to say.

2. Pastimes and hobbies: In my leisure time . . .

☐ I enjoy games like *Scrabble*, *Monopoly*, and *Pictionary*.	☐ I like talking-and-listening games like *Password*.	☐ I prefer to be active, and enjoy participating in sports.
☐ I enjoy movies and television.	☐ I listen to records and tapes, and read novels or poetry.	☐ I like observing the action of ice hockey, races, rodeos, and soccer.
☐ I express myself with my hands through painting, crafts, or pottery.	☐ I express myself verbally, talking or writing to friends.	☐ I prefer the full-body expression of dancing, gymnastics, and swimming.

3. Motor skills: How I feel about my physical self . . .

☐ My fine motor skills are better than my gross motor skills;. I'm good with my hands.	☐ I'm not well coordinated.	☐ I'm very coordinated.
☐ I prefer spectator sports.	☐ I avoid sports and outdoor activities.	☐ I enjoy outdoor activities such as camping, climbing, and fishing.

4. Feelings: Emotionally . . .

☐ I am somewhat inhibited, and do not reveal my feelings.

☐ I readily verbalize emotions and talk about my feelings.

☐ I tend to be impatient and easily frustrated. I am aware of my feelings, but don't necessarily label them.

☐ I am embarrassed by others' emotional outbursts.

☐ I am sympathetic to others' feelings and problems and am a good listener.

☐ I cry and laugh easily, and often swing back and forth between emotional highs and lows.

5. Memory: When remembering . . .

☐ I write down what has to be recalled and find cue cards helpful.

☐ I say aloud what I have to remember.

☐ I remember actions better than spoken or written words.

☐ I form mental pictures.

☐ I talk to myself and almost hear a voice within my mind.

☐ I do not automatically form visual images, and have difficulty recalling facts.

☐ I use a highlighter when going over written material.

☐ I sometimes tape-record material.

☐ I "act out" to help myself remember, and sometimes have difficulty understanding the meaning of what's been read or said.

6. At work: On the job . . .

☐ I need lots of space, and don't like to sit or stand too near others. I work best alone.

☐ I thrive on others' company, don't like to work alone, and like to bounce ideas off others.

☐ I like to be near others but not necessarily to talk. I enjoy working with others

☐ I use a flow chart to help track my work on projects.

☐ I talk to myself when working.

☐ I have difficulty meeting deadlines.

☐ I insist on keeping to the agenda at meetings.

☐ I enjoy business meetings, and like to talk to and hear the views of others

☐ I avoid meetings when possible, and find it difficult to sit and concentrate.

Totals: _____ Looker   _____ Listener   _____ Mover

Chapter Two

Learning Styles in Infancy

In the first weeks of life, babies demonstrate their Listener, Looker, and Mover tendencies through the ways they respond to the people and objects in their very new surroundings. So, parents need not wait to offer the kinds of feedback their infant craves and to begin stimulating his less-preferred senses as well.

This chapter provides descriptions of three infants, each a different type of learner, and compares their development throughout the first year of life. A Learning Style QuickCheck for Infants is included to help you pinpoint *your* baby's learning style (see page 39), and you'll find plenty of ideas to help you start your child on the road toward the learning-style "balance" that will pay him such big dividends later.

A baby's first year is characterized by developmental strides unmatched in magnitude by any other period in childhood. Enjoy each and every one!

A LOOK AT THREE LEARNERS

Michael, Emily, and Aaron shared a hospital nursery and, in their sixth week of life, are physically within a half-pound and a half-inch of one another. But, as you will see, the similarities end there! Already, three distinct personalities have emerged, along with different tolerance levels, different coping mechanisms, and even unique sets of likes and dislikes. All of these traits stem from the babies' inborn learning styles—the way they process the sensory information that bombards them during every waking moment. For the purpose of clarity, our case-study babies possess "pure" learning styles; that is, each exhibits the characteristics of only a visual, an auditory, or a kinesthetic learner.

In reality, probably more than half of all children display the traits of two learning styles. Let's take a look at our three learners.

Six Weeks of Age

Meet Michael. Each morning, six-week-old Michael wakes at daybreak, blinking his brown eyes against the glare of sunlight. As he becomes used to the brightness, he lies quietly, his eyes flitting around the nursery. They first fixate on the stuffed tiger that shares his bassinet, then jump to the dancing bears hanging overhead, then dart toward the patterned quilt and the puffs of blue ribbon with which his mother has adorned the bassinet cover. Soon, they focus on the tiger again.

Michael continues to devour the sights around him until he spies movement in the doorway. He looks intently at the approaching figure, then fixes his gaze on a particularly pleasing sight: his mother's familiar face.

For as long as his eyes are open each day, baby Michael is busy using them to learn about his world. His visual search is constant, for he craves colors, patterns, and movement in much the same way that he craves feeding or holding. This urge to use his eyes comes from within—sometimes subtly, sometimes powerfully. And, from the same inner source comes a built-in safeguard against overstimulation, for when Michael's had enough, he simply shuts his eyes or turns his head. Michael, you see, is a Looker.

Meet Emily. Emily, also six weeks of age, sleeps on, undisturbed by the sunrise, but snaps to attention if the phone rings, the dishwasher starts, or the hallway clock chimes the hour. Just as Michael is enthralled by sights, Emily is drawn to sounds. She tenses in eager recognition of her parents' voices, turns her head toward the faintest noises, shows distress at sudden quiet, and drifts off to sleep to the soft tones of her music box. When her parents announce that it's feeding time, she becomes still and quiet, as though waiting to be lifted. When they sing and talk to her, she coos in response.

Emily's parents have taken to playing a radio in the nursery, since even the drone of a newscaster's voice seems to entertain their baby. By the same token, they've learned to keep her away from noisy gatherings and busy public places because, unable to block out sensory information the way that Michael can, Emily is easily overstimulated. But, the solution to even this problem lies in her penchant for sounds: no matter how tense she becomes, the hum of the vacuum cleaner or fan puts Emily to sleep within seconds.

And, she'll stay that way, sometimes even sleeping through a feeding, as long as the "white noise" continues. She is, of course, a Listener.

Meet Aaron. Aaron was born at the same time as Michael and Emily, but has been rolling from front to back regularly since his eleventh day of life. Wriggly when awake, restless when asleep, Aaron can work free of the tightest of swaddlings, and then, surprised by the sudden freedom of his limbs and coolness on his skin, will sound a protest. His own movements often startle him—he'll jump at the sight of his own fist passing by or at the falling sensation he gets when he flips over. Yet, even at his most relaxed, he's never still, with his fingers stretching, ankles flexing, and neck arching.

Aaron is highly attuned to motion of all types. In fact, he goes absolutely rigid, yelping in anguish, if he's not clutched tightly when carried down a flight of stairs or lowered to his changing table. Though no lullaby or mobile can reach him when he's upset, he relaxes instantly when picked up and held, falling into an almost trance-like state when his skin is stroked. His father's most effective colic remedy is to lie down, hugging Aaron to his chest, while taking long, exaggerated breaths that allow the baby to feel restraint, yet "float along" with each inhalation and exhalation.

Even at this age, Aaron is fun to play with. He can already hold small toys, and he kicks strongly enough to send a beach ball rolling or a rattle jiggling. Like Emily, he has no defense against overstimulation—in fact, he creates it himself—so his parents have learned to keep him calm by rocking and walking him about between feedings and naps. Without a doubt, Aaron is a Mover.

How does *your* baby absorb information? Does he take in the most through his sense of sight, like Michael? Does he tend to rely on his ears for comfort, information, and entertainment, as Emily does? Or, like Aaron, does he favor the sense of touch when exploring his world? To find out, complete the Learning Style QuickCheck for Infants found on page 39, placing a mark next to those behaviors that best describe your baby. When finished, total each column to determine whether your child most clearly prefers looking, listening, or moving.

HOW LOOKER, LISTENER, AND MOVER INFANTS DEVELOP

As you've seen, the differences between Michael, Emily, and Aaron at six weeks of age are already striking. Each baby has his or her own set of responses to people, places, and things—responses deeply rooted in the infant's inborn learning preference. And, as the following descriptions show, these differences become more marked as babies grow and change throughout their first year of life.

Three to Seven Months of Age

Michael. Looker Michael is unusually alert, constantly scanning his surroundings, wide-eyed, for something of interest on which to fix his gaze. Even when nursing, his eyes remain open, first studying his mother's face, then moving beyond. His father usually slips a toy or two into his bassinet at night, and the sight enthralls him for many minutes upon awakening; but Michael's eyes are soon on the move again, searching the nursery for more stimulation. If Michael happens to be on his stomach, he lifts his head and cranes his neck as if to assure himself that his favorite sights are still there. If he's on his back, he gazes in awe at his own fingers or swipes at his crib gym.

At five months, Michael can grab and hold those dangling toys; and, soon after, he becomes adept at handling intricate multicolored items, passing these objects from one hand to the other, and even searching for them briefly when they disappear from view. He's fascinated by the toys bobbing in his bath water and by the goings on outside the picture window. At seven months, Michael begins to babble, but more often sits quietly in his playpen, either looking at himself in his mirror or manipulating the dials and knobs on his *Busy Box.*

Michael's parents describe him as a quiet, contented, but somewhat fearful baby. Because sights, his favorite entertainment, are always available, because he's in no great rush to verbalize or move about, and because he's so highly attuned to his surroundings that unfamiliar faces and places make him uneasy, his parents' description is right on the mark.

Emily. By comparison with Michael, Listener Emily is uninterested in the sights around her. But, even at three months, Emily spends a lot of time in sound play. She babbles, coos, clicks her tongue, buzzes her lips, and uses her voice to attract attention. Her favorite game takes place when her mother or father imitates the sounds she makes; in fact, she's receptive to anyone who tries this.

Sounds are still a source of comfort to Emily. She's content to sit, toyless, for long periods, as long as there's music or conversation around her. When things grow silent, she begins a verbal racket of her own as if to fill the void. She grows quiet at the sound of a familiar voice, seems to anticipate from her mother's intonation such events as bedtime or a ride in the car, and loves to be sung to.

At seven months, Emily takes as much interest in toys as Michael, though she plays with them in a different manner. While Michael likes to put his eyes and fingers to work, Emily is rewarded by the sound a toy makes when she's used it correctly. Unable to squeeze a rubber toy yet, she'll bang it on the floor to hear it squeak. She has just begun to roll over, and cannot yet sit without help.

Emily's disinterest in getting around and delight in noisy toys, babbling, and social games cause her parents to describe her as a friendly, expressive, somewhat uncoordinated baby.

Aaron. At three months, Mover Aaron already shows his moods. He arches his back to show tension, bangs both feet to indicate playfulness, and jerks his head from side to side to pull away or to show frustration. He can still be soothed by cuddling, and is calmest when being walked or swung.

Aaron loves to play with his hands and feet and to explore things with his mouth. He hasn't yet begun to babble, but his rocking indicates that he'll be quick to get around in earnest. And, sure enough, he sits by four and a half months, slides along on his stomach a month later, and crawls during month six, showing no qualms about venturing from his parent's side in his quests. He is unimpressed by even the most fascinating toys, using them only as a brief stopover during his travels. Unlike Emily, he usually ignores background noises.

At seven months, and despite his parents' efforts to engage him in other play, Aaron seems to view his mother and father as "vehicles"— with knees to bounce on, fingers to tickle, and arms to rock—rather than playmates. This, combined with his overall silence and the ferocity with which he practices new skills, causes his parents to describe him as a quiet and single-minded child who is perpetually in motion.

Eight to Twelve Months of Age

Michael. Michael, the Looker, quickly perfects his thumb-and-forefinger grasp, and loves to point with, poke with, and wag his index finger. He frequently amuses himself by filling and dumping containers of small objects, and will hold up his hands for pat-a-cake over and over again. Although he's wary of strangers, he delights in face-making and peek-aboo games involving his parents.

Michael still studies the details of toys and household objects, and though he's never happy for long hearing a story in someone's lap, he'll sit for many minutes examining books and magazines by himself.

Michael remains a quiet baby. He'll clap his hands and wave "bye-bye," but responds to attempts to get him to babble with an engaging stare, rather than words or sounds. Michael can be enticed to crawl around and even to pull himself to a standing position by the sight of an interesting-looking item, but needs adult assistance to take his first steps.

As he approaches his first birthday, Michael is fascinated by detail, both in real life and in picture books; but, so far, his speech is still gibberish. He rarely climbs or makes his way across a room, unless a particularly thrilling sight awaits him; but he loves to experiment, under his parents' watchful eyes, with coin banks, crayons, and stickers. Socializing and full-body play still hold little appeal; but, with toddlerhood just around the corner, Michael exhibits more than ever a Looker's superior eye-hand coordination and penchant for observing.

Emily. Noise-making toys are Listener Emily's favorite playthings during the second half of the year. She particularly enjoys banging on her toy piano, babbling on a plastic phone, and pushing a click-clacking truck back and forth. Games involving noise delight her, as she can already duplicate barnyard calls and street sounds. And, when the game ends, Emily finds a way to keep the noise coming no matter what room she's in, by banging pot covers, throwing toys to the floor, or screeching just for the sheer pleasure of doing so. She also loves her nap- and bedtime stories—though, unlike Michael, she shows little interest in the accompanying picture book.

Emily is somewhat better at filtering out background noise than she used to be, and, while still wary, is not as overwhelmed when out in public. She is very entertained by music and the sounds of children's voices; in fact, she'll stop whatever she's doing to make her way toward the television each time certain familiar commercials are broadcast. Unfortunately, her sleep is still as easily disturbed as her play, so her parents now face a box fan toward the nursery wall and run it year-round in the hopes of drowning out noise.

At eleven months, Emily has already spoken several words and can follow verbal instructions with ease. Although she can certainly crawl, she still shows little need to get around; in fact, her parents can get her to stand only by placing her favorite toys atop the coffee table. Walking, it seems, will have to wait.

As she celebrates her first birthday, Emily still shows no preference for her left or right hand. She now walks alone and climbs stairs with assistance, but still reverts to a hands-and-knees scoot when she wants to get somewhere quickly. Although her limbs may be quiet, her mouth and ears are almost never at rest. Emily fits the profile of a Listener more and more each day.

Aaron. By contrast, Mover Aaron can't seem to sit still! He stands, sidles along the furniture, and walks alone within the two-week period preceding his nine-month "birthday," relying on instincts and a certain fearlessness that Michael and Emily don't seem to possess. Of course, Aaron loves roughhousing and active play, spending at least two hours a day moving between his ride-in coupe and his handlebar-equipped trampoline. He is most cooperative when he's on the move; in fact, his parents have taken to dressing and diapering him wherever he may be at the moment and allowing him to wander about while eating. They've learned the hard way that changing tables and highchairs are not Aaron's strong suit!

Books and small toys are lost on this little Mover, though he does occasionally use them for target practice. And, he doesn't take kindly to car rides, morning naps, shopping trips, or any other activities that force temporary confinement. When rocked in his parents' arms, though, worn-out Aaron sleeps like a stone.

As he approaches the twelve-month mark, Aaron is still the fussiest of the three babies, adept at full-body activity but frustrated to tears by sit-down play. He is physically demonstrative, wanting everything from hugs to back rubs to another child's toy, but he cannot yet express himself verbally. Aaron points, gestures, and grabs frantically for his needs, and is quick to anger when he's misunderstood.

Like other Mover babies, Aaron is also frustrated by his inability to duplicate others' actions in his play. He'd love to use a shovel in his beloved sandbox, twist the dials to work his toy computer, or fit the plastic people into his pull-along school bus, but he still lacks the necessary eye-hand coordination. Yet, even as he exits babyhood, Aaron can be calmed, as always, by a brisk ride in his stroller or on the back of Dad's bike.

HOW TO INTERACT WITH AN INFANT

The descriptions of Michael, Emily, and Aaron clearly show just how different three babies can be. In the very first week of life, their respective learning styles marked each child as a unique individual, and these distinct personality differences held firm throughout infancy.

But, no matter what learning style your infant may exhibit, early-childhood experts agree that you, the parent, are that infant's most important plaything—even during late infancy, when toys begin to claim his attention. The time you spend with your baby each day, be it one hour or twelve, will provide him with a feeling of importance, a healthy sense of routine, and, with a bit of effort, specially chosen sensory stimulation, all of which are vital to his development.

There are certain factors to consider when you're tending to or playing with a small baby—factors that, regardless of learning style, can improve your child's receptiveness and guarantee him your full attention. To help your infant derive the most benefit from your time together, you may wish to keep the following guidelines in mind.

- *Make Your Baby Comfortable.* A baby is happiest when he's recently been fed, rested, and changed, and is comfortably situated away from glaring sunlight and chilling breezes.

- *Make Eye Contact With Your Baby.* It will be easier to keep your child focused on you if you bring him to your level by placing his infant seat on the table beside you, or drop to his level by arranging your activity on the floor. Gazing into your baby's eyes as much as possible and making exaggerated faces while you speak will keep your own attention from wandering and encourage your baby to stare back.

- *Use an Appropriate Voice and Vocabulary.* Since research has shown that infants respond better to higher-pitched tones than to low tones, moving your voice up an octave will hold your baby's attention longer. He'll also be better able to follow your words when you speak slowly and in simple sentences.

- *Eliminate Competition.* Even older babies are distracted by nearby goings on. Before you begin your play, it's a good idea to shut the dog in the bedroom, occupy older children elsewhere, take the phone off the hook, and move away from the window or TV.

- *Keep Your Baby Close to You.* Staying within arm's length of your baby will enable you to offer plenty of soft strokes, encouraging words, and loving smiles, even when you're elbow-deep in a household task.

- *Entertain Your Baby.* Offer your baby plenty of the kinds of stimulation he seems to like best. If you're able to play with him at that moment, this will start things off on a high note. If you're busy with something else, this will help him stay happier for a longer period.

- *Introduce Variety in Your Baby's Play.* Whether your baby is interacting with you or amusing himself, persistence in offering new types of stimulation—music and noisy toys, say, if he tends to favor sights— will help him develop and enjoy different ways of perceiving the world around him.

- *Know When to Quit.* Despite their curiosity, infants are quite susceptible to "stimulus overload." Too much intense play, prolonged concentration, or overly varied stimulation may render your baby cranky and sleepless. You can avoid this by removing his toy or ending your play together before it begins to lose its appeal.

TECHNIQUES FOR AFFIRMING AND DEVELOPING LEARNING SKILLS

As you have seen, parental interaction plays a large part in coloring a baby's sensory experiences. By being aware of his learning style, by examining your own actions toward him, and by offering him playthings selected with his sensory preferences in mind, you can "spoon feed" your baby the kinds of stimulation he adores and bolster what you see as his weaker areas, as well. Whether you're bathing, changing, feeding, playing with, relaxing with, or just working alongside your infant, the way you approach him and the toys you choose can work wonders.

Each of the following sections focuses on building the skills inherent in one of the three learning styles: looking, listening, or moving. First, each section looks at the long-term benefits derived from strengthening those skills. For instance, a child with strong Looker skills often excels at spelling and writing, while a good Listener will have an easy time expanding his vocabulary. Next, a list of suggestions is presented for further developing the skills of a baby who has inborn strengths in that area. For example, you will learn how to enhance Mover skills in Mover babies. Finally, techniques are presented for promoting sensory awareness in those babies whose skills in a given area may need a boost.

Each of these lists is based on years of clinical experience and on toys and activities that my young clients have repeatedly selected as their favorites. My other criteria for an item's inclusion are that the plaything be moderately priced and readily available; that the toy or technique be age-appropriate; and that the suggested activity be either very familiar to parents or—as is the case with "palming" (see page 55)—easily learned from suggested sources. In a few cases, I've indicated that an item can be obtained only through catalogues. In each such case, you'll be able to find the address of the mail-order company in the Resources list on page 265.

You may find that many of the toys listed for the enhancement of an inborn learning skill are marked by the manufacturer as being appropriate for the next higher age group. In my practice, and with safety considerations always a factor, I have found that clients' learning strengths frequently enable them to enjoy these playthings a bit ahead of schedule.

Whenever possible, the suggested activities are multisensory in nature; that is, they activate more than one channel of learning by combining the type of stimulation to which your child needs exposure with his favored form of stimulation. For example, one of my favorite items for strengthening a Looker infant's Listener skills is the lift-and-look book, which allows him to involve his eyes and hands while he gets valuable listening practice. In fact, many toys and activities are useful for strengthening more than one skill. Shelcore's *Musical Pop-Up Piano,* for instance, appeals to Lookers, Listeners, and Movers, and can be used to affirm skills in one learner or to develop them in another. Just remember that when choosing a multisensory activity to strengthen one of your little learner's weak skills, the activity must involve your child's *strong* skill, as well.

Keep in mind that it's perfectly acceptable to borrow ideas from lists meant for other learners, provided you recognize that the activity may be a bit too advanced to be immediately successful, or may simply not appeal to your baby. By all means, though, be creative and flexible—and patient! You may find that the plaything your baby rejects today is simply perfect two months from now, just as you may stumble upon an idea from another learner's list that your baby will absolutely adore. The key, after all, is to have fun with your baby while he gains important skills from your play times.

Building Looker Skills

Well-developed Looker skills lead to strong powers of observation, the ability to remember what is seen, and good eye-hand coordination, all of which are an immense help when a child begins to read and write. No matter what your baby's learning style, he stands to gain either reinforcement or encouragement of his Looker skills from the activities you choose to provide.

Looker infants, of course, possess the above-mentioned abilities from birth, and so will particularly enjoy their parents' attempts to focus on their favored sense. Listener infants are social creatures, and so will probably be most receptive to those Looker activities that are liberally sprinkled with conversation. Similarly, Mover infants will be most interested in sights that are somehow connected to *their* love—physical activity. Here are some ideas.

ENHANCING AN INFANT'S EXISTING LOOKER SKILLS

When holding your baby for a bottle feeding, be sure to switch him from side to side, just as breastfed babies are moved from breast to breast. This will stimulate each of his eyes in turn.

Suspend colorful mobiles over your baby's crib. The use of commercial mobiles made of interchangeable parts or homemade mobiles made of painted clothespins or paper-plate faces will enable you to change the toy from time to time. Of course, any mobile should be kept out of baby's reach and must be removed altogether once he can stand.

Indulge your baby's need for frequent eye contact. Meet his glance, gaze at him, and let him be the one who looks away.

Keep the lights on in the nursery during the early weeks so that your baby can look around whenever he's awake. Once his surroundings begin to distract him and keep him from falling asleep, try a night light instead.

Make a finger puppet by drawing a face on your index finger. Make a game of baby's following the wiggling finger with his eyes.

Place your baby in the center of things, where he can observe family members as they go about their daily activities.

Lullaby Light Show by TOMY projects a revolving display of colorful figures on the nursery wall or ceiling.

Time spent crawling is important to the development of visual skills. Take care not to rush past this stage in favor of baby's standing.

Using photos, make a picture book of the important people in your baby's life—parents, siblings, grandparents, and baby-sitter—and look at the finished book together.

Spend time in front of the mirror with your baby. Make faces, point to the various reflections, "play" with baby's image, and laugh together.

Offer your baby large, washable cloth blocks to study, manipulate, and stack.

Attach a *Busy Box* by Gabriel or an *Activity Center* by Fisher-Price to your baby's crib.

Provide large, colorful rings that stack from largest to smallest.

Offer a chain of colorful *Kiddie Links* by PlaySkool for your baby to pull apart and, later, reattach.

Sit and Play Stroller Toy by Sesame Street attaches to your baby's stroller and offers five activities to involve baby's hands and fingers.

ENCOURAGING THE DEVELOPMENT OF LOOKER SKILLS IN LISTENER AND MOVER INFANTS

Make continuous eye contact with your baby while you feed, diaper, bathe, hold, and talk to him.

Crib Mirror by Sesame Street attaches to the side of baby's crib and offers constant visual stimulation.

Use the *Disney Dreamtime Carousel* by Mattel to project rotating pictures on the ceiling to the tune of "When You Wish Upon a Star."

Play peekaboo with your baby, hiding your face, his face, or a toy beneath your hands or a light blanket and then making it reappear.

Disney Roll 'N See by Mattel inflates to a cylindrical shape, and has windows that encourage baby to peer at the pictures and brightly colored balls inside while he rolls the toy.

Remind baby to *see*. Point out and name household objects, using the word "see" each time. Show exaggerated surprise or excitement, or act out the same with a stuffed animal, when coming upon a special sight.

Play "Where are your eyes?", "Where are the teddy bear's eyes?", "Where are Daddy's eyes?", etc. Cover or close the eyes each time to convince baby of the importance of seeing.

Baby Mickey Glowing Starlight by Mattel is a glow-in-the-dark toy that offers visual stimulation no matter what the time of day or night.

Portrait Teething Ring (through catalogue only) from The Right Start is a colorful, chewable, moisture-proof ring of photo frames. Use it to frame a picture of one of your baby's favorite people, or even his cat or dog.

You can take even a very young baby on sightseeing outings, keeping him in a backpack or your arms for maximum interaction. The sunlight and new sights will offer a variety of visual treats.

Make a game of your pointing to an object and baby's crawling to touch—and, later, retrieve—that object.

Disney Hug Tight Rattle by Mattel has a suction-cup base and contains colorful beads in Mickey Mouse's see-through midsection. This can be attached to the highchair tray for visual stimulation during feedings.

When your baby attempts an eye-hand activity, like stacking or fitting pieces of a toy, provide a commentary on his actions to help keep him interested.

Play with a jack-in-the-box, and encourage your baby to watch for the character's reappearance.

While driving, point out familiar or interesting sights to your baby. Later, ask him to locate them on his own. Don't hesitate to stop the car for a closer look at anything unusual.

Building Listener Skills

Listener skills go hand-in-hand with a child's growing sociability, speech and vocabulary, ability to follow directions, and interest in reading. It stands to reason that a baby whose Listener skills are encouraged will go on to have an easier time making friends and tackling school work than will a child whose Listener skills are weak. All three types of learners, then, will benefit from their parents' attention to this area of development.

The baby whose Listener skills are inborn will enjoy and profit from any opportunity for communication or self-expression. Lookers and Movers, who delight in moving their hands and their whole bodies, will most readily accept those Listener activities that combine action with talking and listening. Here are some suggestions for all three types of learners.

ENHANCING AN INFANT'S EXISTING LISTENER SKILLS

Gently shake rattles, bells, and other noisemakers near your infant's ears.

Leave a radio playing softly in the nursery.

Slip a soft-covered rattle inside your baby's bedclothes, or tie a rattle to his infant seat. This way, his slightest movements will produce a pleasing sound.

Play a tape of lullabies, such as Steve Bergman's *Lullabies From Around the World*, as background music to accompany any activity.

Offer your baby the conversation he craves. Talk to him as you tend to his needs, describing what you're doing, asking him questions, and using any sort of response as his answer.

Sing and chant to your baby. Even the tiniest Listener will respond with excitement to familiar songs and rhymes.

Bring "home sounds" to your baby's attention. Explain in simple words what each whir, beep, ding, and whoosh signifies. For example, "Do you hear the timer? The clothes are dry now," or "Do you hear the noise? Now the dog-food can is open."

Imitating the sounds your baby makes will encourage him to make more. As he grows, make a game of this, taking turns with a pretend microphone.

Chirping Birds by Little Tikes makes a satisfying chirping sound when the birds are lifted from their nest.

Disney Roly-Poly Chime Toy by Mattel sounds a chime when rolled back and forth on its rounded base.

Pretend to talk on a toy telephone, and encourage your baby to do the same. Even simple babbling, if repeated, will model the give-and-take of conversation.

Put life into the stories you read to baby by giving distinctive voices to different characters and using expressive tones.

Musical Teething Keys by Shelcore serves as a teether and a rattle. In addition, baby can make music play by pushing a button on the key ring.

Musical Pop-Up Piano by Shelcore plays three tunes when its keys are pressed.

Play cassettes that were created especially for babies, such as Hap Palmer's *Babysong*.

ENCOURAGING THE DEVELOPMENT OF LISTENER SKILLS IN LOOKER AND MOVER INFANTS

As you cuddle and rock your baby, sing in time to the chair's motions.

Slip a pair of *Foot Jingles* by Sesame Street on baby's feet. Cookie Monster and Big Bird will rattle as he kicks his legs.

Provide your baby with a soft wrist rattle that he can wear on his forearm or ankle.

Listen and Learn Balls by Texas Instruments offer an animal sound and a corresponding picture each time the ball is turned.

Busy Guitar by PlaySkool makes five different sounds to correspond with baby's touching five different places on the instrument.

"Turn on" your infant's ears several times a day. This technique, described by Paul Dennison, Ph.D., in Edu-Kinesthetics' *Brain Gym: Simple Activities for Whole Brain Learning* (Glendale, CA, 1986), involves gently massaging the outer edge of the ears, starting at the top and working down. By doing this, you will stimulate the acupuncture points and bring energy to your baby's ears.

Musical High Chair Toy by Sesame Street fits all highchairs and plays twelve different tunes when baby turns the gears to get the music started.

Use your hands to act out songs as you sing them aloud. For example, "The Itsy Bitsy Spider" can crawl up your baby's stomach, helping him associate the words with the action he loves. Hand gestures can also spice up many ordinary words and phrases, like "good-bye," "all gone," "hot," "cold," "big," and "little."

Disney Musical Crib Rail Rocker by Mattel rocks atop a crib rail while playing a lullaby.

Provide a variety of floating, sinking, and squirting toys during bathtime, and keep up a conversation as baby plays with the various toys.

Animal Sounds Barn by Fisher-Price contains five moveable animals and produces different barnyard noises when baby manipulates the various buttons, levers, and dials.

To help keep baby's interest, simplify the text of picture books to a few words per page.

Disney's See 'N Say by Mattel combines pictures, a pull-down lever, and sounds of all kinds.

Make use of "fun" noises. Animal sounds and expressive sounds that replace words—"yuck," "uh-oh," "brrr," and the like—will probably be attempted by baby before the words themselves.

Use "baby talk" and repetitive syllables to make words easier for your baby to mimic. A train can be a "choo-choo"; an ice cream bar, a "pop-pop"; shampoo, "poo"; pajamas, "pj's"; etc.

Building Mover Skills

Although Mover skills may not be needed for success in academic subjects, children who possess a Mover's speed, agility, balance, and coordination are usually revered by their classmates, and thus gain an early social edge. Mover infants, of course, will be enthralled by any efforts to provide them with the sensory experiences they adore. Listeners, who prefer to talk rather than do, will respond best to verbal coaxing and a play-by-play description of the activity at hand. And Lookers, as always, will get the most from those Mover games and tasks to which visual stimulation has been added. The following ideas may be helpful.

ENHANCING AN INFANT'S EXISTING MOVER SKILLS

Breastfeed your baby, if possible. He'll adore the skin-to-skin contact.

Learn to do infant massage, and treat your baby to this sensory experience often.

Provide a lambskin mat or blanket. This will keep baby cool in summer and warm in winter, and is said to encourage relaxation and sleep.

Bathe with your infant. Holding him on your lap in the tub will maximize skin contact.

Offer crib dolls and stuffed animals for hugging and cuddling.

Attach a crib gym, with suspended rings, bells, and knobs, for baby to grab and kick at.

After carefully checking the interior of an empty appliance carton for exposed staples, put a favorite toy inside to encourage your baby to crawl in, or creep inside the box yourself and invite your baby to follow.

Rocking Pony by Fisher-Price is small enough to offer climbing and rocking fun to any baby old enough to sit without support.

Provide toys your baby can push while standing, like *Corn Popper* and *Musical Chimes*, both by Fisher-Price.

Offer a four-wheel, no-pedal riding toy, such as *Tyke Bike* by PlaySkool.

Place a sofa cushion on the floor, and stay close by while your baby practices climbing up and over it.

Activity Rocker by Today's Kids is height-adjustable, has a dashboard, and makes four "action sounds" to accompany baby's rocking.

Baby Crawl-Through by Shelcore is an inflatable windowed tunnel that encourages creeping and crawling.

Make a game of covering baby's arm, foot, leg, or abdomen with a folded cloth diaper or face cloth and letting him work free of it.

When your baby is in his infant seat, place lightweight toys on his lap or at his feet to encourage kicking.

ENCOURAGING THE DEVELOPMENT OF MOVER SKILLS IN LOOKER AND LISTENER INFANTS

Touch your baby as much as possible—hold him, rock him, hug him, and caress him. When he's not in your arms, keep him near you in his cradle or infant seat for plenty of patting and stroking.

"Wear" your infant in a baby sling or front carrier. This increases skin contact between you and baby and makes him more of a participant in your chores and activities.

Sing while you're rocking and holding baby. The sensations of touch will soon be associated with the comforting sensations of sound.

Supply a large, lightweight, brightly colored ball for baby to roll, kick, and toss.

Allow your baby to move about without the restraint of a walker or playpen.

The *See-Inside Roller* by Lakeshore (through catalogue only) is an eighteen-inch-long inflatable cylinder with a vinyl window that lets baby peek at the balls that rattle and jingle inside. Your baby can crawl alongside or over the top as the toy rolls along.

■ *Touch 'Ems* by PlaySkool are soft, colorful rattling toys with six distinctive textures for baby to feel.

Sit with your baby in a wading pool. Talk about the fun you're having, the toys you're playing with, and the feel of the water.

Provide a set of small sandbox tools—a rake, a ladle, a shovel, and a strainer, for instance—to encourage sand play.

Fill a plastic dishpan with one inch of dry cereal, and give your baby cups and spoons to use in this indoor "sandbox."

As a change of pace from the stroller, pull your baby around in a fenced wagon.

Supply a Bop Bag—an inexpensive inflatable toy with a character's face and a weighted bottom. No matter what your baby does to the inflated bag, it will always return to an upright position.

The Rider/Walker by Clover encourages large-muscle movement by serving as either a riding toy or a means of support for new walkers. It is available as a fire truck, a car, or a police cruiser.

Strap your baby into a helmet and tyke seat, and take a bicycle ride together. Point out the sights along the way.

Talk about your baby's actions and bring his surroundings to his attention. This will reduce his anxiety about attempting large-muscle activities.

As you work and play with your infant, please do not limit yourself to the suggestions above. Toy store inventories change constantly, so it may well be that an item you have decided to purchase now sits alongside a similar toy that's even easier to use or even better suited to your baby. No one knows your child better than you, after all. So, now that you've used the information in this chapter to determine your baby's playing and learning needs, feel free to consider both your own taste and your baby's personality when making toy and technique selections.

Please bear in mind that visible results may be slow when you attempt to encourage an infant's weaker areas. Remember that efforts to round out your child's development contradict his inborn sensory urges. You may not see signs of improvement, or even enjoyment, on your baby's part for weeks. But, gentle perseverance—in small doses—should eventually overcome your infant's resistance.

Remember that your goal is a happy child, not an honors student! Have fun, and enjoy every endearing moment of infancy as you play with your baby.

Learning Style QuickCheck for Infants, Birth to Twelve Months of Age

Directions: Place a check next to all behaviors that are characteristic of your infant. Then, total the checks in each column to determine which learning style he or she favors. You'll probably find that most of your responses are confined to one or two columns, just as in Chapter One's Learning Style QuickCheck for Parents (see page 16).

Looker	Listener	Mover

1. Communication: When my baby wishes to express himself . . .

Looker	Listener	Mover
☐ He points to what he wants.	☐ He babbled early and frequently.	☐ He uses gestures, rather than words.
☐ He responds with gestures, not words.	☐ He said his first word before age one.	☐ He is prone to tantrums.
☐ He plays very quietly.	☐ He follows directions easily.	☐ He shakes his head to indicate "No."
☐ He likes to observe goings on, rather than participate.	☐ He tries to imitate words spoken by others.	☐ He grabs at objects and toys impulsively.
☐ He didn't babble until late in his first year.	☐ He uses inflection when vocalizing.	☐ He rarely babbles at all.

2. Favorite Toys and Pastimes: When my baby plays . . .

Looker	Listener	Mover
☐ He likes dangling toys, color, and motion.	☐ He likes rattles and noisemakers.	☐ He likes being bounced and tickled.
☐ He is visually alert.	☐ He likes rhymes, songs, and finger plays.	☐ He likes to be rocked, cuddled, and held.
☐ He enjoys a *Busy Box*.	☐ He seems to "eavesdrop" on conversations.	☐ He often kicks at his crib mobile.
☐ He looks at picture books.	☐ He babbles to his toys.	☐ He enjoys the swing and bike rides.

3. Motor Skills: When my baby moves about . . .

☐ He watches his hands while playing.

☐ He was slow to sit up, and more interested in babbling.

☐ He sat without support before six months of age.

☐ He reached for objects before five months of age.

☐ He is consumed by talking, not walking.

☐ He crawled before eight months, and walked before age one.

☐ He likes to explore small objects with his hands.

☐ He prefers riding toys that make noise.

☐ He is very active.

☐ He likes to pick up and and place small pieces, and enjoys puzzles and shape sorters.

☐ He uses toys mainly to create sounds.

☐ He used riding toys before ten months of age.

4. Ways to Soothe: When my baby is fussy . . .

☐ He is quieted by the sight of a familiar face.

☐ He is quieted by the sound of a familiar voice.

☐ He is quieted by being picked up.

☐ He is calmed by a familiar toy.

☐ He is calmed by music.

☐ He is calmed by being held and rocked.

☐ He is easily distracted by a change of scenery.

☐ He is easily distracted by a xylophone or piano.

☐ He is easily distracted by a massage or car ride.

Totals: _____Looker _____Listener _____Mover

Chapter Three

Learning Styles in Toddlerhood

As young Lookers, Listeners, and Movers begin their second year, their actions make it clear that they're leaving infancy behind. During this evolution from baby to full-fledged toddler, a child's sensory preferences continue to influence both her development and her responses to the people and objects that figure in her life.

This chapter first describes three different learners in early toddlerhood, and then compares and contrasts their growth during the period from thirteen months to three years of age. A Learning Style QuickCheck for Toddlers is included to help you identify the way your own child absorbs information (see page 63), and lists of suggestions are provided to guide you in enhancing her daily explorations. This chapter also addresses the child-care issue, offering ideas for making your toddler's day-care arrangement as beneficial as possible.

Toddlerhood may be notorious for its parent-child power struggles, but it brings with it just as many exciting social breakthroughs and physical achievements. As you encourage your toddler's growth, take pride in her budding independence, as well!

A LOOK AT THREE LEARNERS

Although they're exactly the same age and have spent their infancy in similar family circumstances, toddlers Tina, Anthony, and Paul are amazingly dissimilar. Where one child seems to excel, another struggles, with their varying levels of development quite naturally dictated by learning style. Given the tremendous impact of a child's inborn preference for sights, sounds, or tactile sensations, it probably won't surprise you to learn that Tina, a Looker, exhibits eye-hand coordination far beyond that of which Anthony and Paul are capable; that Listener Anthony's verbal skills are quite advanced; and that Mover.Paul continues to perform the kinds of physical feats that have astounded his parents from the very first. Although many children exhibit characteristics of more than one learning style and are therefore considered Looker-Movers, for example, or Looker-Listeners, our case-study toddlers display "pure" styles. This has been done to highlight the distinctions between the three sensory preferences. Let's take a closer look at each toddler.

Thirteen Months of Age

Meet Tina. Like infant Michael in Chapter Two, thirteen-month-old Tina displays the Looker style of learning, preferring visual stimulation to any other. Always intrigued by detail, Tina has, until now, been content to sit quietly, exploring with her eyes and hands. But now that she's toddling in earnest, a whole new world has opened to her roving eyes and probing fingers. She has discovered buttons and dials on appliances, cabinet-door handles, the blinds, various cords and wires—all, Tina seems to think, for her personal entertainment. Tina's desire to handle such tempting devices far outweighs any desire to run, jump, or climb; in fact, her sole gross motor effort since learning to walk has been to step atop the baseboard heater in order to reach the drapery tiebacks and peer out the dining-room window.

Tina loves imitative play and tries to duplicate many of her parents' actions with toys. Her long-handled push toy serves as a vacuum cleaner, and her drumsticks as kitchen utensils or hand tools. And, though she makes no move to join in, she also enjoys watching other children at play. When alone, she plays contentedly for long periods with nesting toys, a peg board, puzzles, and other playthings that exercise her eye-hand coordination.

Tina recognizes words as symbols for objects, but rather than speak, will point toward the window or the kitchen when coaxed to say "car" or "cookie." She waves good-bye and throws kisses, but sees no need to accompany these gestures with words. In fact, at thirteen months, Tina's speech—really just occasional babbling—is little different from what it was two months before. Her love for quiet play helps her retain the label of an "easy" baby; but, though she's just a month past her first birthday, there's already a noticeable gap between Looker Tina's visual and eye-hand abilities and her skills in language and full-body activities.

Meet Anthony. Listener Anthony, also thirteen months of age, shares Tina's disregard for active large-muscle play, but lacks her fine motor ability. Shape sorters, snap-together blocks, and stacking toys gather dust on the nursery shelf while Anthony changes the discs on his music-box record player, chats with his dolls, or trails after his parents, eager for conversation. He already indulges in pretense, chanting "A–B–E–B" to a cousin's cast-off book bag before donning it and announcing, "Go gool." Anthony also likes to perch on the stairs in his fire-fighter's hat, alternating the words "My fie duck" with siren sounds. He puts on his best performances for an audience.

When there's no one available to share his play, Anthony keeps the auditory stimulation coming by singing and humming, substituting babbles for words he can't remember. In public, he approaches anyone in his path with keen anticipation of their smiling reactions to his sophisticated vocabulary. Unfortunately, Anthony's sociability now causes problems at bedtime. His radio is no longer an acceptable night substitute for Mom's and Dad's company, so he calls for them many times during the night.

At thirteen months, Anthony walks with a waddling, bowlegged gait. He falls a lot, and so is still hesitant to climb stairs or cross unfamiliar or unlevel terrain. He'll sit on a riding toy if another child joins him in play, but prefers to settle himself beside the supervising parent for a "chat." Indoors and out, conversation takes precedence over physical activity for Listener Anthony.

Meet Paul. Paul, a thirteen-month-old Mover, is quite the opposite of Anthony—largely silent, but never still. He runs, jumps, hops, climbs, kicks a ball, and walks backwards with complete confidence, the faster the better, and has already climbed atop a neighbor's tricycle in a desperate attempt to pedal along. Paul delights in all sorts of physical play—hide-and-seek, the pool and sandbox, his rocking horse, his riding toys, his slide, and the "house" his father made from an appliance carton.

Paul received a toy tool kit for his first birthday and bashes delightedly with the hammer. He tends to ignore the other tools, though, having tried and discarded them in much the same manner he tossed aside spoons and forks, crayons, and other small items that require manual dexterity. Not surprisingly, Paul is a messy eater and an aggressive, daring, somewhat destructive force while at play. Only his teddy bear sleeping companion escapes rough handling. This toy spends the night locked in Paul's arms, and the day hidden beneath his pillow for safekeeping.

As he enters toddlerhood, Paul has a one-word vocabulary—"No"—
and still relies on gestures and howls to convey his wants and needs. As
the gap grows wider between this Mover's motor skills and language
ability, it comes as no surprise that Paul's frustrations are beginning to
take a physical form: daily tantrums.

What type of learner is your toddler? Is she a Looker, like Tina, enthralled by visual stimulation? Or is she more attracted to sounds, like
Listener Anthony, or movement and sensations, like Mover Paul? The
Learning Style QuickCheck for Toddlers on page 63 will provide the
answer. Simply check those traits that are characteristic of your toddler,
and then add the checks in each column. A glance at the totals will tell
you which learning style your child favors, and help you understand her
inborn strengths and weaknesses.

HOW LOOKER, LISTENER, AND MOVER
TODDLERS DEVELOP

The pictures that have been painted of Tina, Anthony, and Paul clearly
show the distinctions that exist between the three types of learners at the
start of toddlerhood. The fact that these three children absorb information about their world through the sense dictated by their learning style
has caused them to develop different skills at surprisingly different
paces. You'll see from the accounts that follow that this trend will
continue as Tina, Anthony, and Paul move through toddlerhood.

Sixteen Months to Two Years of Age

Tina. As Looker Tina passes the sixteen-month mark, her words begin
to flow. Easy-to-picture words come first, like "dog," "shoe," and "car,"
and the word "see" is soon added to form two-word sentences about the
all-important sights in Tina's environment. Her first three-word sentence, also used frequently, reflects both Tina's liking for solitude and
her ability to persevere: "No—Tina do!"
    When at play, Tina continues to explore with her eyes and hands.
When Tina's parents try to read to her, she insists on holding the book
herself so that she can look ahead and back as she pleases. Tina loves
blocks, a pull-toy duck whose wings and feet move as he does, puzzles,
her toy farm, and anything with intricate parts. Her current favorite
plaything is a child's jewelry box with doors, drawers, and a lid that lifts
to reveal a mirror and a spinning ballerina.

Tina even manages to incorporate sights into her outdoor play. Although still uninterested in riding toys—she's more likely to turn her trike over to watch the front wheel spin—she simply adores sightseeing strolls to the local mall, to a nearby nature preserve, or just through the streets of her town. Tina plays with a ball, but more to watch the colors blend as it rolls than for exercise; she uses a swing, but on her stomach so that she can twist around and then watch the world spin by; and she plays in the sandbox, so long as there's a basketful of intriguing-looking sand toys beside her.

In a group, Tina still keeps to herself. She likes her own space, pulls away from being touched, and keeps her emotions so much in check that the yelling or crying of other children actually alarms her. (She relies on fleeting facial expressions to indicate her own surprise or displeasure.) Despite her penchant for being alone in a roomful of children, Tina is fascinated by the activities and various interactions that take place within her play group. In fact, on most mornings, she devotes more time to observation than to actual play.

Anthony. Unlike Tina, who labors to produce words, Listener Anthony imitates everything he hears and quickly builds a grammatically correct sentence around almost every new word in his vocabulary. His sentences provide him with a strong sense of self, as in "No way, Daddy," "I do it fust," or "Dat *my* toy car." By eighteen months of age, Anthony possesses a huge, clear vocabulary, and uses such adultlike inflection and articulation that he's often mistaken for a much older child.

As he moves through early toddlerhood, Anthony continues to love being read to; in fact, if no one is available to oblige him, he'll sit with an unopened book in his lap, naming the various characters and their actions. Lately, he's discovered the art of storytelling, and he and his father exchange tales whenever they're working side by side or traveling in the car. Aside from books, Anthony's current favorite toys are a mock pay phone, a toy cassette player, and various dolls and figures with whom he can act out daily events.

Anthony is a sedentary toddler, uneasy about climbing, swinging, or traversing the stairs. His avoidance of gross motor activity often borders on the comical, for he'll strike up conversations with or otherwise attempt to distract the adult at hand solely to avoid taking his turn in a game. At home, he needs help with zippers, clasps, and even the Velcro closures on his sneakers, but will dictate exactly what the assisting adult should do.

Not surprisingly, Anthony loves to socialize. He approaches both friends and strangers with greetings and questions, clearly enjoying every moment of conversational give-and-take. If, as often happens,

Anthony's playmates can't quite keep up with his verbal ability, he simply directs his attention towards the adults. At age two, Anthony mixes happily with the children in his play group, but quickly loses interest whenever an activity doesn't provide the noise or conversation he craves.

Paul. Mover Paul is constantly on the go, and shows little interest in communicating. At sixteen months, his vocabulary is limited to "Ma," "Da," and an occasional "No!" tossed over his shoulder as he whizzes by whomever calls out a greeting or request. Paul, you see, is far too busy to listen. In fact, he is past twenty months before his language skills begin to emerge in the form of terse action words like "go," "run," and "hide." Paul seems to struggle with the formation of each word, opening his mouth and thinking hard before uttering a sound. Needless to say, Paul is quite anxious when the thought he wants to communicate is particularly important to him; frustration and tantrums are becoming more and more frequent.

Unlike Tina, who is very entertained by quiet play, and Anthony, who wanders between activities but makes important social connections along the way, Mover Paul derives little benefit from toys and indoor play. His favorite game is something his parents call "dump and toss," in which Paul empties cabinets, unloads shelves, or dumps dresser drawers. Sometimes he flings the contents into his wagon and races around the house, playing garbage man; but more often, he just moves on to the next room, leaving a huge mess in his wake. Paul's parents have tried in vain to discourage this practice, for Paul is very quick and methodical about his mess making and just loves the bending, twisting, and throwing involved.

Outdoors, Paul fares much better. He loves roughhousing of all sorts, as well as any activity that involves pushing, kicking, throwing, and pounding. He began pedaling a tricycle well before age two, is fearless aboard a slide or jungle gym, and has learned the rudiments of "pumping" to keep a swing going. Paul likes to engage the neighboring kindergartener in play by daring the boy to chase or race him. Of course, the five-year-old possesses a physical edge, and Paul, already overstimulated by all his running around, winds up flinging himself on the ground and howling in frustration because he simply can't keep up with his friend.

When Paul socializes, he relies on action—chasing and grabbing— rather than verbal interplay. He is quick to join any loud, wild activities that he didn't initiate himself, and just as quick to recruit additional playmates. Paul's characteristic exuberance turns to tears at the slightest hint of anger, and he is learning to evoke similar emotional responses from others by goading them. At two years of age, his gross motor actions and rough-and-tumble sort of socializing seem to his parents to be more characteristic of a three-year-old.

Two-and-a-Half to Three Years of Age

Tina. Looker Tina began using three- and four-word sentences before she was two years of age, but six months later, she still omits sounds and parts of speech on a regular basis. She says, "Dat paint boo" for "That paint is blue," for instance, and "Can' fine ma bankie" for "I can't find my blanket." Always on the alert for familiar sights, Tina has begun to recognize and read "Dead End" and "Stop" signs, as well as department-store and fast-food-restaurant logos. Naturally, she relies on visual cues like color, shape, and letter configuration rather than phonics in order to do this; but Tina is nonetheless proud to show off her talents.

Tina spends much of her play time with her chalkboard, her doll house, and the collection of puzzles her mother borrows each week from a local toy library. She has discovered the joys of arts and crafts, and frequently asks to use paints, crayons, and markers. Tina has also become fascinated by board games. She likes to watch others play, and when no one's around, she likes to set up the playing pieces by herself and pretend she's a participant.

Tina continues to demonstrate excellent fine motor skills. She has been successful in all her early efforts with scissors, crayons, and clay. In fact, at two-and-a-half years old, she is able to draw recognizable shapes. Tina is a stickler for details when it comes to artwork. You can count on her to add chocolate chips to a modeling-dough cookie, or a tail to one of her animal creations. Tina's gross motor development continues at a much slower pace. It's not surprising that it takes some coaxing to convince her to try a full-body activity like climbing or riding a tricycle; even then, she quickly loses interest.

As she approaches her third birthday, Tina still prefers solitary play to games involving other children. She seems distressed by their noise and commotion, and is put off by impulsive hugs, hand holding, and similar social overtures for which toddlers are known. However, she is beginning to enjoy the different reactions she can elicit by making a silly face or by deliberately putting a puzzle piece in the wrong place. At three, Tina is still a confirmed Looker—quiet, content, strong on visual and fine motor skills, and weak in social and gross motor areas.

Anthony. While Tina's speech is still fairly primitive, Listener Anthony has become quite the conversationalist. Now that he understands the concept of tense, he peppers his speech with words like "yesterday," "tomorrow," "already," and "yet." Anthony also has an amazing memory for words. He mispronounces a few, but never fails to use them in the proper context. Anthony is also beginning to understand that letters make up words, and will shout, "N-O spells No!" or make reference to his "N-A-P nap."

At age two-and-a-half, Anthony loves pretend play. He drags his stuffed-animal friends into his playhouse several times a day and stages a three- or four-way "conversation" to fit the fantasy of the moment, but he's just as happy role-playing without props or companions. These days, a children's tape recorder is Anthony's favorite toy. He sings, chants nursery rhymes, and tells stories into the microphone, and enjoys the playback just as much as the recording session. He also spends a lot of time working with his realistic-sounding toy tools and using the siren on his pressure-sensitive toy ambulance.

Like Tina, Anthony would never choose gross motor play over other types of activities. When he absolutely has to indulge in full-body play, you can rely on him to talk himself through each and every step. His artwork is often creative, and almost always story-related, but very, very primitive. As he approaches three years of age, Anthony ignores puzzles, shape sorters, and, in fact, the majority of his toys. As you can see, motor skills are not this toddler's strong suit.

Socially, however, Anthony shines. Not only does he talk and reason when it comes to his own conflicts, but he uses his conversational skills to help his playmates resolve their problems, as well. Anthony is very much at ease with verbal instructions and helps his friends in this area, too. He loves the limelight, has a flair for the dramatic, and can be a bit bossy when organizing a game or assigning roles for one of his imaginary dramas. If the activity turns physical, however, Anthony's Listener-borne confidence vanishes, and he quickly removes himself from the area. Like Tina, Anthony displays the same strengths and weaknesses at age three that he did in infancy, for his language skills far surpass his motor ability.

Paul. At two-and-a-half years of age, Mover Paul's lagging verbal skills cause him increasing frustration. When he wants to convey a need, he does so in an almost frantic fashion, having learned to anticipate misunderstanding and delayed gratification. Paul's vocabulary is growing, though not nearly fast enough to keep pace with his increasingly sophisticated thoughts, but his speech is filled with the sort of verbal shortcuts you'd expect from someone a year younger. He omits words and ending sounds, saying "Scoo" for "Excuse me," and "Wan joo" for "I want juice." Because many parts of speech are ignored altogether, Paul's sentences are still limited to two or three words.

As this little Mover grows, he needs more and more space to play. Enthralled, as always, by full-body activity, Paul pushes, chases, runs, climbs, and jumps at every opportunity. When the weather curtails his outdoor fun, you can find him moving furniture and piling up toys indoors as he imitates a delivery man or mechanic. Paul rarely sits down, and when he does, it's either to roll his collection of cars across a table top or to watch some cartoon superhero perform fascinating physical feats.

Paul's own gross motor skills continue to amaze his family. He can climb to the low branches of a tree, maneuver a scooter, and, with an adult hand to hold, roll along on a pair of skates—all before his third birthday. Lately, he has taken to imitating a preteen neighbor's karate moves. Fine motor tasks frustrate Paul terribly—for instance, he still switches hands and grips his crayon in a thumbs-up fist when attempting to draw—so Paul avoids these activities at all costs.

As he leaves toddlerhood behind, Mover Paul has many friends. Since he's faster than most children his age and has little patience with timidity, most of his favorite playmates are a year or two older than Paul. He is particularly well liked by the boys in his play group, and they follow his lead just as he follows the six-year-old next door. But for all his athleticism, Paul remains moody and emotionally needy. He will not sleep without the blanket and rag doll that have shared his bed since infancy, and he craves his parents' and teachers' patient reassurance to see him through his frequent episodes of frustration, embarrassment, and wounded feelings. Like that of his Looker and Listener counterparts, Mover Paul's uneven development continues to be dictated by learning style.

LEARNING STYLE AS A CHILD-CARE CONSIDERATION

These days, it's more the exception than the rule for a child to spend her entire toddlerhood at home in the primary care of a parent. Day-care centers, family day-care homes, baby-sitters, and trusted friends and relatives all figure largely in the lives of today's young children. Certainly, any parent who is returning to work will review child-care options carefully before doing so. But did you know that when making such arrangements, your toddler's learning style merits as much consideration as cleanliness, safety, and affordability? Understanding how your child learns best, as indicated by the Learning Style QuickCheck for Toddlers (see page 63), can help you select the child-care environment that best meets her developmental and emotional needs.

Child-Care for Lookers

During toddlerhood, Lookers tend to be much like Tina, our case-study child—quiet, serene, and very good at entertaining themselves. To avoid your Looker's being lost amidst children whose behavior commands more attention and more assistance, you might wish to seek out a child-care setup that stresses interaction with care givers and doesn't routinely leave passive children to their own devices simply because they seem content.

Since a Looker toddler will benefit from daily exposure to activities that exercise her less-favored senses of hearing and touch, it's important that her child-care environment offer all types of music, a safe area for outdoor play, and occasional messy activities like painting and water play. To indulge her fascination with intricate toys, the opportunity to select playthings from a varied collection should also be available.

At first glance, a Looker toddler may seem ideally suited to an in-home, one-to-one baby-sitting arrangement. After all, this would place her in a quiet setting with no competition for use of her beloved toys. However, it's important to also encourage development of her physical and social skills. For this reason, you might wish to consider a family day-care setting for your Looker if she is to be cared for outside the home. If she is to be cared for at home, enrollment in a play group might be the answer.

Child-Care for Listeners

Like our Anthony, Listener toddlers are usually expressive, social, somewhat uncoordinated children who thrive on talking, singing, and playing with others. They do well in group situations, and relate just as well to the adults around them as they do to other children.

Many toys are unappealing to a Listener toddler, but, if you place her in daily contact with playmates who *do* enjoy them, you may tempt her to give them a try. It's also a good idea to match her with a child-care setup that offers numerous opportunities for indoor and outdoor physical play.

Safe areas in which to throw balls, ride trikes, run, and climb will encourage the sort of full-body play from which she shies away. And, finally, it's important that a Listener toddler feel free to express herself, with frequent permission to act silly and be loud.

If you're satisfied that the care giver or staff that will interact with your toddler is knowledgeable, nurturing, and unflappable, a young Listener should fare quite well in either a day-care center or a family day-care home.

Child-Care for Movers

Like Paul, most Mover toddlers speak very little and prefer to express themselves physically by means of impulsive hugs, joyful jumps, foot stamping, and tantrums. They're a bit haphazard when at play, hopping from one activity to another and leaving quite a mess in their wake, and they tend to be emotionally needy. It's wise to consider a Mover's activity level and moodiness when making her child-care arrangements.

Because a Mover's physical ability overshadows her language and fine motor skills, it's particularly important to provide her with a care giver who freely offers affection, support, and comfort during times of frustration. A daily routine that is constant and offers plenty of time for transition between activities can give the Mover toddler a reassuring sense of control over her environment. She needs room—and freedom— to roam, exposure to both full-body play and eye-hand activities, and lots of adult patience regarding food spills, strewn toys, primitive artwork, and toilet training. An in-home baby-sitter or a family day-care setup that includes four or less children would be ideal for affording the quantity and type of attention a toddler Mover needs to keep frustration at bay.

Sharing Information About Learning Style

Once you've settled your toddler into the child-care setup that best meets everyone's needs, you'll no doubt establish regular communication with her care giver. Naturally, frequent contact—whether by note, phone, scheduled conference, or a daily exchange at the door—will provide valuable information about your child's time away from you. But, familiarity with a toddler's learning style will help you take these talks one step further. You see, once you determine that your toddler is, indeed, a Looker, Listener, or Mover, you will be able to share certain observations and suggestions that may prove vital to the child's development. If your toddler spends part of the day in someone else's care, you may find it easier to guide her toward well-rounded development if you first consider each of the following aspects of her behavior and then discuss your thoughts with her care giver.

Behavior Patterns

How does your toddler act when you're at home with her, as opposed to when she is in someone else's care? Do all involved adults get the same impressions about her language and motor skills, her level of self-confidence, and her ability to socialize? If a toddler is at ease in her care giver's presence, you can expect her to "be herself." Ask the care giver to fill out the Learning Style QuickCheck for Toddlers (see page 63) to see if your results agree.

Kinds of Play

When in the care of others, does your toddler gravitate toward the same toys and activities each day? Are these toys predominantly Listener items, like musical instruments and talking toys? Does she prefer such Looker toys as puzzles and blocks? Or does she spend her time at Mover activities—speeding about on a riding toy or popping in and out of a playhouse? Your toddler probably favors the same types of toys while at home with you, and stands to benefit from exposure to playthings that will stimulate her other senses. You may wish to offer her care giver a few suggestions from the lists at the end of this chapter.

Social Behavior

How and with whom does your toddler interact while you're away from her? Does she prefer to play alone, or does she seek the company of other children? Depending on your child's play habits, you and her care giver may wish to encourage a bit more interaction by selecting a relatively passive playmate to join in some of her activities. Or, you might see a need to expose her to the joys of solitary play, either by creating a private, special sitting area, or by introducing a daily quiet play time.

Language

Does your toddler communicate as well with her care giver as she does with you? Requests for "bowly" or "goosh" may be enough to send *you* heading for the kitchen, but to avoid frustration on your child's part, it's a good idea to translate her home vocabulary for those who care for her. You might also wish to exchange information on any special tactics that seem to encourage improvements in your toddler's speech.

Motor Skills

What are your toddler's current physical capabilities? Is she more active with you than with her care giver? Less active? Does she prefer full-body play, or would she rather work with her hands? If your child has recently shown interest in a new skill, both you and her care giver should provide encouragement. If your child tends to avoid physical activity, you can share ideas about how to entice her to try different types of play.

TECHNIQUES FOR AFFIRMING AND DEVELOPING LEARNING SKILLS

A toddler needs no formal instruction to learn about her world. Whether she spends the day with a parent or a care giver, she'll absorb plenty of important information through play and sensory experience. But, when the adult in charge makes a toddler's learning style a factor in the selection of her toys, her activities, and her outings, the child will be gently guided toward well-rounded development, and will acquire skills that are sure to prove invaluable during her academic years and beyond.

Each of the following sections explains the importance of sharpening the skills associated with one of the three learning styles: looking, listening, or moving. You will then find lists of toy and technique suggestions, grouped according to whether the particular activity enhances already strong learning skills or develops weaker ones. The toys and techniques suggested for learning-skill enhancement have been based on, say, a Looker's visual acuity or a Mover's natural coordination. The suggestions for skill development involve multisensory activity—auditory *and* tactile stimulation, for instance. As such, the play ideas are intended to overlap with your toddler's inborn strengths, so that she remains involved while you explore new territory together. Choose your favorite ideas and give them a try!

Building Looker Skills

The Looker skills acquired during the early years help a child to recognize, recall, and reproduce what she sees through such fine motor endeavors as drawing and painting. The toddler who lags behind in this area usually finds intricate toys, puzzles, crayons, tools, and even eating utensils to be objects of utter frustration. But the toddler whose eye-hand skills are affirmed or improved through specially chosen experiences approaches both these and later visual tasks with more interest, more confidence, and more success. Looker toddlers will delight in *any* visual stimulation parents can provide, while Listeners and Movers, whose skills in this area can use an extra boost, will do best when Looker activities are tied in with their preferred senses: hearing and touch. You may find some of these suggestions helpful.

ENHANCING A TODDLER'S EXISTING LOOKER SKILLS

Offer a shape-sorting toy, which requires your toddler to insert a shape into a matching opening.

Provide snap-together *Duplo* blocks by Lego or *Wee Waffle Blocks* by Little Tikes to encourage use of the eyes and hands together.

Make a photo album of people and objects familiar to your child, and look at it together often.

Offer a set of different-sized toy barrels for your child to stack and fit inside one another.

Provide a peg board with fist-sized pegs.

Encourage your child to scribble in various art mediums—chalk, crayon, washable marker, and the like—on different-colored papers.

Give your toddler plenty of magazines to use as often and in whatever way she wishes.

Watch for birds, cats, squirrels, or other animals. Make a game of your toddler's finding for herself what you've already spotted and described.

Keys of Learning by PlaySkool helps a child match colors and shapes by fitting large, colorful keys into different-shaped keyholes.

Encourage your toddler to pour water from a plastic pitcher into plastic cups.

Show your toddler how to pump the handle of a top to make it spin.

Outline a table setting of plate, cup, fork, and spoon on paper. Let your toddler "set the table" using real utensils.

Buckle your toddler into her highchair and give her a bowl of fist-sized novelty magnets to stick on the refrigerator door.

Arrange to exchange puzzles with several friends so that your toddler always has several "fresh" ones to play with.

Play with PlaySkool's *Mr. Potato Head* together to give your child practice manipulating small pieces.

ENCOURAGING THE DEVELOPMENT OF LOOKER SKILLS IN LISTENER AND MOVER TODDLERS

To rest and refresh her eyes, encourage your child to "palm," as described in Celestial Arts' *Natural Vision Improvement* by Janet Goodrich (Berkeley, CA, 1986). Hold her hands, palms up, in front of her. Place the center of her cupped palms over her eyes to shut out all outside light. Then, tell her to close her eyes for about ten seconds.

Study an object together. Then hide it, close your eyes, and take turns describing the object to each other.

Tell your child a story in the dark. This will encourage her to envision details.

Roll a large lightweight ball to each other. Remind your toddler to keep her eyes on the ball.

Find a place outdoors to lie down and watch the clouds together.

Play store, exchanging pretend money for pretend items. This encourages visualization.

Provide fist-sized easy-grip crayons.

Offer your child materials like glue sticks, felt scraps, washable markers, and other fist-sized items to be used for simple crafts.

Work together with clay and modeling dough.

Visit a local sporting event—a high school soccer game is fine—and encourage your toddler to watch for various details.

Buy puzzles with knobbed pieces for easy insertion and removal.

Magna Doodle by Tyco is an erasable magnetic drawing board that works both fingers and arms.

Invest in a lift-and-look book, such as G.P. Putnam's Sons' *Spot Goes to the Farm* by Eric Hill (New York, 1987), and share it with your toddler.

Post Office by Fisher-Price has a dial, a lever, slots, and doors contained within a mailbox-shaped carrying case.

Encourage play with two-inch collectible cars, some of which change color with variations in temperature or convert with a few twists into an entirely different object.

Building Listener Skills

A toddler calls upon her Listener skills when she speaks, when she plays, when she interacts with others, and when she learns from the sounds around her. Listener, Looker, and Mover toddlers can all profit from activities that call upon the sense of hearing. Listeners benefit because these experiences affirm an inborn strength; Lookers and Movers, because their ability to communicate and socialize improves along with their growing auditory skills. Just as with Looker skills, the toddler who already possesses this learning style will need no prodding to play with games and toys that stimulate her preferred sense. Lookers and Movers may need some convincing, though, and this is best accomplished by incorporating sights, motion, or touch with whatever Listener activities you suggest. These ideas may help.

ENHANCING A TODDLER'S EXISTING LISTENER SKILLS

Provide a pair of sturdy headphones so that your toddler can listen to music whenever she chooses. Collect cassettes of children's music for use in the car and at home.

Provide plenty of opportunities for your toddler to socialize with other children by enrolling her in a play group or by scheduling regular play dates with the children of friends.

Encourage language development by asking your toddler to describe, explain, and otherwise expand on what she says.

Expand your child's vocabulary with a book like Western Publishing's *Golden Picture Dictionary* (Racine, WI, 1989), which has over 2,500 pictures of such uncommon words as oboe, unicycle, and yak.

Speak to your toddler in fairly complex sentences, giving lots of detail. This will encourage her to do the same.

Make it a practice to ask your child to relay messages to her other parent, her siblings, or her friends.

Set aside a special time of day for reading aloud. Let your toddler select a favorite book, and ask questions to help her express her feelings about it. For example, you might say, "What did you like best about the puppy?"

Buy or make a tape of household sounds like the dishwasher, the dog's bark, the telephone, footsteps on the stairs, the doorbell, and the vacuum. Play the tape back, and ask your toddler to identify the various sounds.

Get in the habit of talking about what you're doing as you do it. For example, you might say, "Daddy is going to wash the car. First, I use the hose to put water in a bucket. Then, I need bubbles. What can I use to make bubbles?" Involve your toddler in the conversation.

Make a chalkboard picture according to your toddler's specifications. Ask her what she'd like you to draw, and have her dictate the size, color, shape, and location of each detail.

Invest in a Golden Sound Story by Western Publishing. You might try *Mickey's Birthday Surprise* or *The Sesame Street Pet Parade* (Racine, WI, 1991). These books have built-in voices and sounds, which your toddler can activate by pressing pictures that match those scattered throughout the text.

Play a modified version of "Simon Says" by asking your child to follow the usual commands without visual cues from you.

Make a game of giving your toddler silly directions, like "Put the washcloth on your head," "Stand on top of the book," or "Put this toy under the chair."

Check your local library, YM-YWCA, or YM-YWHA for toddler story-time programs in which you can involve your child.

Encourage your toddler's auditory memory by turning ordinary activities—dressing, meal preparation, and bathtime, for instance—into sing-alongs.

ENCOURAGING THE DEVELOPMENT OF LISTENER SKILLS IN LOOKER AND MOVER TODDLERS

Make it a practice to speak to your toddler slowly and in short, simple sentences.

When your toddler mispronounces a word, repeat and affirm your child's thought while pronouncing the word correctly. At a pond, for example, your toddler might point and say, "Guh, kack kack." You can respond, "You're right! The duck says 'quack, quack.'"

Make hand puppets for yourself and your toddler by sewing two buttons on a sock to look like eyes. Have the puppets talk to each other.

Stage a make-believe tea party. To encourage conversation, ask questions of your toddler, like "Do you want hot tea or cold tea?" or "How many cookies would you like?"

Create a special story corner with a beanbag chair or soft rug and a cart or bin for storing books. Encourage your toddler to sit with you while you tell stories and read aloud to him.

Play supermarket with your toddler, using goods from the kitchen. Take turns being the shopper and the storekeeper, and make conversation while you play each part.

Keep television to a minimum, and encourage talking, music, and reading in its place.

Browse through mail-order catalogues together. Your discussions about the pictured items will be great vocabulary builders.

Bring-Along-A-Song by TOMY is a child-sized mock cassette player that plays four nursery rhymes and has colored push buttons.

Pop-up, scratch-and-sniff, and lift-and-look books are perfect for active storytelling.

Hide somewhere in the house, and make a game of your child finding you by following the sound of your voice.

Hide a treat, and give your toddler verbal instructions for finding it.

Watch a video created especially for children, and sing songs from the video during other times of the day.

Big Bird Talking Phone by Sesame Street is a push-button instrument that features pictures and voices of the Muppet characters.

Plan special outings to help build your child's vocabulary. There's a great deal to talk about at a pet shop, firehouse, park, or post office.

Building Mover Skills

Well-developed Mover skills give even small children the confidence they need to get the most enjoyment from group situations. The coordinated toddler usually emerges as the first, the quickest, and the best at physical activities, becoming a magnet of sorts for her playmates. As such, all toddlers, regardless of learning style, can profit from large-muscle activity. This is simple enough with Mover toddlers, who will be thrilled with any sort of body contact and gross motor play you suggest. Listeners and Lookers, though, will probably need some encouragement in the form of either conversation or visual stimulation, as the case may be. Perhaps you'll be able to use some of these suggestions.

ENHANCING A TODDLER'S EXISTING MOVER SKILLS

Place materials of different textures in a pan, sandbox style. Rice, beans, water, and oat flakes are great fun to scoop and pour.

A backyard swing set offers the opportunity for frequent active play.

Shoe-box-sized cardboard bricks or Little Tikes' *Giant Waffle Blocks* are great for building and toppling.

For variety, exchange riding toys with friends' children.

Enroll in a parent-and-child swim class.

Throwing, catching, and kicking sponge *Nerf* balls is great exercise for toddlers.

Invest in a *Sure Hit Batting Set* by Lakeshore (through catalogue only). The set includes a ten-inch ball, a foam bat, and a batting tee.

Be sure to provide your toddler with plenty of holding, rocking, and stroking.

Enroll your toddler in a kiddie gymnastics program, or provide a tumbling mat at home for rolling and somersaulting practice.

Practice climbing up and down stairs with your toddler, placing just one foot on each step and moving the other foot ahead to the next step.

Assign your toddler her own garden spot in which she can dig, squirt the hose, play with rocks, and pull weeds.

Tot Trike by The Toy Factory is a good first tricycle for toddlers. It has two front wheels for extra stability.

Invest in a wagon or stroller so that your toddler can give rides to her favorite doll or stuffed animal.

Provide a child-sized broom, rake, watering can, and shovel to encourage your toddler's imitative play.

ENCOURAGING THE DEVELOPMENT OF MOVER SKILLS IN LOOKER AND LISTENER TODDLERS

Provide an inflatable outdoor pool to promote water play. Naturally, an adult should always be in attendance.

A playground is the perfect place for hesitant toddlers to observe, and eventually attempt, such large-muscle feats as climbing and balancing.

March to music, alternating arms and legs, to improve your child's coordination.

Cozy Coupe by Little Tikes is a toddler-sized car that is propelled by a child's footsteps, rather than pedaling.

Make a balance beam from a two-inch by four-inch board. Lay the board on the ground, and encourage your toddler to walk along with arms outstretched.

Provide a steel-framed riding pony for climbing, bouncing, and rocking.

Create a special outdoor play area for your toddler, equipped with his own toys, to encourage active play.

Make a game of pantomiming such everyday actions as vacuuming, shaving, or opening a window, and have your toddler guess what you're doing.

Sing and act out the classic song, "This is the way we sweep the floor (touch our toes, climb the stairs, etc.)."

Play "marching band" with rhythm instruments like wood blocks, a drum, cymbals, or a triangle.

■ Provide a wheelbarrow to encourage outdoor play. Suggest that your toddler cart various items around the yard.

■ Make a playhouse, complete with doors and windows that open and shut, from an appliance carton. Encourage your toddler to crawl inside as you play "family" together.

■ Play with a set of *Catch-It Critters*, distributed by Toys to Grow On (through catalogue only). The Velcro inside these mitts makes it easy for your toddler to catch the ball.

■ Add a visual and auditory touch to tricycling by decorating your child's trike with colored spoke covers, a basket, handlebar grips with streamers, a horn, and a bell.

■ *Easy-Set Bowling* by Fisher-Price has a large ball and a stand with indentations in which to set each of five brightly colored pins.

As you scan the above lists and your neighborhood toy store for those activities that would best suit your toddler, other skill-building ideas may strike you. I urge you to try them out! You've already identified your child's learning style, and you've also learned how to blend what she likes with what she needs. Most important, you know her temperament better than anyone, so don't be afraid to experiment with variations. After all, no single idea is right for every parent and child.

Although you may find that your toddler takes to a new toy or technique immediately, it's just as likely that she will resist or ignore a new item or activity the first few times you try it. Please don't be concerned. You can expect visible improvement of your toddler's weaker skills to take some time. Remember that your primary goal is a confident, well-rounded child. And, as you gently shape your child's learning experiences, also keep sight of a second goal: an improved parent-child relationship that's shorter on frustration and longer on good old-fashioned fun!

Learning Style QuickCheck for Toddlers, Thirteen Months to Three Years of Age

Directions: Check all the statements below that are characteristic of your toddler. Then, total the checks in each column and compare your totals. Typically, most of your responses will be in one or two of the categories, providing a clear picture of your toddler's preferred learning style.

Looker	Listener	Mover

1. Communication: When my toddler wishes to express herself . . .

Looker	Listener	Mover
☐ She has a small vocabulary.	☐ She has a large vocabulary.	☐ She relies on nonverbal communication.
☐ She speaks in short sentences.	☐ She combines words into sentences that are easy to understand.	☐ She speaks very little.
☐ She confuses the order of words in sentences.	☐ She likes to talk.	☐ Her speech is difficult to understand.

2. Favorite Toys and Pastimes: When my toddler plays . . .

Looker	Listener	Mover
☐ She likes shape sorters and stacking rings.	☐ She enjoys being read to.	☐ She often chooses the sandbox and outdoor activities.
☐ She often chooses to play with blocks.	☐ She learns nursery rhymes and the words to songs easily.	☐ She pulls things out of drawers and off shelves.
☐ She likes crayons, paper, and paints.	☐ She likes records and tapes.	☐ She takes toys apart.

3. Motor Skills: When my toddler moves about . . .

Looker	Listener	Mover
☐ She likes to use her hands and fingers in play.	☐ She concentrates on language rather than full-body play.	☐ She especially likes to climb.
☐ She looks around while riding the swing.	☐ She has limited coordination.	☐ She is well coordinated.

4. Social Skills: When my toddler is around other people . . .

☐ She often pulls away from being touched.

☐ She likes to be close, but prefers talking to touching or holding.

☐ She likes to be rocked and held, and always wants more.

☐ She uses facial expressions to reflect happiness, sadness, and anger.

☐ She changes the volume of her speech according to her mood.

☐ She seeks out hugs.

5. Emotions: When it comes to my toddler's feelings . . .

☐ She is not very emotional.

☐ She expresses her feelings with dramatic flair.

☐ Her feelings are easily hurt.

☐ She seems surprised by the outbursts of other children

☐ She uses names for feelings, such as "happy" or "sad."

☐ She is prone to frequent and surprising outbursts of joy and anger.

6. Memory: When my toddler learns . . .

☐ She remembers faces.

☐ She adds words to her vocabulary quickly.

☐ She imitates the actions she sees, such as washing the car.

☐ She remembers activities best after seeing them.

☐ She remembers a word or name after hearing it only once.

☐ She remembers activities best after doing them.

Totals: _____Looker   _____Listener   _____Mover

Chapter Four

Learning Styles in the Preschool Period

Between the ages of three and five years, a child makes tremendous strides toward independence. He still requires lots of reassurance and support from his parents, and even more frequent guidance and instruction, but what he learns during the preschool period helps a child bridge the gap between the emotional neediness of toddlerhood and the relative self-reliance he'll have to draw upon when he begins school.

Most of the experiences that bombard the preschooler during these important months are a function of his learning style. As was true during infancy and toddlerhood, from ages three to five, a child's inborn sensory preference can cause his perceptions to be quite different from those of his peers and playmates. This is because preschool-aged Lookers, Listeners, and Movers continue to be drawn to and responsive to very different types of stimulation, even when their surroundings are the same.

This chapter introduces you to a Looker, a Listener, and a Mover at the start of the preschool period. Comparisons of each learner's development from age three to age five are also provided to demonstrate the impact of learning style on a child's different skill areas.

Preschool programs and their accompanying social experiences can play a big part in a three- or four-year-old's development. This chapter explains how to make your preschooler's learning style a factor in your selection of his school, in your reinforcement of the learning he does there, and in your discussions with his teacher. The chapter concludes with lists of easy-to-implement ideas, grouped according to learning style, for building up your preschooler's weaker skills while providing him with plenty of opportunities to play at the activities he loves best. A Learning Style QuickCheck for Preschoolers is included to help you determine your child's learning-style preference (see page 87).

The child who enters the preschool phase of life may still seem very much a toddler. But, by the end of this phase, both feet are firmly planted in childhood. Have fun with your preschooler as he travels the meandering path that will lead him to the social and academic challenges of kindergarten.

A LOOK AT THREE LEARNERS

Elena, Rachel, and William are all three years of age. Each child has caring and involved parents, a middle-class home life, and a school-aged sibling. All three children are veterans of baby gym, story time, and parent-child activity groups; and all will attend preschool next fall. But, as you will see, similar backgrounds do not necessarily yield like children. Because our three preschoolers have different learning styles, from the very first, the children have responded to, absorbed, and processed the information from their surroundings in diverse ways and at varied speeds. As a specialist in communication disorders, I see many children who exhibit combinations of learning styles—Looker-Listeners, for instance, or Looker-Movers—but, for the sake of clarity, you will see that each of our case studies demonstrates characteristics of a single learning style. Let's look at our three learners.

Three Years of Age

Meet Elena. Looker Elena is a quiet but contented child. Her speech and vocabulary are within normal range for her age, but Elena keeps to herself, just as she did throughout babyhood. Working alone, she produces tremendous quantities of artwork, which she displays all over the house. Elena can draw or paint a person, a tree, a flower, a house, and a variety of animal-type creatures, all in detail. She also loves cutting and pasting and working with clay. Unfortunately, Elena's dexterity doesn't carry over into gross motor areas. Her climbing, hopping, and other full-body efforts are still hesitant and somewhat clumsy.

Elena has recently discovered fashion dolls. She delights in matching the little outfits, and does more dressing and undressing of the dolls than actual pretend play. Elena is also a great fan of her library's children's room, which has a separate magazine and puzzle area, papier-mâché replicas of various storybook characters strung from the ceiling, and a rug modeled after a giant game board. Every visit she makes is a visual treat.

Just as she always has, Elena learns best by observing. She is quick to say "Show me" or "Let me see" when she doesn't understand something, and gets many play ideas by watching other children. In a Looker's typically reserved fashion, though, Elena waits till that child is elsewhere before trying the activity herself. She can recognize and read the logos on various delivery trucks, can spot words like "library," "school," and "deli," and can spell out her name with magnetic letters. At age three, Elena is the very picture of a preschool Looker: visually oriented, good with her hands, and somewhat below the norm in gross motor and social skills.

Meet Rachel. Rachel, a Listener, is just four days younger than Elena. She, too, avoids gross motor activities when she can, well aware that they're not her strong suit; in fact, Rachel has begun to volunteer her services as "judge" or "audience," depending on which part assumes the most sedentary role in the activity at hand. This satisfies Rachel's need to socialize without demanding too much running around on her part. Rachel's fine motor coordination is on a similar level, so she frequently asks for help with the eye-hand portion of activities, requesting, for instance, that her parents "Draw some characters for my story" or "Build a block house for my circus animals."

Rachel's verbal skills are quite advanced for a child of three. She knows scores of rhymes, chants, and jingles, and she sings—on key—to almost every activity. She can also recite her street address and phone number, as well as the names of family members. Rachel is fascinated by words; in fact, when she hears something new, she'll ask for a single repetition and then immediately assimilate it into her vocabulary.

When it comes to play, Rachel's current favorite pastimes include joke- and storytelling, playing "Mommy" or "school," and listening to all types of music. Because children her age find her somewhat bossy, and because older playmates provide conversation better suited to her sophisticated tastes, Rachel often trails after her big sister's friends. But the lagging fine and gross motor skills that are so typical of a young Listener keep Rachel from really enjoying *either* age group's games and fun.

Meet William. Like Rachel and Elena, Mover William is three years of age. However, gross motor activities pose no problem for him. He loves to run, climb, wrestle, and play "karate." In fact, William is so given to full-body movement that he simply cannot sit still for table play or stories. Within minutes, he's rolling or crawling around on the floor, instead.

At play time, William ignores puzzles, games, paper and crayons, and small toys in favor of his fleet of construction trucks, his bicycle, and his growing collection of sports equipment. He manages to turn even his sister's playthings into Mover props: her purse becomes his mailbag; her dolls, his victims or "bad guys"; her doll stroller, his snowplow; and so on. Although he's too restless to sit for very long, William still enjoys an occasional stroller ride himself. He is patently uninterested in drawing, bead stringing, or any other activity involving eye-hand coordination, for these pose quite a problem for him. At night, he spurns books and stories in favor of a back rub and lots of hugs.

At three years of age, William still speaks in two- and three-word sentences. He thinks hard before uttering all but the simplest words, yet still mispronounces many of them. William becomes understandably upset when he can't express himself, crying, stomping, and shrieking in frustration. Tantrums, which have been part of his behavioral repertoire for almost two years now, still occur daily. The give-and-take of ordinary conversation is much too fast for William, and he loses interest almost as quickly as he tunes out instructions, lectures, and even the briefest of monologues. This little Mover will soon be entering preschool with excellent full-body coordination, but with verbal and fine motor skills that lag far behind those of most of his classmates.

Does your preschooler seem most tuned in to visual stimuli, like Looker Elena? Does he react to and learn from sounds, like Listener Rachel? Or is he most like Mover William—highly sensitive and in perpetual motion? The Learning Style QuickCheck for Preschoolers on page 87 will tell you how your child learns. Simply check off the characteristics that best describe your child, and then total each of the three columns: Looker, Listener, and Mover. The column with the most checks is the category into which your little learner fits.

HOW LOOKER, LISTENER, AND MOVER PRESCHOOLERS DEVELOP

You've seen that their diverse learning styles have led Elena, Rachel, and William to become strikingly different three-year-olds. The way these children absorb, process, and respond to environmental information is still determined by the sensory preference each possessed at birth. As you follow our three learners throughout the preschool period, you'll see that the developmental differences that exist at age three only become more marked with the passage of time.

Three-and-a-Half to Five Years of Age

Elena. As she moves through the preschool period, Looker Elena continues to express herself in short, unelaborated sentences. Even at home, she rarely volunteers information, and must be coaxed to provide details about school and play dates. Elena plays regularly with one neighboring child; when several are present, she usually retreats to the sidelines to watch for a while before joining in their games. Elena's gross motor skills are now acceptable for her age, though she's far better at swatting or bouncing a ball than at activities like running or hopping, which involve full-body coordination.

Since so many gross motor activities call for either socializing or getting dirty—neither of which thrills her—Elena gravitates toward art projects and solo play. She enjoys board games and puzzles, and has taken to building projects—high-rises, bridges, and castles—from a variety of blocks. Elena takes pride in her precise coloring and skillful cutting and pasting, and presents each masterpiece to her mother for display.

Elena has a carton of "favorite" picture books and has begun to sight-read words that crop up with any frequency—mom, dad, yes, no, dog, cat, and the like. She also employs her memory when reading whatever street and traffic signs she passes. Lately, Elena has become fascinated by the details on automobiles, and she can now discriminate between different makes and models by their trunk and hood ornamentation, wheel covers, or taillight configuration. In fact, one of her favorite games is to "match" passing cars to those of people she knows. "There's a car like Grandma's, only blue!", she may shout. Or, "David's mom has that same car, only her lights aren't broken."

At preschool, Elena never commands the limelight. Here, as at home, she is attentive but quiet, busying herself with solitary games and projects. Her sophisticated artwork stands out from that of her classmates, and she is one of the few preschoolers who can print the entire alphabet—neatly—from memory. By her fifth birthday, Elena can print the names of all her classmates, and about a dozen other words, as well. As her very rewarding preschool experience ends, Elena looks ahead with excitement to the challenges of kindergarten.

Rachel. Listener Rachel is as much a chatterbox as Elena is reserved. She uses elaborate sentences and multisyllabic words, and astounds her teachers and classmates daily with such vocabulary gems as "binoculars," "wigwam," and "diagonal." When she's not taking the lead in home or school discussions, Rachel can usually be found relating every detail of a story or reciting some rhyme or song—verbatim.

It comes as no surprise that Rachel delights in group activities and considers almost everyone her friend. Because her advanced verbal skills make her a natural organizer and ringleader, Rachel's earlier tendency toward bossiness flourishes during her preschool years. Accustomed to assigning roles and detailing instructions, she is quick to "tell" on friends or classmates who don't follow the rules.

Rachel still shows little interest in arts and crafts or intricate toys. She cannot yet print, and when asked to draw, dashes off a simple picture and then dresses it up with an accompanying story. She seems to view painting, drawing, and cutting and pasting activities as opportunities for socializing, and is more concerned with the nitty-gritty of conversation than with completing the project at hand. Rachel has come to enjoy time spent on the playground because of the opportunities for interacting with friends. As she does at home, Rachel attempts to control her group's play verbally, as in, "Let's pretend we're the three bears walking back to our home, which is here, under the slide. You be the mother, you be the father, and I'll be the little baby bear." If the game takes a more physical turn, with the "bears" chasing one another or careening down the slide, Rachel usually makes her way indoors—just as she does when the weather happens to turn a bit too hot, cold, damp, or windy to suit her.

At preschool, Rachel separates easily from her parents. She is helpful, personable, knowledgeable, and so eager to read that she grabs every opportunity to ask what labels, posters, and notes "say." Of course, Rachel consistently receives glowing reports from her teachers. Like Looker Elena, Rachel will enter kindergarten with confidence and eager anticipation born of a positive preschool experience.

William. Unlike talkative Rachel, Mover William's more rudimentary speech is labored and difficult to understand. He mispronounces sounds, misinterprets some of what is said, fails to grasp common expressions, and has trouble recalling spoken instructions or details. Even at five, William still relies on body language to communicate, grabbing, hitting, and pushing before it occurs to him to express his needs in words. Still, he is a sensitive child, easily hurt himself, and alert to, if not always considerate of, the feelings of others. Just as he has since babyhood, William constantly seeks out body contact with family, friends, and teachers; in fact, he is often reprimanded for his habit of bestowing overexuberant bear hugs upon his peers.

William is extremely well coordinated. The training wheels on his bicycle are long gone, and he can climb a pole, kick a football, and swing a racket as well as boys two years older. Brave and daring, William takes the lead during most outdoor play, with the habitual disarray of his clothing serving as testimony to his activity level. William has become more interested in art projects of late, but likes to work "big." Easel and mural projects are much more to his liking than cutting and pasting, partly due to the fact that he has yet to designate a dominant hand. William has already abandoned any attempts at neatness; in fact, the messier the activity, the better he likes it. You can count on this little Mover to throw down his fist-clutched crayons when the finger paints appear. Few of his creations make it to the refrigerator door, though. Usually, they're dropped, torn, or forgotten.

Preschool presents a problem for William because he simply doesn't have the patience for the sit-down activities that constitute so much of the curriculum. Class discussions, story time, work sheets, sing-alongs, and many art projects exact a heavy toll on a child who would prefer to be running about. Since he lacks the visual and auditory skills needed to print a number, learn a song, or recite the alphabet, William quickly turns his attention to diversionary activities—making animal noises, throwing paper, or tickling his classmates. Not a morning has passed during which William hasn't required discipline of some sort, and his teachers have grave reservations about his preparedness for kindergarten.

LEARNING STYLE AS A PRESCHOOL CONSIDERATION

A generation ago, preschool was somewhat of a luxury; today, most parents view it as an important step in a child's progression toward school readiness. A year or two spent in the company of qualified adults and a roomful of busy three- or four-year-olds teaches a child a great deal about separating from his parents, responding to different authority figures, focusing on and completing tasks, and functioning as part of a group.

With luck, the school you select for your preschooler will exercise all of his developmental areas—physical, social, emotional, and intellectual—rather than focusing on the more formal class work he'll face as a kindergartener. Since most children aren't really ready to read or write until they're past the age of five, any preacademic work that's covered should be presented in the spirit of play. Of course, the bottom line is that preschool will have to be fun if your child is to enjoy going there!

Assuming that your community offers a choice of schools, what else should you look for? Now that you've pinpointed your own child's learning style with the Learning Style QuickCheck for Preschoolers (see page 87), you'll be able to make a more informed choice. These general guidelines may help you.

Preschool for Lookers

During the preschool years, the quiet, visually oriented Looker learns by first observing and then imitating what he sees. He's perfectly suited to classrooms in which there are different learning centers—science and math tables, a reading corner, a dress-up center, a block area, and the like—from which he can choose. Naturally, he'll gravitate toward puzzles, games, building sets, and other forms of solitary play every chance he gets, so it will be helpful if classes are small and there's an extra adult or two on hand to note his habits and occasionally steer him toward group activities. A preschool setting that emphasizes cooperation and offers daily exposure to music, as well as provisions for outdoor and other full-body play, will stimulate a Looker's less-favored senses of hearing and touch and, as a result, help him gradually strengthen his Listener and Mover skills.

Preschool for Listeners

The sociable, talkative Listener learns by putting what he hears to work. He'll flourish in any classroom with materials for dramatics—a puppet theater, a housekeeping corner, a mock store, or a make-believe post office. And, for a Listener, a piano, rhythm instruments, and cassette player should be viewed as necessities rather than frills.

A Listener preschooler rarely accepts things at face value, and he'll feel most free to ask the questions, rattle off the instructions, and offer the explanations so characteristic of his learning style in a permissive classroom atmosphere in which individuality and independence are highly regarded. Since he's likely to ignore the chalk, stamp pads, blocks, trucks, and *Tinkertoys* that are provided during free play time, the Listener will benefit from daily gym and crafts periods or from other teacher-directed opportunities to exercise his large and small muscles.

Preschool for Movers

The Mover preschooler learns best what he experiences with his whole body. For him, the school facilities are an important consideration, for more than anything else, the Mover needs space—floor space, a gym, and a play yard in which to roam free. He'll find only frustration with a teacher who heavily emphasizes paper-and-pencil tasks or sit-and-listen activities. More than either of the other learners, the Mover needs a setting in which different ability levels are expected, accepted, and used as a basis for personalized activities. It's wise to remember that the Mover's awareness of his lagging skills is usually keen. The smaller the pupil-teacher ratio in his preschool, the more much-needed support and attention he'll receive.

Though he should feel free to be messy until his maturing fine motor abilities permit neater work, the Mover still needs encouragement in the use of his small muscles. Simple crafts that emphasize free expression rather than duplication of a teacher's prototype can gradually stretch a Mover's eye-hand capabilities, as can almost any free-time activity that's made into a game—piling checkers into a tower, for example. Moreover, the Mover stands to benefit from a classroom atmosphere in which cooperation, assistance, appropriate conversation, and other social skills are painstakingly taught and rewarded.

Sharing Information About Learning Style

Once your child is enrolled in a preschool setting that's well suited to his learning style, it's important to enlighten the teachers about how he best learns, plays, and socializes. From the beginning, parents can mention that their child seems to be a visual, auditory, or kinesthetic learner. If the teacher is familiar with the learning-styles theory, the terms "Looker," "Listener," and "Mover" will crop up on their own, and parents can freely discuss the specifics of their child's learning preference. If not, parents can simply describe the child's learning strengths and weaknesses and then mention a tactic or two with which they've had success at home. For instance, you might say to the teacher, "Kerry remembers everything she sees, but she seems hesitant to talk, and doesn't enunciate her words as well as the other children do. Recently, we began a homemade 'word book,' in which we paste photographs of new vocabulary words. Now, Kerry seems more interested in using new words."

No doubt, conclusions about your child's learning needs would eventually be reached by the preschool staff, anyway. But early communication may spare a Looker child from weeks of being overlooked, or prevent a Mover child from initially being coerced into sit-down activities that he's simply not equipped to handle. Happiness and well-rounded development should be the goal of every preschooler's parents and teachers, and this goal is most likely to be attained when adults share the following information.

Learning New Skills

How does your child learn best? If he's a Looker, like Elena, he will learn best when provided with demonstrations or illustrations that he can copy. If he's a Listener, like Rachel, he may need detailed spoken instructions and verbal reinforcement. A Mover, like William, generally requires the most assistance. Because of the Mover's inability to pay attention within a group and to process information spoken across a room, teacher and child or parent and child often have to perform the new skill together.

Correcting Behavior

What approach seems best when correcting your child's behavior? Often, a warning glance is all that's required to set a Looker preschooler back on track. Listeners, of course, respond best to explanations and to such verbal validations of their own protests as, "I'm sorry you're tired. Maybe you'd like to take a rest *after* you pick up the toys." Movers, who thrive on action, often need to have their inappropriate behavior redirected to some acceptable action. Karate kicks of a block tower can be redirected toward a Bop Bag; the need to lie on a table can be refocused to a beanbag chair. Movers also need more touching—more hugs, more lap time, more by-the-shoulders steering—than other learners.

Kinds of Play

How does your child like to play? At school, he probably gravitates toward the same types of toys and games that he chooses at home. It's also likely that these activities and playthings are a clear reflection of his learning style. Lookers, for example, often love building sets, while Movers prefer riding toys. You may wish to exchange suggestions with your child's teachers about games, activities, and techniques that have been used successfully to strengthen your child's weaker skills.

Observations About Development

Are there aspects of your child's development that warrant attention? Does he sufficiently communicate his needs? Are his fine and gross motor skills significantly behind those of his classmates? Does he have the ability to listen and pay attention for short periods of time? You might wish to exchange observations about your child's development with his teachers and compare notes periodically about his progress in these areas.

Support Services

Are speech, hearing, and vision screening available at your child's school? If so, it would be a good idea to take advantage of these services. And, should further evaluation be recommended, it would be best to follow up immediately rather than delay and, thus, risk a widening of the gaps in your child's skills.

TECHNIQUES FOR AFFIRMING AND DEVELOPING LEARNING SKILLS

As the preschool-aged child becomes more independent of his parents, grows comfortable with the preschool staff, and acquaints himself with his classmates, he becomes part of a world of rapidly expanding horizons. Between time spent playing alone and time spent with parents and teachers, a child is—with luck—treated to sensory experiences that are both constant and varied. And, when a preschooler's learning style becomes a consideration in the planning of his daily activities, he receives healthy measures of both the stimulation he craves and that which he needs to bring weaker skills up to par.

The sections that follow describe the benefits of developing those skills that are part of the three learning styles: looking, listening, and moving. In the case of each style, this is followed by a list of toys and techniques meant to strengthen the skills of children who show a preference for that style. Then, suggestions are presented for developing a similar sensory awareness in children who possess one of the other two learning styles.

The ideas for learning-style affirmation include toys and games that tax a learner's strengths. The suggestions for developing lagging skills have been selected because they are multisensory. That is, they employ two or more senses simultaneously—one of which, in this case, is the sense your child needs to develop. Those multisensory activities and materials that involve your child's preferred sense are, of course, the ones that will work best for him.

As you peruse the lists, looking for ideas suited to your child, remember that *fun* should be your main criterion. Please enjoy yourselves, whether the activities you choose are for your child's use alone or for the two of you to try as a team.

Building Looker Skills

Children rely on their Looker skills when they observe, memorize, and recreate. These are the skills that give certain children the edge when it comes to reading readiness, artwork, and paper-and-pencil tasks. While good eye-hand coordination and the willingness to persevere at a task both come naturally to the Looker child, they can also be developed in other learners when the right play experiences are provided. Of course, preschool-aged Lookers will be the most receptive to activities involving visual stimulation; after all, these children are naturally inclined to use their eyes and hands. Listeners, who much prefer socializing to solitary play, but can certainly use some fine motor development, may find their interest piqued by toys and games built around conversation. Movers, who also need help with visual and eye-hand skills, will be happiest about those Looker activities that are the least restrictive. The following ideas should help you strengthen your child's visual abilities.

ENHANCING A PRESCHOOLER'S EXISTING LOOKER SKILLS

■ Provide a fishing set with a pole and line containing a magnet or hook that your child can use to catch brightly colored toy fish.

■ PlaySkool's classic *Tinkertoys* is a building system with colorful, diverse pieces and illustrated instructions for assembling various creations.

■ Little, Brown, and Company's *Find Waldo Now* (Boston, 1990), as well as other books in Martin Handford's *Waldo* series, has Waldo and other unusual characters waiting to be found somewhere in each illustration—on a busy street, in outer space, in a prehistoric scene, and the like.

Take your child for a walk around the block. When you return, ask him to "palm" (to learn how, see page 55) and, while his eyes are closed, answer questions about what he saw, like, "What color was the big moving truck?" or "Was the mail carrier wearing a hat?"

Lego Basic, a building set by Lego, contains doors, windows, wheels, and hundreds of primary-colored interlocking pieces.

Provide different-colored and different-sized beads and cord for your child to use in creating bracelets and necklaces.

Keep a variety of simple board games on hand. By all means, play the games with your child, but also permit him to use them by himself in his own imaginative fashion.

Teach your child to recognize various geometric shapes—hexagons, ovals, trapezoids, and the like—by playing with a puzzle-like shape-sorter toy. PlaySkool's *Form Fitter* and L'il Hands' *Shape Sorter Bucket* are two examples.

Big Bird's Match Game by Sesame Street uses a windowed game board to sharpen memory and matching skills. Players must remember what is behind each window as they try to find characters that are alike. Different theme cards can be slipped behind the windows to add variety to your child's play.

Offer your child a collection of small objects, and make a game of sorting them according to color, shape, or size.

Provide a *View-Master* viewer, which has reels of television and movie characters appearing in 3-D. The pictures change with the flick of a lever.

PlaySkool's classic *Mr. Potato Head* has plastic bodies with holes for the insertion of brightly colored facial features and accessories.

Play-Doh by Kenner makes a variety of different play sets—a bakery, a fast-food store, a diner, and a "fun factory," for instance—that enable the child to press, roll, and slice colored modeling dough into diverse forms.

Besides providing color-matching practice, *Gazoobo Shape and Sort Key House* by Chicco can be used as a puzzle, a shape sorter, or a series of keys and locks.

The Glo-Doodler Fun Slate by Color Forms allows a child to draw with a special pen and create pictures that glow.

ENCOURAGING THE DEVELOPMENT OF LOOKER SKILLS IN LISTENER AND MOVER PRESCHOOLERS

Allow your child to dial numbers on the telephone. As you call out a number, he can hold the receiver and either dial or push the corresponding button.

Provide a brush, a cup of water, and a paint-with-water book. Since the colors appear as soon as water touches the page, your youngster's finished picture will look great every time.

To encourage coloring, cutting, and pasting, provide a child-sized table and chair at which your preschooler can work.

Large, soft sidewalk chalk is perfect for drawing and scribbling on driveways or cement. Your child's creations will last until the next rainfall.

Duplo blocks by Lego are the big brothers of the classic Lego blocks. The pieces snap together and come in a variety of forms and sizes, without being so small that they frustrate children with an unsteady hand.

A chalkboard affixed to the wall at your child's height will encourage drawing, particularly when you leave him daily picture messages and encourage him to do the same for you.

Finger painting on large sheets of paper gets the eyes and hands working together, and allows your child to be as messy as he wants.

Little Tikes' *Wee Waffle Town* and other waffle-block sets encourage less-adept fingers to build and create. The sets come with people, cars, trees, doors, windows, and primary-colored snap-together squares.

Trainer scissors, with two sets of finger holes, enable an adult hand to guide a child's hand as it makes those first scissors cuts.

Invent lots of "pretend" scenarios to encourage visualization. Your child can be the gas station attendant, the postal worker, the waiter, or the shopkeeper, and you can be the customer. Few props are needed as you act out your parts together.

Place several small toys in a bag. Ask your child to slip his hand into the bag and identify the toys by touch. Once he guesses, he can remove the toy to see if he was right.

Jumbo-sized crayons, which are much easier to manipulate without breakage than their standard-sized counterparts, are available in most variety and toy stores.

To encourage drawing, provide "fun" writing implements like glitter pens, scented markers, neon-colored pencils, four-color pens, and character pencil toppers.

Make a game of scribbling on blank paper and then examining the results for hidden "pictures." Take turns pointing out what you see in each other's creations.

Make it a habit to pore over photo albums together, recounting the stories behind your child's favorite snapshots.

Building Listener Skills

Because socialization is so important to a preschool-aged child, Lookers, Listeners, and Movers can all benefit from building those skills that facilitate conversation and social behavior. At the same time, encouraging a child's self-expression and reliance upon auditory memory helps him vent frustrations and prepare for the academic work that awaits him in kindergarten. Offering a Listener child a toy or activity that taxes his verbal skills is a simple matter, of course. You won't find the going as easy if he's a Looker or Mover; but, chances are he'll be most receptive to Listener games and playthings that also call his favored sense into play. Here are some skill-developing suggestions for all three types of learners.

ENHANCING A PRESCHOOLER'S EXISTING LISTENER SKILLS

Continue the practice of regularly scheduled story times. Encourage your child to relate part of the story or to fill in a blank as you tell it, as in, "When Goldilocks sat in Baby Bear's chair,————." Pause long enough for your child to explain what happens next.

Sesame Street Inter-Com Telephone Set by Ideal contains two plastic phones linked together by thirty feet of cord. This toy enables children to enjoy "long-distance" conversation.

Make it a practice to attend children's concerts and storytelling festivals. The combination of music and words is very stimulating to Listeners.

Listening Lotto, distributed by Lakeshore (through catalogue only), offers playing boards of pictures that correspond to sounds on a tape. If, for example, your child hears a baby's cry, he covers the picture of the baby on his card. The tape contains forty-eight sounds altogether.

The Fisher-Price *Tape Recorder* has excellent sound reproduction and easy-to-push buttons. Your child can listen to prerecorded tapes or make tapes of his own.

Most public libraries schedule story hours for preschoolers. This opportunity to hear a tale and sing a few songs—all in the company of other young children—will delight Listeners.

Several companies—Sony, Panansonic, and Sanyo among them— make an inexpensive headphone radio. This all-in-one listening device is perfect for preschoolers.

Just for fun, make it a practice to make up poems and rhymes as you travel in the car or work at a task together.

Familiarize your preschooler with the world of poetry by borrowing and reading aloud collections from your library's children's section.

Look through magazines together, and take turns making up stories about the people in the various pictures.

The Fisher-Price *Wireless Microphone* is a battery-operated toy that transmits your child's voice over FM radio.

Start a tradition of family sing-alongs, during which you can teach your child words to songs from your own school days.

Video Technology's *Electronic Junior Jammer* is a cassette player that plays ten nursery-rhyme melodies and comes with a "DJ's Manual."

Teach your child how to select and borrow records and cassettes from the library. Doing so will provide him with the largest and most varied selection of songs and stories possible.

PlaySkool's *Alphie II Computer Learning Toy* "talks" to the child as it sharpens his prereading skills.

ENCOURAGING THE DEVELOPMENT OF LISTENER SKILLS IN LOOKER AND MOVER PRESCHOOLERS

Mattel's *See 'N Say* and PlaySkool's *Sounds Around* have dials to spin and levers to press to start the toys "talking." Several varieties of each are available, covering everything from nursery rhymes to ABC's.

The game cards in Milton Bradley's *Sesame Street Light and Learn* contain printed instructions that you can read aloud to your child. As he selects a game card and then moves Big Bird around the battery-operated board in search of number, shape, or letter matches, you can name and count the pictures together.

Read picture books to your child about things that move—trains, planes, construction vehicles, and fire trucks. He'll love stories with built-in action.

Keep hats, badges, toy tools, and other dress-up accessories on hand, and encourage both conversation and the assumption of various roles as you and your child stage a bank robbery, perform a highway repair, attend a birthday party, or go on a big-game hunt.

What's Wrong?, distributed by Lakeshore (through catalogue only), is a set of picture cards with such obvious mistakes as a telephone with a banana for a receiver, or a man bathing in his clothes. As your preschooler points out what's funny about each picture, you can ask him to describe or explain what he sees.

Your child will get practice recognizing colors, shapes, and numbers with Western Publishing's Golden *Big Bird Beep Book* (Racine, WI, 1989). Questions are asked, such as, "Can you find the yellow flower?" or "How many carrots are there?" The child touches an electronic wand to his chosen response and waits for an answering beep.

When your preschooler accompanies you on an errand, bend the rules and, when appropriate, allow him to explore, touch, and taste the things you encounter en route. The more involved he is in the outing, the more likely he'll be to respond to your questions and conversation with dialogue of his own.

Use a table top as a puppet theater, and encourage your child to speak for the characters in the shows you create together.

Teddy Ruxpin by Worlds of Wonder is an easy-to-operate cassette-playing stuffed bear with a moving mouth and eyes. Each of the story cassettes is accompanied by a colorful picture book.

Look for books that have accompanying animals or other props that your child can hold or use to act out the story. *Paddington Bear* and *The Velveteen Rabbit*, both distributed by Troll Learn & Play, are examples of book-and-animal sets.

Treat your child to a new vocabulary word each day. You can start by presenting, defining, and acting out the day's word, and then attach a related picture to the refrigerator or your child's lunch bag. Be sure to use the word in conversation as many times as possible.

Try embellishing nursery rhymes with movement. As you chant "Jack and Jill," for example, you can clutch a pretend bucket, skip about, and then tumble down. During "Little Miss Muffet," you can encourage your child to sit, use an imaginary bowl and spoon, and then leap up in fright.

Milton Bradley's *Candyland* and *Chutes and Ladders* are classic beginner board games that involve counting and color matching, as well as use of the hands and the imagination. As you play these games with your preschooler, be sure to count aloud and discuss where the playing pieces are headed.

■ Sit with your child during a broadcast of *Sesame Street*. The fast-moving skits are great fodder for laughter, singing, conversation, and number and letter practice.

■ Join your child in pretend play with a farm, an airport, or a marina play set. Encourage him to make up a story and provide the voice of one or two of its characters as you set up the scenery and play with the various pieces.

Building Mover Skills

Well-developed Mover skills have little to do with a child's conversational ability, attention span, or other classroom "pluses." But, by preschool age, the agile and coordinated child exudes a sense of confidence that puts him in the lead both in the gym and on the playground. It follows, then, that a body image and an overall athleticism that are improved by exposure to large-muscle activities will stand every preschooler in good stead.

A child who's a Mover will, no doubt, be a willing participant in any gross motor game or technique you wish to try, simply because these activities appeal to his inborn sensory preference. In contrast, Lookers and Listeners will be navigating foreign waters each time they attempt full-body play; but you can make the going a bit easier for them by building in some of the visual and auditory stimulation they adore. You should find some of these ideas helpful in encouraging your child's Mover skills.

ENHANCING A PRESCHOOLER'S EXISTING MOVER SKILLS

■ Provide your child with knee pads, a helmet, and a pair of ice, roller, or in-line skates.

■ Encourage your preschooler to walk, hop, and twirl on a ground-level balance beam. A street-side curb or a two-by-four placed on the grass can serve the purpose.

■ Seek out a cargo net, knotted rope, or rope ladder for your child's climbing practice.

■ *Bag of Feelies*, distributed by Lakeshore (through catalogue only), contains ten pairs of textured pieces. One of each pair is placed in a cloth bag; the other is left out for the child to feel and then match with its hidden mate.

PlaySkool's ten-inch *Play Cycle* is a safe, sturdy first bicycle, complete with rugged training wheels.

Access to an outdoor swing set encourages a child to hoist himself into a swing and then pump his legs to get in motion.

Several companies make a Bop Bag, which is a sand-weighted inflatable toy with bounce-back action. This is the perfect target for venting frustrations or just-for-the-fun-of-it rhythmic punching.

Dance and exercise with your preschooler, encouraging him to move at different energy levels to different tempos.

A two-sided easel, comprised of both a clipboard and a chalkboard, will allow your child to involve his whole body in various large-sized projects.

Giant Tumble Balls, distributed by Lakeshore (through catalogue only), come in three sizes—nineteen, twenty-four, and thirty inches—and can be rolled, bounced, kicked, or ridden on after inflation.

For no-miss dunking, present your child with a height-adjustable basketball net and a foam basketball.

Tonka makes a realistic heavy-duty mixer, dump truck, and crane that are perfect for use in sand, dirt, leaves, and pebbles.

Provide your child with a lightweight nylon tent, or just tack an old blanket to a fence, for all kinds of outdoor play.

Jumpin' Jiminy Bounce by Natural Science is a thirty-six-inch soft, rounded trampoline that's ideal for preschoolers.

Lakeshore offers five-inch plastic *Safety Stilts* (through catalogue only) with a stable, no-slip base and adjustable handgrips.

**ENCOURAGING THE DEVELOPMENT OF MOVER SKILLS
IN LOOKER AND LISTENER PRESCHOOLERS**

A selection of pool toys—floats, swim rings, rafts, and ride-on inflatable animals—make water play almost irresistible.

Play catch with a large, soft *Nerf* ball. Stand very close to your child as you aim the ball into his outstretched arms. As his skills improve, you'll be able to move farther apart.

Offer one of the widely available games in which Velcro-covered balls are tossed at a large, colorful target. This safe variation of darts encourages throwing practice because a "hit" is almost guaranteed.

Make a couple of paper pompoms and encourage your child to play cheerleader, with lots of running, jumping, bending, and stretching.

Teach your child the movements to various hand-clapping games, like "Pat-a-Cake" and "A Sailor Went to Sea, Sea, Sea."

Cap Toys' *Official Crunchball* is a baseball set with a soft, oversized, fabric-covered bat and ball.

Offer your child the chance to ride the coin-operated horses, race cars, and boats so often found outside supermarkets.

Introduce your child to gardening. Weeding, raking, planting, watering, and watching over a special garden spot will appeal to all types of preschool learners.

Create an inviting outdoor play spot that's just for your child. If you vary the accompanying toys, he'll vary his activities, as well.

Soft Sport Ring Toss Set by Franklin can be played indoors or out. It has a soft, squeezable post, base, and rings.

Seek out a two-step flight of stairs on which your child can practice climbing and jumping.

Provide a collection of washable cars and trucks for your preschooler's indoor and outdoor use.

■ Give your child a paintbrush and a bucket of water, and ask him to "paint" the fence, the steps, or the sidewalk.

■ Fisher-Price's *Fun With Food Supermarket Cart* comes with two baskets, plastic groceries, and play money.

■ Your preschooler can be the navigator or the passenger when you provide a child-sized wagon for his outdoor use.

When selecting activities and playthings for your preschooler, keep in mind that flexibility is important—even vital. Naturally, no two children will be ready for a given toy at exactly the same time, nor will they derive equal enjoyment from it even when its introduction is timed exactly right. A trip to the toy store may well convince you that a different toy from the one I've recommended will achieve the same developmental purpose while being much better suited to the tastes of you and your child. You are certainly the best judge of your youngster's temperament, so I urge you to trust your instincts in modifying my suggestions or in borrowing ideas from the lists compiled for other types of learners.

It's also important that you not expect overnight success in your efforts to round out your preschooler's learning skills. The fact is that many weeks may pass before you first notice that there's a new sureness to his grip, that he's becoming more observant, or that he's relying more frequently on verbal rather than bodily expressions of his wants and needs. But rest assured, the changes *will* come in time, bringing with them a satisfying sense of achievement that will put smiles on both of your faces!

Learning Style QuickCheck for Preschoolers, Three to Five Years of Age

Directions: Review the following lists of behaviors, checking off those that are characteristic of your child. Then, total each column and compare the results. In most cases, you'll find your responses concentrated in one or two of the columns. The learning style listed at the top of that column is the learning style of your preschooler.

Looker	Listener	Mover

1. Communication: When my preschooler wishes to express himself . . .

Looker	Listener	Mover
☐ He speaks in short sentences, using simple language.	☐ He talks a lot and uses complete sentences.	☐ He uses brief sentences and searches for words.
☐ He is fairly quiet.	☐ He relates stories in detail.	☐ He communicates with body movement and facial expression rather than words.
☐ He communicates through drawing and painting.	☐ He enjoys conversation.	☐ He sometimes talks to inanimate objects.

2. Favorite Toys and Pastimes: When my preschooler plays alone . . .

Looker	Listener	Mover
☐ He likes beads, blocks, puzzles, and crayons.	☐ He makes up stories.	☐ He likes to play outside.
☐ He likes watching TV and films.	☐ He likes books, tapes, and music.	☐ He heads for tricycles, bicycles, and other wheeled toys.
☐ He enjoys drawing, coloring, and crafts.	☐ He likes being read to.	☐ He loves to climb.

3. Motor Skills: When my preschooler moves about . . .

Looker	Listener	Mover
☐ He cuts, colors, and prints with ease.	☐ He prefers talking to fine or gross motor activities.	☐ He runs, jumps, and climbs with coordination.
☐ He isn't particularly active.	☐ He loves to talk about the work he produces.	☐ He prefers active play to sit-down activities.
☐ He can draw a recognizable person.	☐ He talks and instructs himself while drawing.	☐ He does not yet draw or print anything recognizable.

4. Social Skills: When my preschooler mixes with other children . . .

☐ He's one of the quiet ones.

☐ He makes conversation easily.

☐ He is very sociable.

☐ He often pulls away from being touched.

☐ He is sometimes bossy.

☐ He enjoys their company.

☐ He observes before joining in a game.

☐ He takes charge during pretend play.

☐ He relates physically, with lots of touching.

5. Formal Group Settings: When my preschooler is at day care or school . . .

☐ He likes working on individual activities, like cutting and pasting.

☐ He likes to talk in front of the group.

☐ He likes active group games.

☐ He prefers to watch others play rather than participate.

☐ He prefers to play in groups rather than by himself.

☐ He fidgets and squirms during sit-down activities.

☐ He needs time to feel comfortable.

☐ He is attentive and follows directions well.

☐ He sometimes indulges in distracting or attention-getting behavior.

6. Emotions: When it comes to my preschooler's feelings . . .

☐ He has trouble expressing emotion.

☐ He uses names for his feelings, like "angry" or "happy."

☐ He is very easily hurt.

☐ He is startled by the outbursts of others.

☐ He is very vocal and dramatic.

☐ His moods are often extreme. He can be angry one moment, and laughing the next.

☐ He finds conflicts fascinating to watch.

☐ He uses words to settle disputes.

☐ He seems to crave the reassurance of hugs, smiles, and praise.

7. Memory: When my preschooler learns . . .

☐ He remembers activities best after seeing them.

☐ He adds new vocabulary words daily.

☐ He imitates the actions he sees.

☐ He learns colors, numbers, and letters quickly.

☐ He memorizes songs and rhymes quickly.

☐ He remembers activities best after trying them out.

☐ He recognizes product and chain-store logos.

☐ He loves to ask and answer questions.

☐ He is most attentive when he can play an active part in the lesson or exercise.

Totals: _____Looker   _____Listener   _____Mover

Chapter Five

Learning Styles in Kindergarten

The kindergarten year provides a child with gentle exposure to academic work within a play environment. Few five-year-olds are ready to learn from work sheets, books, or blackboard lessons; but a kindergarten atmosphere of exploration, experimentation, and discovery provides the perfect transition from the freedom of preschool to the relative regimentation of the elementary grades.

Just as it has since infancy, in kindergarten, a child's inborn sensory preference determines what she notices and how she absorbs and responds to that information. Depending on learning style, you'll find that some five-year-olds are instinctively drawn to the sounds, some to the movements, and others to the sights that surround them. This, naturally, colors what, how, and when they learn.

Chapter Five presents three different learners—a Looker, a Listener, and a Mover—at the beginning of the kindergarten year, and follows and compares their differing rates of development between ages five and six. A Learning Style QuickCheck for Kindergarteners is included to help you pinpoint your own child's sensory preference (see page 117).

This chapter also explores the effects of learning style on a child's kindergarten experience, and offers ideas on the types and durations of programs best suited to each learner. Finally, you'll find lists of toys and activities that will provide the kinds of play that your child finds most appealing while bolstering her weaker skills, as well.

Kindergarten is a time of tremendous social growth as children replace some of their attachment to Mom or Dad with close friendships and pupil-teacher relationships. At school, kindergarteners become part of a world designed especially for them—a world that encourages them, informs them, and teaches them to cope with the structure and teacher expectations they'll face in grade school. Make the most of the kindergarten experience, for though it spans only ten months, your child is likely to seem eons wiser at its conclusion!

A LOOK AT THREE LEARNERS

Nicole, Brendan, and Robby turned five years old during the summer that preceded kindergarten. The children live in similar neighborhoods, have several friends who reside within walking distance of their homes, and have toddler siblings. Each attended preschool last year and enjoyed various community children's programs, as well. Despite our case studies' common backgrounds, however, you'd have to look hard to find three children that are less alike!

You see, Nicole, Brendan, and Robby were born with different sensory preferences; that is, each child instinctively responds to a different element—be it sight, sound, or motion—within the same environment. Take the three to a horse farm, for example, and you'll soon find Robby astride a fence, flicking imaginary reins; Brendan executing near-perfect snorts and whinnies; and Nicole staring intently at everyone and everything that crosses her path.

Five years of this sort of inborn response have caused the three children to develop an array of learning skills at vastly different paces. Of course, many children are combination learners, and display the traits of two, or even three styles. For clarity, however, our case-study children have only one style each. Let's take a look at our three learners, and examine the role that sensory preference has played in each child's adjustment to kindergarten.

Five Years of Age

Meet Nicole. Nicole is a Looker—a quiet, solemn child who is given more to observation than conversation. When she does speak, her sentences are simple and direct, with little inflection and few accompanying gestures. Nicole rarely exhibits excitement, fury, or other mood extremes. More often, milder emotions are displayed with widened eyes, a furrowed brow, or the set of her jaw.

At play time, Nicole can usually be found drawing and coloring, poring over picture books, or making an elaborate creation from snap-together blocks. Generally she prefers to play by herself, but occasionally she joins a friend for a table-top or card game. "Go Fish" and *Chutes and Ladders* are among her favorites, but she insists on playing by the rules. If her playmate gets the giggles and starts to make her playing piece "dance," or if she suggests that two-of-a-kind is better than four-of-a-kind, Nicole walks away in a huff. Her need for order carries over to her appearance, as well: Nicole is extremely fussy about her clothing, her hair, her room, and her work space.

Nicole is not a risk taker, nor is she particularly quick or agile, so she rarely seeks an active role in outdoor play. Her excellent eye-hand coordination enables her to excel at T-ball, but she is annoyed by most of her other gross motor performances. As a Looker, she gets much more enjoyment from watching other children run, climb, and play ball than from trying to join in their games. Nicole is a standout at fine motor activities, however. She can print the entire alphabet from memory, and she produces artwork that is remarkably neat. She has the skill and patience to play marbles and pick-up sticks, and she assembles jigsaw puzzles as quickly as many adults!

Nicole has been in kindergarten for only three weeks, but she has adjusted beautifully. Her classroom, adorned with papier-mâché animals and decorations of every kind, is a nonstop visual treat. And, there are shelves of games and puzzles and a crafts table towards which Nicole makes a beeline at every opportunity. As a pupil, she is reserved, but very agreeable. She rarely volunteers answers or information, but she cooperates when called upon. Though Nicole enjoys watching her classmates at work and play, she's still somewhat daunted by the sea of new faces and the level of activity in the room. When the bustle and confusion become overwhelming, Nicole usually makes her way to the teacher's side, where she watches and waits until things quiet down again.

Nicole's social and gross motor skills could be better, but she's likely to succeed in kindergarten on the strength of her Looker abilities alone. Her self-control, visual acuity, and sense of order will stand her in good stead in any classroom!

Meet Brendan. Listener Brendan is as effusive as Nicole is reserved. He expresses his feelings easily, using the same adultlike speech he has relied upon since toddlerhood, and understands slang and colloquial phrases that go right over the heads of most of his classmates. When the teacher calls out, "Hold your horses!" on the playground, Brendan is one of the few who stop dead in their tracks. Most of the others crane their necks in search of four-legged animals. Brendan uses sentence context to determine the meaning of an unfamiliar word; seconds later, he can usually spout a precise definition of his own making. He is somewhat haphazard about his appearance and his work and play areas, but there is always a reason for the disorder: "These trucks *have* to stay on the floor, because it's rush hour and traffic isn't moving."

Needless to say, Brendan makes friends easily. He loves to lead activities, assign roles, and set rules. On the playground, you'll often find him speaking for the quieter children and bossing anyone who'll allow it, for few of his peers can match his verbal skills. Brendan needs encouragement to use playground equipment for its intended purpose; for example, he'd rather use the monkey bars as his store or castle than for climbing. You see, gross motor play doesn't provide the same opportunity as pretense for Brendan's beloved socializing. When no playmates are available, he usually heads for the television or his collection of audio cassettes.

Brendan's fine motor skills are about average for a five-year-old. He likes arts and crafts and table work, but more for the chance to sit with his friends than for the production of a particular masterpiece. He has difficulty printing letters and numbers from memory; his efforts at writing his name are usually accompanied by mumbled self-reminders, like "Make a stick, and then a loop and a loop." Letter sounds, however, pose no problem; Brendan is able to sound out many three- and four-letter words.

At school, Brendan's favorite activity is Circle Time, during which the class sits together for a lesson, a story, or a song—usually led by Brendan! He loves the limelight, and proudly displays his understanding of weather, time telling, and the calendar. During free time, Brendan is quick to persuade classmates to share the various play centers with him, for he loves their company. Brendan's penchant for sounds means that he can be easily distracted from work and play. A passing lawn mower, corridor noises, or the sounds of another class on the playground all cause his attention to wander from what he's doing; but Brendan follows directions so well that he gets back on track pretty quickly.

Overall, Brendan's visual and gross motor abilities are acceptable, but nowhere near the level of his Listener skills. However, his superior language ability and outgoing personality may be all he needs to make his kindergarten year a positive experience.

Meet Robby. Robby, a Mover, is having a much tougher time adjusting to the relative confines of his new classroom. His rudimentary speech is difficult to understand, and he is quick to tune out the conversation of others. Since Robby discovered that silly behavior wins the laughter of his classmates, poking, noise-making, and face-making have become much more rewarding than whatever activity is on hand! Robby doesn't always respond when called upon, either, for he often becomes so involved in creating distractions that he doesn't hear the teacher's voice. The most effective way to get him back on track is to steer him, physically, with a grip on his shoulders.

Indoors or out, Robby plays long and hard, stopping only when exhaustion reduces him to tears. His dangling shirt tails, untied shoes, and torn pants are testimony to his activity level. His favorite games have lots of action and few rules; tag, hide-and-seek, and foot races are daily "musts"! Robby can always find companions on the playground, but since he's faster and more coordinated than most, they eventually tire of losing and wander away. Robby is hurt and angered by their departure, but he doesn't possess the social skills that could keep his playmates from leaving.

Robby's efforts at printing his name are hurried and primitive. Most of his letters are off the line, and some are reversed. He is often confused by the names and order of alphabet letters; the fact that they make sounds baffles him completely.

Since sitting still is a problem for him, Robby has little interest in artwork. He can think of a dozen reasons for leaving his seat—a sudden thirst, a broken pencil, the need to use the bathroom, and the desire for a closer look at a truck driving by the window are just a few on his list. And, when he's exhausted these excuses, Robby will crawl around on the floor in search of shoelaces to yank or ankles to tweak. With all of these distractions, it comes as no surprise that Robby rarely finishes a project.

Robby feels just as confined when he is steered toward his classroom's science center, library corner, or puzzle table, and wanders away at every opportunity. He's the first in line, however, for any gross motor activity—Indian dancing, for example, or distributing boxes of crayons—and he lives for the time his class spends outdoors or in the gym. Unfortunately, his lack of self-control and short attention span have already made him a frequent guest of the classroom's time-out corner. It's unlikely that Robby's kindergarten year will provide him with benefits like those enjoyed by Nicole and Brendan.

How does your kindergartener learn? She may rely on visual stimulation, like Looker Nicole. She may be very verbal and drawn to sounds and language, like Listener Brendan. Or, she may be like Mover Robby—a physical child who is highly attuned to motion and touch. A Learning Style QuickCheck for Kindergarteners has been provided on page 117, to help you make this determination. Simply review the behaviors in each of the QuickCheck's three columns, marking each that seems to describe your child. Since most of your responses will be concentrated in one or two categories, the column totals will provide a clear indication of learning style.

HOW LOOKER, LISTENER, AND MOVER
KINDERGARTENERS DEVELOP

Nicole, Brendan, and Robby are at very different points of development simply because each child learns in a manner unlike the others'. The children's ability to follow directions, remain attentive, and recall what they've seen and heard are all functions of their diverse learning styles— styles that are already causing them to cope differently with the kindergarten experience. As we continue our learners' stories and follow their progress throughout the school year, you will see that the various imbalances in Nicole's, Brendan's, and Robby's development continue to color each child's learning and behavior.

Five-and-a-Half to Six Years of Age

Nicole. Nicole has become a bit more sociable during the course of the school year. She is still reassured by first watching a game or activity before actually participating, but now joins in more readily than in the past. Nicole has become friendly with two of her classmates and, outside of group activities, doesn't seem to feel a need to mix with the rest of the children. She remains an observer on the playground, since most outdoor activities are too rough or too dirty for her liking. When she tires of watching, you can count on Nicole to head toward whichever activity requires the most eye-hand coordination. Marbles and ring toss are frequent choices.

Nicole's fine motor skills are quite advanced. She was the first of her friends to learn to button, lace, zip, and tie, and continues to produce the precise work her teacher has come to expect. Her efforts at printing the alphabet are frequently displayed as models for the other children, and her artwork is easy to recognize due to her use of outlining, shading, and brilliant colors. Nicole is equally neat about her appearance, and thrives on the order and routine of a typical school day.

Reserved and polite, Nicole remains a child of few words. Her sentences lack verbal detail, but she pronounces almost every word correctly because of her long-time habit of observing other speakers. Nicole's teacher encourages the use of inventive, or phonetic, spelling in the composition of one- or two-line "stories." But since Nicole relies on memorization rather than a sounding-out approach to reading and is bothered by the misspellings that seem to leap at her from her paper, most of her efforts contain only two or three words. The accompanying illustration provides any missing details.

Just as she "sees" words in her mind before reading or writing them, Nicole uses visual strategies to learn other things. She learned her phone number only after carrying it on a slip of paper for weeks; she can tell left from right because her right arm faces the teacher's desk when her class rises for the Pledge of Allegiance each day. Nicole is adept at premath activities, like counting, sorting, and categorizing, because each requires the visual and fine motor skills that come to her so naturally. Though she has trouble listening for long periods of time—she tends to daydream and then leap back to attention when she sees her classmates moving on to a new activity—her kindergarten year has served to reinforce the skills and behavior that made her such a willing student in the first place! It's very likely that Nicole will have just as easy a time in first grade.

Brendan. Kindergarten is also a positive experience for Listener Brendan; in fact, the daily group activities and instant availability of playmates serve as the perfect showcase for his verbal skills! Brendan is equally comfortable interacting with children and adults. He continues to take the lead during discussions and storytelling, voicing his opinions with confidence and using multisyllabic words and adultlike phrases that leave his classmates open-mouthed and envious.

Whether working or playing, Brendan has come to enjoy fine motor activities. His printing and artistic efforts are still quite ordinary, but he recognizes that most projects and games afford additional opportunities to socialize. Even when the teacher calls conversation to a halt, Brendan guides himself through the task at hand with whispered instructions, just as he has since toddlerhood. Saying things like,"Q is like O, but has a little squiggle on the bottom," helps keep his attention focused on his work.

Because Brendan has yet to develop confidence in his gross motor skills, he still shies away from playground equipment and rough-and-tumble games. At recess, you're more likely to find him giggling with his friends than running races. Not surprisingly, Brendan readily joins any games that involve conversation. He loves to play "The Farmer in the Dell," "Giant Steps," and "Bluebird, Bluebird."

In the classroom, Brendan is adept at following even three-part instructions. He can count to one hundred with accuracy, and can also recite the days of the week, the months of the year, and the four seasons. His printing is laborious and his efforts at spelling poor, but Brendan's teacher encourages his newly discovered love of communicating with others through crude notes. Another favorite kindergarten activity is a weekly program during which two other classes join with Brendan's for songs and stories. During free time, Brendan heads for the listening corner, where headphones, books, cassettes, and records are available, or the drama center, which contains furniture, dress-up clothes, and various grown-up "props" for pretend play.

Occasionally, Brendan must be reprimanded for the inevitable results of his advanced language skills: calling out answers, eavesdropping, and chatting during quiet time. Background noise and the conversation of others continue to act as a magnet for Brendan's attentions, particularly during seat work, so his art and pencil-and-paper efforts are frequently interrupted. But, a few words from the teacher or his own recollection of her earlier instructions is all it takes to set Brendan straight. Overall, he is an asset to his class; and, like Nicole, he finds kindergarten exciting. Brendan can't wait for first grade, when he can be among friends for the whole day!

Robby. Mover Robby's efforts at communicating have not greatly improved during his kindergarten year, and this is a source of embarrassment whenever other children correct his grammar and pronunciation. When Robby protested, "He taked free crowns!" after a classmate helped himself to some extra Crayolas, his remark met with a humiliating chorus of "It's *crayons*, not *crowns*!" In light of Robby's slow progress in language areas, his teacher has referred him to the speech-language pathologist for an evaluation.

Robby is always in a hurry, and has little patience for seat work. His efforts at drawing and printing his name are awkward and rather sloppy, peppered with letter reversals and unrecognizable forms. He has better luck controlling chunky pencils and crayons than ordinary slim ones, but his overzealous cross-outs and erasures, combined with his habit of wandering away from the table, practically guarantee a ripped or unfinished product! Robby hasn't yet learned to read numbers or letters, because he simply cannot remember what each looks like. The fact that letters have accompanying "sounds" remains a mystery to him.

Robby continues to thrive on movement. He is devastated each time he learns that it's not a gym day, and whenever rain threatens the class's outdoor play. As always, he loves to run and chase; for this, he is still held in high regard—on the playground, at least—by most of his male class-mates. During the year, however, some of the gentler children began to shun him as their earlier awe turned to scorn for his inability to sit still and pay attention. Many of Robby's peers are now also annoyed by his tapping, wiggling, poking, and noise-making—habits that cause their teacher to take time out for a reprimand from almost every activity.

Overall, Robby has made little social or academic progress during his kindergarten year, and is already becoming somewhat hardened to perceived failure and the disapproval of his teacher and classmates. His parents are rightfully concerned about his ability to handle a full day of school in first grade.

LEARNING STYLE AS A CONSIDERATION IN KINDERGARTEN

Despite the recent proliferation of toddler and preschool programs and the importance placed on school readiness by today's parents—most of whom are kindergarten veterans themselves—organized kindergarten remains optional in many states of the union. Nevertheless, if for no reason other than the accompanying social benefits, the vast majority of five-year-olds attend some sort of formal school program. The following discussions will help you select the type of kindergarten class—and the type of teacher—that would be best for your little learner, and will guide you in working with your child's teacher to prepare your child for her first year of elementary school.

Choosing the Best Kindergarten Class for Your Child

Depending on where you live, of course, the kindergarten possibilities open to your child may range from just one—that within your public school system—to dozens, including church and temple programs, boarding schools, academic preparatory schools, specialized kindergartens for the gifted or challenged, and programs that, like Montessori, espouse a par-ticular teaching method. Needless to say, children's kindergarten experi-ences can differ greatly according to the school in which they are enrolled. Even within a single town, school hours, facilities and supplies, regula-tions, parental involvement, teacher credentials, and methodology are usually far from uniform!

If you have the luxury of considering more than one program for your child, remember that the *teacher's* learning style can have a tremendous influence on things like classroom arrangement, the design and presentation of lessons and activities, and the teacher's interaction with pupils. As is the case with parent and child, a teacher's learning style can either complement that of the child or create the potential for friction. For this reason, it often pays to learn whatever you can about the classroom practices of available teachers.

To illustrate this point, try to imagine your five-year-old learner under the tutelage of the three teachers profiled below. Their credentials may well be identical, but you're likely to feel that one teacher would be a much better "fit" for your child than the others.

Mrs. Combs, a Looker. Mrs. Combs runs a structured, orderly kindergarten. She keeps a large illustrated list of classroom rules posted by her desk, and reviews the list at least twice a week. She writes the class's daily schedule on a nearby chalkboard, next to a colorful chart listing the names of that week's classroom helpers.

Mrs. Combs feels it's important for children to have their own "space" at school, so she assigns a labeled coat hook and shelf area to each student and adheres to the traditional use of desks. At music and story time, her pupils sit on carpet squares arranged in two concentric circles. During group lessons, a rectangle of red tape that adorns the floor near the bulletin board enables the children to sit in an orderly fashion.

Most kindergarten teachers employ the concept of a morning Circle Time. Mrs. Combs uses her Circle Time to fill in the weather chart and calendar, present flannel-board stories, and show samples of what the class will be doing that day. Naturally, visually oriented Mrs. Combs has a magnificent classroom, with coordinated decorations covering every available space. She makes frequent use of filmstrips, videos, work sheets, and arts and crafts of every kind. Her classroom has its own computer; to help her pupils memorize the keyboard, Mrs. Combs provides each child with a paper copy for his or her desk. The class is often encouraged to dictate sentences and stories, which Mrs. Combs copies onto huge sheets of lined easel paper and uses for reading practice.

Naturally, Mrs. Combs makes neatness a priority. She praises the children for coloring within the lines, for printing with precision, and for helping keep the classroom clean. The best of her pupils' work is displayed on a hallway bulletin board, and she frequently offers work and project samples that the children can copy. Her penchant for orderliness extends beyond the classroom, as well. The children line up, boy-girl-boy-girl, when moving from place to place, and are encouraged to stay to the right of a certain silver line that runs the length of the hallway. Mrs. Combs is a highly organized and thoroughly dedicated teacher; but it's easy to see that Mover children, in particular, would have a difficult time adhering to some of her teaching methods, expectations, and classroom policies.

Ms. Perez, a Listener. At first glance, Ms. Perez's classroom seems busier and noisier than that of Mrs. Combs. Ms. Perez feels that working at round tables, rather than in rows of desks, will encourage conversation and cooperative behavior among her students. Mrs. Perez likes to teach the class as a group; when it's time for such a lesson, the children cluster together on the floor at her feet. Like Mrs. Combs, Ms. Perez also has a list of class rules. Rather than displaying them on a chart, however, she has worked them into a song that the children sing almost every day. Ms. Perez is also less formal about class jobs, for she prefers that all her students share responsibility for a tidy classroom.

Ms. Perez uses Circle Time to read aloud and teach songs to her pupils. An accomplished storyteller, she uses her voice, her dramatic flair, and even some amateur guitar strumming to spin amazing tales that rivet her young students to their places. Ms. Perez looks for feedback and encourages discussion, but she insists that the children take turns, and asks that they sit quietly and listen when someone else has the floor.

Ms. Perez makes frequent use of oral directions, first making sure she has her class's attention and then requesting that the children repeat her instructions. She asks a lot of questions during the course of the day, and when forming small groups to work on projects, she pairs the most sociable children with the most quiet in an effort to help the latter "open up." Ms. Perez shows her Listener tendencies by the kinds of activities she encourages. Show and Tell, Sharing Time, and circle games like "A Tisket, A Tasket" are all part of her routine. She often uses songs and role-playing to introduce new concepts or to reinforce the old.

Ms. Perez teaches a phonics approach to reading: she trains her pupils to listen for and remember the various letter sounds, and employs games and songs to make the job easier. Wishing to encourage the children's composition efforts in every possible way, Ms. Perez has taught them to use inventive spelling—the writing of words as they sound to the child—and leaves pencils, markers, and paper in many places around the room. One of the highlights of the kindergarten year is the class play, a much-rehearsed effort that is short on costumes and props, but long on dramatics. This allows each student a moment in the spotlight. Ms. Perez is a highly creative teacher, but her theatrics and her emphasis on self-expression might well be troubling to Looker or Mover kindergarteners.

Mr. Warner, a Mover. Mr. Warner's classroom has little in common with that of Mrs. Combs or Ms. Perez. Mr. Warner's students have no assigned work spaces; instead, they are encouraged to perform tasks and tackle various activities wherever they feel most comfortable. If a child feels like stretching out on the floor to read, fine! If someone else decides to carry his tray of clay from the art center to the windowsill, that's acceptable, as well. Needless to say, the appearance of Mr. Warner's room ranges from messy to downright chaotic, but he doesn't mind a bit. His own Mover tendencies ensure permission to roam!

Mr. Warner's daily Circle Times are brief, and usually employ movement and music. He starts with an "electric hello," during which each child in turn faces his neighbor for a greeting and handshake. Mr. Warner then gives a quick summary of the day's events and leads some bending and stretching exercises before sending the group on to another activity. Often, Circle Time is the only portion of the day the class spends together; Mr. Warner encourages individual work and the self-selection of games, toys, and projects. While the children roam freely among the classroom's learning centers, Mr. Warner himself moves from pupil to pupil, lending a hand or teaching a skill as necessary.

This kindergarten class takes as many field trips as the teacher can organize. During weeks when nothing special is scheduled, Mr. Warner leads an adventure in the school yard or an excursion to the farthest reaches of the building. Mr. Warner's students are among the youngest in the school, but they're the first to point out the basement entrance, the freight elevator, and the gymnasium's supply room.

Mr. Warner places less emphasis on reading and math readiness than on building his pupils' self-esteem. Children who treat each other well are roundly applauded, and the teacher is quick to offer a pat on the back or a ruffling of the hair to students who reach a personal goal. Mr. Warner employs lots of multisensory and manipulative materials. To reinforce the alphabet, for example, he uses letters cut from sandpaper or letter cookies baked by the class. As might be expected, Mr. Warner is quick to veer from his intended daily program to take advantage of a special event. He might suggest soap-flake snowmen on a snowy day, or he might initiate a crawling race to help celebrate the birth of a baby sister or brother.

Mr. Warner's kindergarten is certainly the least restrictive of the three and makes the most allowances for a Mover's sensitivity and need to wander. But, it's quite likely that the lack of structure would frustrate a Looker child, just as the infrequent social opportunities would unsettle a Listener.

Clearly, every teacher's learning style colors his or her classroom setup and teaching practices, and, depending on the style possessed by a particular kindergarten pupil, the same classroom can be either an ideal learning environment or a place of frustration. If you have no choice regarding your child's kindergarten placement, obviously, you can do little more than share your knowledge of her strengths and weaknesses with the teacher while reinforcing at home the material presented at school. You can also remain alert for signs of discontent or frustration on your child's part, so that you and her teacher can cooperate in a search for solutions. When there are several kindergarten options available, however, it would be wise to let your child's learning style guide your final decision.

Kindergarten for Lookers

Looker children thrive in a classroom that offers lots of the hands-on materials that tap their visual and eye-hand skills. Puzzles, kits, craft supplies, blocks, and games are all favorites of the Looker. In fact, these children enjoy success in nearly every school setting because they are self-directed, attentive pupils who enjoy working alone. Neither the academic demands imposed by private schools nor the full-day schedule now followed by many kindergartens across the country pose a problem for the Looker child. Naturally, most Looker children are happiest with a teacher who is a Looker as well, for they may be made uncomfortable by the emphasis that Listener teachers place on verbal activities or by the lack of structure found in many Movers' classrooms.

Kindergarten for Listeners

Listener five-year-olds also do well in almost any kindergarten setting, because they possess the auditory skills needed to follow directions, communicate easily, and master beginning reading skills. A full-length school day rarely proves too taxing for a Listener; instead, it affords extra time for the socializing she loves. Like Looker children, Listeners can usually meet private schools' academic and behavioral expectations. Listener and Mover teachers are both fine choices for a Listener kindergartener, who might be somewhat frustrated by a Looker teacher's emphasis on neatness, visual tasks, and routine.

Kindergarten for Movers

A Mover kindergartener needs a teacher who can tolerate her high activity level and inability to stay with an activity for more than a brief period. A teacher who is herself a Mover would be the ideal choice, simply because the teaching methods of both Lookers and Listeners so often require a level of organization and attentiveness completely foreign to the Mover child. A Mover might also do well in a private kindergarten that provides one-to-one instruction geared toward special learning needs. She would probably not fare as well in an academically challenging program; since the Mover's slowly developing visual and auditory skills make reading and writing exercises in frustration, disruptive behavior would almost certainly result. Naturally, half-day kindergarten programs are the best option for the busy Mover. Some parents choose to delay their Mover's kindergarten entrance until age six in an effort to circumvent academic and behavioral problems. Doing so gives the child's weaker skills extra time to develop.

Working With Your Child's Teacher

No matter what your kindergartener's learning style, you can help her prepare for the more structured environment, the increased academic demands, and, in many cases, the longer school day of first grade by keeping abreast of her progress in the various skill areas. This is best accomplished by posing direct questions to the kindergarten staff, assessing the resulting information, and then acting on whichever of the teacher's recommendations seems appropriate. In many cases, remedial help will be available within the school. If not, you'll be steered toward the proper personnel in the community. (See Chapter Nine, "Learning Problems and Possibilities," for more information on learning problems.) The following questions should make you privy to a wealth of important information about your child's kindergarten progress.

- Is my child making steady, even progress, or has she reached a plateau in a particular area?

- How are my child's social skills? Has she formed special friendships? Does she share, cooperate, participate, and ask for help when she needs it?

- Does my child pay attention during group lessons?

- Can my child start a project and see it through to completion?

- Does my child show any signs of vision, hearing, or speech problems?

- Are my child's reading- and math-readiness skills sufficient for success in first grade? If not, why not, and how can these skills be improved?

- What are the teacher's recommendations for at-home reinforcement of specific learning skills?

It's important for parents to remember that each learning style has built-in strengths and weaknesses. Listeners, for example, learn to read with ease, but usually struggle a bit with math activities. Most Movers lag behind in several academic areas, but possess a physical confidence lacking in Lookers and Listeners. It's wise to keep your expectations realistic while encouraging your kindergartener to be proud of any and all of her accomplishments.

TECHNIQUES FOR AFFIRMING
AND DEVELOPING LEARNING SKILLS

You've seen that inborn learning patterns influence what, how, and how quickly a five-year-old learns. Without gentle intervention, the inequalities that exist among a child's skill levels at the beginning of her kindergarten year will, in all likelihood, still be present in June! However, if learning style is made a factor in the selection and presentation of a child's toys and experiences outside of school, you can expect her to travel a long way toward more balanced learning. Auditory skills can be sharpened, visual strategies can be taught, and socialization can be encouraged—all through gradual exposure to activities that tap existing learning strengths and pair them with less-favored but equally important activities.

What follows are three sections, each of which first explains the importance of developing the skills associated with one of the learning styles: looking, listening, and moving. In the case of each style, this is followed by a list of games, toys, and activities meant to strengthen the inborn skills of children who favor that style. A second list presents multisensory ideas for developing these skills in children who possess one of the other learning styles, and who will enjoy the most skill improvement when a troublesome concept or task is approached through their preferred sense.

I urge you to introduce these activities in the spirit of recreation, for your kindergartener may already feel taxed by her hours of formal schooling. At home, she may prefer to relax and just play! The following ideas should please both of you in that they combine skill-building with fun.

Building Looker Skills

The kindergartener with well-developed Looker skills is usually a model pupil—quiet, observant, orderly, and patient. Very adept with her hands and possessing a sharp visual memory, a Looker often reads and writes well ahead of schedule.

Because reading and writing are an important part of every academic subject, it stands to reason that every child who is exposed to activities designed to strengthen visual skills is likely to enjoy a corresponding improvement in school work. While this improvement is most easily achieved with Lookers, who are sight-oriented by nature, Listener and Mover children can be expected to gain even more from the development of Looker skills. And, of course, there are many ways to tailor Looker activities to the sensory preference of your kindergartener.

ENHANCING A KINDERGARTENER'S EXISTING LOOKER SKILLS

■ Provide an ever-changing array of puzzles by borrowing from the library, trading with friends, recruiting hand-me-downs, and encouraging your child to mount and cut up pictures for use as homemade jigsaw puzzles.

■ Begin a simple scrapbook about a subject that interests your child. She can start by collecting, cutting, and pasting photographs, illustrations, and large-type words on sheets of colored paper. The pages can then be strung together with bright ribbon or yarn.

■ Check toy and school-supply stores for connect-the-dot workbooks.

Once your child has drawn the lines needed to complete the picture, she'll have something new to color.

Play simple card games with your child, such as "Go Fish," "Crazy Eights," and "Old Maid."

Encourage your child to create pictures with parquetry blocks or a magnetic mosaic set.

Video Technology's *Whiz Kid* is a perfect first computer for five- and six-year-olds.

With *Light Brite* by Milton Bradley, your child can insert colored plastic pegs into a picture outline that has been mounted above a small bulb, making the entire picture "light up."

Offer a paint-by-number or color-by-number set, which allows your child to produce detailed, professional-looking results.

Parker Brothers' *Boggle Junior* has labeled picture cards, below which the child must reproduce the same word using letter cubes. A timer and an optional word-cover add an element of difficulty.

Perfection by Milton Bradley is a timed puzzle. The child sets the timer and hurries to insert an array of shapes and forms into their proper places before the timer's shutoff causes them to pop back out again.

Buy a paddle to which a ball has been attached by a long rubber string. This toy is an old-fashioned way to challenge a child's eye-hand coordination.

Mona Brookes' *Drawing With Children*, published by Jeremy P. Tarcher (Los Angeles, 1986), teaches children to perceive objects as combinations of five basic shapes. Encouraging the use of these shapes in your child's drawing will enable her to tackle more difficult subjects with more sophisticated results.

Prang's *96 Crayons* contains many unusual shades that will delight your young artist. Fluorescent yellow, limestone gray, and melon are just a few.

The Games Gang's *Pictionary Junior* uses children's own drawings as clues to words and phrases.

Domino Rally by Pressman involves the construction of a domino run, complete with stairs, curves, and various "trick" devices. The beginner set is perfect for five-year-old eyes and hands.

ENCOURAGING THE DEVELOPMENT OF LOOKER SKILLS IN LISTENER AND MOVER KINDERGARTENERS

Provide an inexpensive camera so that your child can photograph the important people in her life and start her own photo album.

School-supply stores carry workbooks of simple mazes to which you can add stories—"The poor, confused rabbit is lost in the forest. Let's help him find his family"—or action—"Let's race this pencil around the track without crashing into any walls"—to increase the mazes' appeal.

Rent children's videos. Movers love cartoons and action stories, while Listeners like interesting characters and story lines.

Provide a *View-Master* viewer. Most of your child's favorite stories and characters are available on picture reels.

During a quiet moment, do visualizations together. You might say, "Let's close our eyes and pretend we're in your room. Can you see your bed? What color is your blanket? What pictures are on the wallpaper?"

Make it a practice for family members to share last night's dreams over breakfast or to recall their favorite day's events at bedtime.

Provide a kaleidoscope. You and your child can take turns hunting for the different shapes and patterns, and describing what you see.

Milton Bradley's *Don't Break the Ice!* requires no reading. Children use tiny mallets to knock plastic cubes from a raised frame. The object of the game is to select cubes that enable the Iceman, who rests above, to stay in place.

To encourage the use of scissors, draw a heavy black shape—a square, rectangle, or oval—around those more-complicated forms and figures that would frustrate your child. Encourage her to cut along your outlines.

■ *Stamp-A-Story*, distributed by Troll Learn & Play (through catalogue only), contains thirty-two rubber picture stamps, an ink pad, and an idea book. Your child can create a story, note cards, gift wrap, and the like.

■ Spice up a game of checkers with *Dino Checkers*, distributed by Childcraft (through catalogue only). In this game, the stegosaurus team takes on the brontosaurus team on a checkerboard made to look like prehistoric terrain.

■ Take a pair of binoculars to a sporting event, and encourage your child to use them to view the game and her surroundings.

■ Kenner's *Play-Doh Fun Factory*, which includes a device that presses the dough into ten different shapes, will encourage your child to work with different colors.

■ Make simple matching exercises for your child by lining one edge of a sheet of paper with groups of dots, dice-style, and the opposite edge with corresponding numerals. Encourage your child to match the pairs by drawing lines from one to the other. (She can also match upper-case letters with lower-case letters, or pictures with their corresponding initial sounds.)

■ Provide coloring books with a theme that appeals to your child. Nursery rhyme and story coloring books are perfect for Listeners, while most Movers like books about vehicles and travel or popular super-heroes.

Building Listener Skills

Listener skills are what help a five-year-old follow directions, remain attentive, comprehend the basics of phonics, and foster friendships through conversation. Therefore, every kindergartener, no matter what her learning style, stands to gain from activities that exercise her language and auditory skills.

Naturally, Listener children are the easiest "sell" for parents wishing to offer sound-related games and toys, as these activities appeal to a

Listener's favored sense. Expanding the Listener skills of Lookers and Movers takes a bit more creativity, but can usually be achieved by pairing Listener activities with a bit of the stimulation the child prefers. For example, playing "Simon Says" combines listening and moving. Here are some suggestions to help you stretch your own child's Listener skills.

ENHANCING A KINDERGARTENER'S EXISTING LISTENER SKILLS

Make up a game in which each player repeats and embellishes the words of the previous player. Try something like, "I'm going on vacation, and in my suitcase, I will pack . . . ," or, "I'm building a sandwich, and inside, I will put. . . ." As each player adds a suggestion, the responses grow longer. This memory game encourages a child's auditory recall while eliciting conversation.

Games such as Trivia Games' *Tot Trivia* will stretch your child's vocabulary and increase her knowledge of general information.

Enlarge your child's vocabulary development by substituting specific names for generic terms. Flowers, for instance, might be referred to as "jonquils," "pansies," "geraniums," or the like.

Permit your child to answer the telephone at home. You may wish to practice various greetings and responses beforehand on a toy telephone.

Tongue Twisters, distributed by Childcraft (through catalogue only), is a game in which children listen to an amusing tongue twister—"Wiggly worms wear woolly hats in winter," for example—and then match what is heard to pictures on a game board.

When traveling by car or taking a walk, encourage your child to count aloud as high as she can go.

Select books to read aloud that are a bit beyond your child's intellectual level. Often, this introduces her to new concepts, causing her to think in new ways.

Seek out beginning reader books that teach basic reading skills through phonics, or "sounding out." *Books by Bob* by Bob Book Publications (West Linn, OR, 1990) is an excellent starter set.

Provide a set of toy walkie-talkies, and exchange messages with your child from different parts of the house.

While you watch from nearby, allow your child to place her own order at a store counter or purchase her own movie ticket. Practice at home first to build her confidence.

When you're working or playing side by side, make a game out of naming words and their opposites—"black/white" or "over/under," for instance.

Ask your child to dial the local Time and Temperature number, and have her repeat to you the information she receives.

Treat your child to a few vocabulary words from a foreign language. *Berlitz Jr. Language Programs* include simple workbooks and tapes in French and Spanish.

Tell a "round robin" story. One person starts a story, stopping after a few sentences. Then, someone else adds to it without repeating the previous player's words, and so on. The story doesn't have to make sense!

Encourage your child to write letters using inventive spelling— words spelled as they sound—and her own illustrations. Help her mail the letters, and ask a few family members and friends to write back.

ENCOURAGING THE DEVELOPMENT OF LISTENER SKILLS IN LOOKER AND MOVER KINDERGARTENERS

Provide a tape player and an action story on cassette. Earphones will help your child focus her attention.

When reading a story together, point to the pictures and ask your child to help tell the story. You can prompt her by inserting transitional phrases, like, "The next thing that happened was . . ." or "At last. . . ."

Choose action stories about adventurers, sports figures, and "bad guys" for Mover children. Lookers most enjoy fantasy stories, with elves, fairies, and other magical characters that can come alive in the child's imagination.

Play "Simon Says" for listening practice. Movers, especially, will love obeying Simon's various commands: "Touch your toes," "Jump up and down," "Turn around three times," etc.

Make a Word Book with your child by cutting out pictures of unusual or favorite items—armoires and canopy beds, or ships and planes—and pasting them in a scrapbook.

When you say a word that's new to your child, define it in the same sentence, as in, "Those twinkling lights are blinking on and off."

Make a game of identifying things by their sound alone—a jackhammer on the next street, or a nearby woodpecker, for example—or purchase a sound-and-picture matching game that provides these noises on tape. *Listening Lotto*, distributed by Lakeshore (through catalogue only), is one example.

Play "What Am I?" with your child, asking her to identify an object from the image created by your words. You might say, "I'm round and fairly flat, with a handle and a cover. I'm silver, and I sometimes get very hot. Can you guess what I am? I'm a frying pan!"

Portable Party Mike, distributed by Troll Learn & Play (through catalogue only), is a hand-held microphone with sixteen different settings to transform your child's voice into that of a chipmunk, a rock star, etc.

Questron's *Little Q* is a hand-held wand that beeps or buzzes in response to matches made in a picture book. Be sure to ask your child to say the pictures' names aloud.

Rebus stories have tiny pictures within the text, each of which stands for a word in the story. Ideals Publishing's *The House That Jack Built*, by Elizabeth Salconer (Nashville, 1990), and Alfred A. Knopf's *Pony and Bear Are Friends*, by Sigrid Heuck (New York, 1990), are examples of two rebus books that can be found in many libraries and bookstores. Encourage your child to "read" these stories along with you.

Schedule a weekly trip to the library, and encourage your child to pick out stories to be read to her at home.

Offer some examples of rhyming words. Then say a word and ask your child to think of a rhyme as quickly as she can. Then switch roles.

Mr. Music Maker's *Telephone Intercom Set* contains two hand-held units, complete with signal alerts, that are connected by thirty feet of wire for all kinds of play.

A set of toy dishes and utensils can help your child verbalize the roles of baker, chef, or storekeeper.

Building Mover Skills

While Looker and Listener skills come into play in the classroom, Mover skills are what enable a child to shine in other areas—areas important to her social, if not her academic, well-being. Kindergarteners who display a Mover's coordination, agility, and speed are gym-class, backyard, and playground standouts who attain a certain satisfying status that only the admiration of peers can bring.

Movers, certainly, will greet with delight any parental attempts to increase tactile stimulation. By working in an auditory or visual element, you're likely to see similar improvement in the gross motor skills of Listeners and Lookers. These ideas should help you encourage Mover skills in your five-year-old learner.

ENHANCING A KINDERGARTENER'S EXISTING MOVER SKILLS

Teach your child to use a jump rope and a *Hula Hoop*.

Help your child plant her own garden in a barrel or a corner of the yard. Provide a child-sized rake, hoe, shovel, and watering can.

Encourage outdoor play by offering sprinklers, water guns, and toys like Wham-O's *Slip and Slide* in summer; and sleds, child-sized snow shovels, and ice skates in winter.

Kick, pass, and throw a child-sized football or soccer ball.

Make a parade by marching and playing rhythm-band instruments.

The *Nerf* foam basketball is safe and fun, and there's even a suction-cup net available for indoor play.

Purchase a pair of child-sized in-line skates, and accompany your child down the street or to the local rink.

Play a game of charades, using exaggerated body movements to depict words, animals, and occupations.

Enroll your child in a swimming program at the local YM/YWCA or YM/YWHA.

Introduce your child to miniature golf. Many cities and towns even have indoor courses for foul-weather play.

Provide your child with her first organized-sports experience by signing her up for a community soccer or T-ball team.

Jog around the block or take a hike together.

Check with your local bowling alley to see whether it provides "bumpers"—guards that deflect the ball from the gutter. If so, take your child bowling!

Teach your child to play "High Water, Low Water." In this game, a rope is stretched between two players who instruct a third player to jump over the rope by saying "high water," or to crawl beneath it by saying "low water."

When your child plays in a sandbox, provide an accompanying bucket of water to add a new, if somewhat messy, element to the experience.

ENCOURAGING THE DEVELOPMENT OF MOVER SKILLS IN LOOKER AND LISTENER KINDERGARTENERS

Enroll your child in a gymnastics class or beginner swim class, first making sure that the teacher has a gentle approach and discourages competition.

Draw a hopscotch board on the sidewalk, and teach your child to play.

Turn a nursery rhyme or familiar story into a mini-drama, and act it out with your child. Demonstrate that gestures can be used to communicate, in place of words.

Encourage outdoor play by offering a three-wheeled scooter, or a bicycle with training wheels.

Suggest that your child invite neighborhood children to her yard for active games like tag or hide-and-seek.

Pretend to be a certain animal, and invent a story line to go with your pantomiming: "Come on, little frog. Let's jump over to that puddle and see if any other frogs are there."

Workshop by Little Tikes is a child-sized workbench that contains plastic nails, nuts, bolts, and screws, as well as the necessary tools.

Fun Jumpers by G. Pierce Toy Company are jumping shoes that look like frogs. They enable a child to bounce around on large rubber-covered springs.

Use a yardstick or broom handle to play "Over and Under the Stick." Encourage your child to climb or jump over or slide beneath a stick, which you can alternately raise and lower.

Take your child to the park or playground frequently. This will delight her social side while encouraging gross motor play.

Ask your child to help you with heavy cleaning or yard work. Keep a conversation going during your efforts.

Suggest slow-moving games, like backyard croquet, or games that require as much luck as skill, like dropping pennies into a jar at the bottom of a water-filled bucket.

Convince your child that her doll or bear needs some fresh air. Accompany her as she pushes or pulls the toy in a stroller or wagon.

Invest in a toy delivery truck, emergency vehicle, mail truck, or school bus, and encourage your child to act out story lines with it.

Pack some flashlights into a backpack and accompany your child on an after-dark adventure. You can catch fireflies, stargaze, and chase each other's shadows en route.

As you scan the above lists of toys and activities, remember that they are intended only as guidelines to help you round out your kindergartener's learning skills. If a suggested toy happens to be something that you can recall disliking as a child, or if the presence of an exploring baby in the house makes you extra cautious about toy purchases, feel free to pass certain items by! Similarly, if an activity from a skill-enhancement list aimed at other learners seems ideal for your child, don't hesitate to give it a try. Certainly, your discretion and knowledge of your child's tastes should be a factor in the toy-selection process. It's not necessary, nor is it advisable, to bombard her with every suggested item!

Be aware that you may not see immediate improvement in your child's learning skills. In fact, depending on her personality, learning style, and initial skill level, it may take many weeks to effect a noticeable difference. But, regardless of whether improvement takes five days or five months, offering the right activities and playthings *will* round out your kindergartener's academic and social development, boosting her self-esteem in the bargain.

Learning Style QuickCheck for Kindergarteners, Five to Six Years of Age

Directions: Check each of the statements below that best describes your child. Then, total each of the three columns and compare results. You're likely to find your responses concentrated in one or two columns, clearly indicating the learning style possessed by your kindergartener.

Looker	Listener	Mover

1. Communication: When my kindergartener wishes to express herself . . .

Looker	Listener	Mover
☐ She uses simple language.	☐ She uses adultlike speech patterns.	☐ Her speech is difficult to understand.
☐ She mispronounces some words and sounds.	☐ She uses sentences that are structurally correct.	☐ She speaks in short, grammatically incorrect sentences.
☐ She omits adverbs and prepositions.	☐ She tells elaborate stories.	☐ She acts out events instead of talking about them.

2. Favorite Toys and Pastimes: When my kindergartener plays . . .

Looker	Listener	Mover
☐ She likes puzzles and board games.	☐ She likes records and tapes.	☐ She likes to play outdoors.
☐ She enjoys computers and calculators.	☐ She likes books and fantasy play.	☐ She enjoys swinging, sliding, and climbing.
☐ She learns new things by watching.	☐ She learns new things by listening to instructions.	☐ She finds full-body uses for almost every toy.

3. Fine Motor Skills: When my kindergartener uses her hands . . .

Looker	Listener	Mover
☐ She prints neatly.	☐ She has acceptable printing.	☐ She finds printing very difficult.
☐ She cuts, colors, and pastes with ease.	☐ She talks to herself while working.	☐ She reverses many letters and numbers.
☐ She produces neat, attractive artwork.	☐ She produces acceptable artwork.	☐ Her artwork is very messy.

4. Gross Motor Skills: When my kindergartener moves about . . .

☐ She chooses table games over outside play.

☐ She does more talking than actual playing.

☐ She prefers outside play to table games.

☐ She chooses games such as badminton, which requires eye-hand coordination.

☐ She chooses games such as "Bluebird" and "Simon Says," which involve verbal interaction.

☐ She is very well coordinated.

☐ She likes games with set rules, such as "Mother, May I?"

☐ She talks herself through activities.

☐ She never walks when she can run or climb.

5. Social Skills: When my kindergartener mixes with other children . . .

☐ She tends to be a loner within groups.

☐ She thrives on her friendships.

☐ She is sociable, but not very verbal.

☐ She watches to see what's expected of her before taking part.

☐ She may get into trouble for too much talking during class time.

☐ She may get into trouble for poking and hitting during class time.

☐ She warms up slowly to new people.

☐ She often answers for others and is somewhat bossy.

☐ She likes to roughhouse.

6. Emotions: When it comes to my kindergartener's feelings . . .

☐ She is not very emotional.

☐ She talks freely about her emotions.

☐ She is emotionally needy and easily hurt.

☐ She has trouble understanding others' emotional outbursts.

☐ She confronts others about her feelings.

☐ She reacts with anger rather than shame or regret when disciplined.

7. Memory: When my kindergartener learns . . .

☐ She reproduces letters and numbers from memory.

☐ She learns best by rote. She knows her address and phone number.

☐ She has trouble remembering.

☐ She remembers what she has been shown.

☐ She knows the sounds made by the letters of the alphabet.

☐ She is easily distracted.

8. At School: When my kindergartener is in the classroom . . .

☐ She dresses neatly and likes to stay clean.

☐ Her appearance is neither messy nor overly neat.

☐ She is unconcerned with her appearance, and often appears bedraggled.

☐ She keeps her work area very neat.

☐ She has to be told to clean up her work area.

☐ She works amidst a huge mess, cluttering her work space within minutes.

☐ She chooses blocks, puzzles, or arts and crafts during free time.

☐ She is attentive and agreeable.

☐ She is very active during play.

☐ She warms up slowly to new situations.

☐ She leads most discussions, and often reports misbehavior to the teacher.

☐ She fidgets and squirms when seated.

Totals: _____Looker   _____Listener   _____Mover

Chapter Six

Learning Styles in First Grade

No matter what type of preschool or kindergarten experience a six-year-old may have under his belt, first grade represents a radical change. Spending over thirty hours a week away from home is often a novel experience in itself, even before academics, art, music, and physical education are added to the picture. First graders must assume a degree of responsibility for their behavior, possessions, movement about the school building, and completion of tasks that, until now, rested on the shoulders of their teachers.

Some first graders are better equipped to cope with this new responsibility than others. You see, organizational, academic, and social skills—all of which result from years of learning and playing according to inborn sensory preferences—differ greatly among six- and seven-year-olds. Children who have been visually oriented since birth, for example, usually learn beginning reading and writing skills with ease. Yet, these Lookers' conversational skills may not approach those of a child naturally attuned to the auditory, and Lookers also lack the superior coordination of a child who favors touch and movement.

Chapter Six illustrates exactly how learning style colors the first-grade experience by following the development of three children—a Looker, a Listener, and a Mover—throughout the course of their school year. A Learning Style QuickCheck for First Graders is included to help you identify the way your own child absorbs information (see page 153).

This chapter also takes a subject-by-subject look at the relationship of learning style to first-grade school performance, and suggests ways to effectively communicate with your child's teacher. Tips are included to help you select extracurricular activities with an eye to learning-style enhancement, and strategies are presented to help your child apply his preferred way of learning to the mastery of reading, writing, spelling, and math. Finally, you'll find lists of specially chosen toys and techniques, designed to sprinkle your child's at-home play time with activities that will encourage his interests and strengths while improving those weaker skills that are part and parcel of his learning style.

Whatever a child's first-grade experience may be, his time at home is an important component of the "big picture." For some, home provides relief from a stressful academic pace or a level of socialization that is at once fascinating and overwhelming. For others, it may be a place that's too quiet or offers limited opportunities to burn off energy. Making your child's at-home learning a low-pressure, made-to-order, fun experience, while allowing him plenty of unstructured time, will enable him to be most receptive to your skill-enhancement efforts and help you both get the greatest benefit from the time you spend together. Enjoy!

A LOOK AT THREE LEARNERS

Christopher, Angela, and Thomas have just begun first grade. The three children are veterans of the same preschool and kindergarten classes, and happen to be almost exactly the same age; each child turned six in early July. Despite these similarities and further likenesses stemming from their home environments, the children entered first grade with three distinctly different sets of expectations and readiness skills. It is their inborn learning styles that have made the difference. Christopher, you see, is naturally drawn to the visual aspects of his surroundings; Angela responds to language and sounds; and Thomas responds to motion and touch. Not every child exhibits the traits of a single learning style in this manner. Looker-Mover and Looker-Listener combinations, for example, are not at all unusual. However, for the sake of clarity and to highlight the characteristics of each type of learner, our case-study children will each display a "pure" style. Let's take a look at our three learners as they begin their adjustment to the first grade.

Six Years of Age

Meet Christopher. Looker Christopher has a highly developed sense of order. Before he leaves for school each day, he checks his room to make sure that his toys and possessions have been neatly put away. When he arrives at school, he goes straight to his desk to organize its contents.

Christopher is equally fussy about his personal appearance. He selects his outfits carefully and becomes quite upset if his clothing gets wrinkled or soiled.

Christopher is a loner. Reserved by nature, he does not make friends easily; he is happiest playing by himself because doing so frees him from the strain of socializing. Christopher enjoys the role of observer. He is fascinated by the interactions and play of other children, but remains on the sidelines as though unsure of how to join in their games.

Christopher's gross motor skills are about average for his age. But, rather than engage in full-body play, he is certain to find and devote his attention to some visual aspect of the activity at hand. When he's at the shore, he shuns the water, preferring instead to write in the sand. When he goes bowling, he shows more interest in the automatic scoring device than in taking his turn. At the park, he sits motionless on a swing, eyes darting back and forth so as not to miss anything. Wherever there's noise, activity, and the potential for messiness, you'll find a somewhat daunted Christopher watching intently from a safe distance.

Christopher's fine motor skills are excellent. He loves to draw and write, for he finds his sophisticated finished products very gratifying. Not surprisingly, Christopher's superior eye-hand coordination makes him a whiz at video games and the computer. He is also adept at mazes, connect-the-dot pictures, and pencil-and-paper games of every kind. And Christopher adores picture books, as he has since babyhood, and greatly enjoys playing cards and board games. Building sets and children's quiz shows and magazines take up the remainder of Christopher's play time.

At the start of first grade, Christopher has quite a large "sight" vocabulary—that is, he can recognize a number of words from memory. He doesn't hesitate to guess at unfamiliar words, but is rarely correct unless the words appear in the context of a sentence. Christopher can add and subtract up to ten with accuracy by envisioning a line of sequential numbers and moving an imaginary "counter" ahead or back as needed. He is also quick to grasp new concepts because he is able to commit to memory everything he is shown.

Christopher's adjustment to first grade has so far been slow. He has trouble listening for long periods, but even when his attention wanders, his good behavior and respectfulness continue. Although at first Christopher was tense and silent much of the time, he is now beginning to feel more at home with his new teacher and classmates, and, as a result, more tolerant of group activities. Certainly, some of his skills are stronger than others. Still, Christopher stands to gain a great deal from first grade on the strength of his visual orientation alone.

Meet Angela. Listener Angela's work and play areas are as cluttered as Christopher's are tidy. To her, the game at hand is much more important than the surroundings in which it takes place; and besides, much of her pretense involves a myriad of props and players, be they real or stuffed. Children gravitate toward Angela, for they admire her self-assurance and the ease with which she talks to older children and adults. Angela usually turns her own adoring gaze toward the friends of her ten-year-old sister. Because she copies their clothing and hair styles and mimics their speech, Angela has become somewhat of a trend setter among the first-grade set.

Angela's sophisticated vocabulary and confident demeanor make her a "natural" at masterminding role-playing games. She loves this sort of play, and the fact that she usually reserves the role of Queen, Boss, President, or Leader for herself adds to her enjoyment. When she's alone, Angela gravitates toward the TV, the tape player, and her toy microphone.

Angela's fine motor skills—cutting, coloring, printing, and the like—are acceptable for her age. At school, she often heads for the crafts corner during free time, not necessarily to work, but because there's always a group gathered there with whom she can try out her play ideas. Her own artistic efforts are not particularly detailed or imaginative, but she's good at instructing other children. Things are not much different out-doors, for there, again, Angela views play time more as a means to socialize than as exercise.

Angela is very much at home in first grade. Reading poses no problem, because our Listener's knowledge of the different letter sounds enables her to sound out even multisyllabic words. Math comes just as easily because of her immediate recall of addition and subtraction facts. The teacher encourages Angela's outspokenness about her opinions and feelings, but has to reprimand her almost daily for general talkativeness and a tendency to speak for everyone in her class. Angela's auditory recall enables her to follow even the most complicated directions, but it comes as no surprise that social Angela is quickly bored with seat work and individual projects. Nevertheless, Angela is so rewarded by her everyday academic success and built-in circle of friends that she can't wait to get to school in the morning.

Meet Thomas. First grade is not as much fun for Mover Thomas. In fact, it's more of an ordeal. This active, sensitive six-year-old chafes at the constraints of classroom life and is repeatedly frustrated when his efforts to "buck the system"—by falling back on the full-body activity he craves—meet with failure.

Thomas tends to mumble when he speaks, mispronouncing words

and using short, poorly sequenced sentences. When he has an urgent need to communicate an idea, you can count on Thomas to express himself physically rather than verbally. The urge to push, grab, hug, and wrestle strikes him long before he thinks of talking things out. Naturally, many of Thomas's classmates keep their distance for fear of becoming one of his targets. The other children are, in fact, slightly horrified by Thomas's shenanigans and the frequency with which he is scolded by the teacher.

Things are different at home and outdoors, for where there are obstacles to scale and balls to throw and kick, agile Thomas emerges as a leader. He has a group of pals who meet each day on the playground for races or a game of tag. And the neighborhood boys flock to Thomas's backyard, because, when school's out, that's where you'll always find him, climbing trees, tackling a buddy, or playing war. Most of the boys' parents, unsure of how to deal with Thomas's frequent tears and wild behavior, discourage his presence in their homes.

Thomas has trouble with printing. He holds the pencil incorrectly and presses so hard that he snaps not just the point but often the pencil itself. Many of his letters are reversed, and none is properly shaped or sized. Art projects, free-time activities, and any class work that requires sitting still are nonstop struggles for Thomas, for he has trouble staying with any task that doesn't allow him to move about. So far, Thomas has enjoyed only two class activities—the creation of a "Things With Wheels" mural, which focused on a favorite topic of his and enabled him to roam while working, and the class's train trip to a duck pond several towns away.

Thomas cannot read yet. He recognizes his name and that of his brother, but because he still confuses the letters of the alphabet and has trouble remembering their sounds, he can neither recall nor sound out other words that he encounters. He can manage simple addition by counting on his fingers, but he can't envision number groupings the way Christopher can and is completely baffled by math word problems.

Thomas is well aware of his academic shortcomings, but is powerless to change his activity level and attention span. In school, he requires a place to work where he cannot create too many distractions for others, a place to calm down when he becomes upset, and lots of support and encouragement in the form of pats, hugs, and handshakes. First grade promises to be quite a trial for Thomas.

What kind of learner is *your* first grader? Is he a Looker, attracted to color, movement, and shapes, as Christopher is? Is he more like Listener

Angela, highly attuned to sounds and language? Or is he drawn to sensations and motion, much like Mover Thomas? The Learning Style Quick-
Check for First Graders on page 153 will give you the answer. Just review
the traits in each of the three columns, checking any that are characteristic
of your first grader. After you total the checks in each column, you should
have a clear picture of your child's sensory preference.

HOW LOOKER, LISTENER, AND MOVER
FIRST GRADERS DEVELOP

At age six, Christopher, Angela, and Thomas's various aptitudes and
weaknesses—all of which are determined by the way each child has absorbed and responded to environmental stimuli since birth—are already
obvious. As we follow our learners through their first-grade year, you will
see that without intervention, each of them will succeed in those subject
areas that "fit" with his or her learning preference. But, by the same token,
the children's struggles will persist—and, in fact, increase—in subjects that
call for skills they do not naturally possess. Let's see how Christopher,
Angela, and Thomas fare as they move through the first grade.

Seven Years of Age

Christopher. Throughout the school year, Christopher continues to prefer
his own company to group play. He has one special friend with whom he
plays during free time, but if that child is absent or tries to vary their games
by introducing a new rule or a third child, Chris wanders off in search of a
solo activity. When spoken to, Christopher expresses himself clearly but
simply. Yet, despite his reticence, Christopher is roundly admired for his
prowess at computer and video games—prowess assured by his superior
eye-hand coordination.

Chris's parents encourage his creative side. They have enrolled him in
a drawing class, and they make sure that he has plenty of models and
craft supplies to keep him busy at home. And, of course, Christopher
remains interested in books, magazines, board games, and card playing.

This spring, at his parents' urging, Christopher joined a T-ball team.
He is certainly no star in the making—in fact, he hates getting sweat and
dust on his uniform and is almost always "out at first"—but Chris adores
playing the role of statistician when it's his turn on the bench. With
T-ball, just as in other areas of his life, Christopher has a great concern
for the rules of the game.

Christopher's progress in reading has slowed somewhat. Without the sounding-out skills needed to master phonics, he cannot decipher the two- and three-syllable words that have cropped up in his reader. Chris still relies on visual memory when the text is simple, and this same ability comes into play when he enjoys comics and the puzzle and hidden-message books his teacher provides for free-time use.

Christopher is enjoying great success with math. He adds and subtracts quickly and accurately, because he can envision groups of numbers in his mind. He has immediate recall of the names and meanings of the symbols for addition (+), subtraction (–), and equals (=), and has quickly grasped the idea behind geometric shapes, graphs, and measurements. He is adept at completing the dittos and workbooks that confound so many of his classmates, and he delights in his teacher's use of visual feedback—stars, stickers, and written words of praise.

Christopher is still an observer. He is particularly attuned to the misbehavior of others, and has taken to biting his nails during tense moments. Christopher becomes impatient with long listening tasks and has trouble absorbing complicated instructions. When Chris is taught, he requires a demonstration instead of verbal directions.

At year's end, Christopher's teacher notes that he sometimes seems to tune her out with a blank stare or closed eyes. (Actually, he is at work forming mental images.) She mentions that he is a perfectionist and should be less critical of himself and more assertive about his ideas, rather than parroting what he deems to be a "proper" opinion. It appears that Christopher will need help with his social and auditory skills to ensure his becoming a happy, confident second grader.

Angela. As Listener Angela moves through first grade, she becomes more sociable than ever. She has play dates almost every day—in fact, she hates to play alone—and attends a constant round of birthday parties and sleep-overs. She makes and receives phone calls quite regularly, and impatiently counts the days between Brownie troop and church school meetings. Angela continues to be talkative to a fault, for her impulsive chattiness often disturbs the teacher's lesson or her classmates' work. Nevertheless, she expresses herself beautifully, voicing sophisticated opinions in precise adultlike language.

Angela's fine motor skills have changed little since September. Her printing and artwork are acceptable, nothing more. She still reverses an occasional letter, and seems unaware of misspellings in her written work. She is enrolled in a crafts class, but attends only when her friends do, because her real interest lies in scheduling after-class play dates.

Outdoors, Angela likes activities that she can share with her friends, like skating, bicycling, and jump rope games. She signed up for a soccer team earlier in the year, but was bored by practice sessions and found the pace of the games so difficult to follow that she eventually dropped out.

Angela's sounding-out skills have kept her at the top of her class in reading. She is particularly good at reading aloud, but as the books become more difficult, Angela is losing her place on the page with increasing frequency. She has similar trouble following the lines of problems printed on math work sheets, though she rarely makes an error when the class does their addition and subtraction aloud or solves word problems as a group.

Angela still asks a lot of questions and makes occasional inappropriate comments in class. She is as distracted as ever by noise and talking, and has great difficulty keeping her mind on visual tasks for more than a few minutes. Angela's teacher suggests that the child learn to become more organized, and mentions that Angela's school work would improve if she expended less energy on socialization and more on her written work. It appears that Angela, like Christopher, would profit from some skill development before tackling second grade.

Thomas. As the school year progresses, Mover Thomas becomes somewhat more communicative. He is still difficult to understand, but his sentences are longer and he uses his hands to help convey difficult messages. Nonetheless, Thomas is not very articulate. Rather than grope for an elusive word, he refers to objects in general terms, like "The thing over there," or "My whatchamacallit."

Thomas has become a tease. He seems to have a sixth sense that enables him to zero in on a child's sore points, and he enjoys wrinkling the paper of a neighboring neatnik or placing his chair a scant inch away from that of a child who needs a lot of space. When Thomas's classmates are working, he often intrudes with a bear hug, a poke, or a tug of the hair.

Thomas shows great pride in his accomplishments on those occasions when he completes an assignment, but becomes frustrated and angry when he finds that he can't sustain such a work pace. These days, Thomas's printing is more legible, but he is a long way from keeping his letters within the confines of the lines, and he still reverses many letters when printing from memory. Few of Thomas's written words are spelled correctly, for he hasn't yet grasped the phonetic skills necessary to make an educated guess. Not surprisingly, Thomas still reads on a level appropriate for a kindergartener. Even at the school year's end, he has a very small sight vocabulary, and loses his place on pages with more than one line of copy. Lately, he has taken to trailing his finger along the page to follow each sentence word by word.

Thomas uses his fingers in math, as well. In an effort to reinforce the concepts of addition and subtraction, his teacher has provided a number line and an abacus at the back of the room. While these are somewhat helpful to Thomas, they provide new distractions in that he now has a built-in excuse to walk around instead of working at his seat.

As he approaches seven years of age, Thomas loves skateboarding, karate, and soccer, though he frequently ignores the rules inherent in the latter two. He signs up for a team sport every season and is usually the undisputed star of the team, but his coaches will all attest to the fact that during practices and games, Thomas is always either making or getting into some sort of trouble. He simply cannot tolerate waiting of any sort.

Thomas has begun to visit the school's speech-language pathologist for help with pronunciation. He has little difficulty with the twenty-minute sessions, mainly because he is the only student present and is helped to concentrate on his work by the therapist's unwavering attention. In class, he finishes his work only when the teacher stands beside his desk to keep him at his task. Thomas loves physical education, art class, and the hands-on projects his class does during science lessons; he loathes the sitting and listening required by music class. Thomas's teacher is rightfully concerned about his inability to adhere to rules, keep track of belongings and assignments, and remember the sequence of months-old routines. Much of Thomas's behavior and many of his skills are more typical of a four-year-old, and his teacher makes an end-of-year recommendation that he be evaluated for possible learning disabilities and placement in a transitional class before advancing to second grade. (For an in-depth look at learning problems such as Thomas's, please refer to Chapter Nine, "Learning Problems and Possibilities.")

THE RELATIONSHIP OF LEARNING STYLE TO A FIRST GRADER'S SCHOOL PERFORMANCE

The academic and fine arts material covered during the primary grades can be divided into Looker and Listener subjects. Only physical education employs a child's Mover skills. Because different senses and learning skills are called into play during class time, each lesson's appeal to a child is largely dependent on his inborn learning preference. The discussions that follow separate first-grade Looker subjects from Listener subjects while describing the visual or auditory components of each area of study. Sample first- and last-quarter reports cards are also provided to illustrate the different academic experiences faced by Lookers, Listeners, and Movers.

Looker Subjects

Considering the many visual aids used in academic work, it's easy to see why Looker skills are so necessary for classroom success. *Spelling*, for instance, is primarily a visual exercise. At first, most Listener children are good spellers, for their reliance upon sounding-out skills is sufficient to reproduce the simple one-syllable words that constitute the bulk of beginner readers and basic writing exercises. But, the English language is awash with exceptions to the rules of phonics, and it is the Looker, able to envision a word's spelling in his mind's eye, who remains a good speller.

Handwriting is also a subject at which Lookers excel. For beginning writers, in particular, a good visual memory is needed to recall the various letter and number shapes before putting pencil to paper. Well-developed eye-hand coordination is then necessary to reproduce the letters and numbers exactly as recalled. These skills also serve Looker children during *art* class. When designing and creating a project, Lookers are able to envision a finished product before putting their deft hands and fingers to work to give their plan life.

Math requires Looker skills in addition to the Listener skills described on page 131. Looker children can recall the symbols used in addition and subtraction (+, −, and =), and use them as visual cues to the operation being performed. Lookers can make immediate sense of graphs, and can call to mind pictures of number values—two stacks of six blocks each, for example, when adding six plus six. Children with strong Looker skills can also easily visualize various geometric shapes and form mental images of the actions involved in story problems: "Jim had six apples but gave two to Meg. How many does he have left?"

Listener Subjects

Of all the subjects that require Listener skills, perhaps *reading* is the most essential. The mastery of reading requires that a child tune into and discriminate between different letter sounds, and then blend these sounds to form spoken words. Even when reading to himself, a child "speaks" each word in his mind. Surprisingly, the earliest readers are usually Lookers, who recognize printed words by sheer visual recall. However, Looker children eventually fall behind their classmates as the reading material becomes progressively more difficult. As sight readers, they can pronounce only those words they have seen before. They lack the Listener skills needed to deal with unfamiliar letter combinations.

Primary music is also a Listener subject. In most cases, the teacher first tells the story behind each new piece of music. The children are then expected to listen to instrumental compositions and memorize lyrics and tempos that become longer and increasingly complex as the school year progresses. Children with below-average auditory skills are hard pressed to listen and vocalize in this manner. In fact, even Listeners may have trouble with either music reading or tone recognition, as each skill originates in a different brain hemisphere, and the two hemispheres are not always equally developed.

Math, or at least a portion of it, comes easily to the Listener child. His well-developed auditory memory and quick grasp of language concepts enable him to process the information contained in story problems—for instance, Jim's sharing his apple supply with Meg. The Listener also has immediate recall of such math-related words as "quarter," "circle," and "o'clock"; can easily memorize the basic rules of addition and subtraction; and comprehends the terms "more," "less," "plus," "minus," and "equals."

Typical Report Cards for Lookers, Listeners, and Movers

Now that we've examined the skills called into play by each subject studied during the first grade, it would be helpful to return to each of our three learners and objectively assess his or her academic performance. Let's imagine for a moment that Christopher, Angela, and Thomas are classmates. The types of first-grade report cards each learner can expect at the end of the first and final marking periods are detailed below. If you imagine further that each grade of "E" means "Excellent," "AA" means "Above Average," "A" means "Average," and "I" means "Improvement Needed," you'll get a clear picture of the learning-skill differences among the three children. Particularly in Christopher's and Angela's cases, you'll also see evidence of academic plateaus, or the leveling off of progress in certain subjects.

FIRST-GRADE REPORT CARDS FOR LOOKER CHRISTOPHER

First-Quarter Report		*End-of-Year Report*	
Reading	E	Reading	A
Spelling	E	Spelling	E
Math	E	Math	E
Handwriting	E	Handwriting	E
Art	E	Art	E
Music	AA	Music	A
Physical Education	A	Physical Education	A
Conduct	E	Conduct	E

Quiet, intense Christopher displays his first-quarter report card with pride, for here is visible proof of his academic ability and self-control. Music and physical education are the only two subjects in which he is not consistently at the top of the class. Later in the year, Christopher is disappointed to find that his reading grade has dropped from "Excellent" to just "Average," but sounding-out skills are being called into play more and more during reading class, and phonics does not come easily to Lookers. Christopher's music grade also falls, reflecting his boredom and frustration with that class's increasingly complex auditory slant.

FIRST-GRADE REPORT CARDS FOR LISTENER ANGELA

First-Quarter Report		*End-of-Year Report*	
Reading	AA	Reading	E
Spelling	E	Spelling	A
Math	E	Math	E
Handwriting	A	Handwriting	A
Art	A	Art	A
Music	E	Music	E
Physical Education	A	Physical Education	A
Conduct	AA	Conduct	A

Angela's report cards are quite typical of a first-grade Listener. Her work in math and music is consistently good, and her reading skills improve throughout the year as phonics begins to play a larger role. On the other hand, she becomes weaker in spelling as the words she encounters begin to defy the rules of phonics upon which she has always relied. Angela's "Average" grades in art, physical education, and handwriting reflect her average motor skills. Because her sociability and chattiness occasionally approach a disruptive level, her conduct grade drops to just "Average" by year's end.

FIRST-GRADE REPORT CARDS FOR MOVER THOMAS

First-Quarter Report		*End-of-Year Report*	
Reading	A	Reading	I
Spelling	I	Spelling	I
Math	A	Math	I
Handwriting	A	Handwriting	I
Art	A	Art	A
Music	A	Music	I
Physical Education	E	Physical Education	E
Conduct	I	Conduct	I

Thomas's report cards tell the whole story. His performance in physical education is always outstanding; his conduct is always a problem. Thomas's academic skills are already a bit below the norm at the time of the first-quarter report, but his teachers choose to be positive and assign him "Average" grades in reading, math, handwriting, art, and music. By the end of the school year, however, Thomas has made so little progress that the gap between his abilities and those of his classmates has widened, and an "Improvement Needed" grade is the only recourse. In art, where Thomas is freer to move about the room, he enjoys some success despite his weak fine motor skills; thus, his maintenance of an "Average" grade in this subject.

WORKING WITH YOUR CHILD'S TEACHER

In this chapter, we've seen three first-grade classmates who are very different learners. Christopher learns best by visual means, and, despite his determination and penchant for organization, still needs help with certain aspects of his school work. Angela, who is most responsive to sound and language, is also a good student. However, she has an entirely different set of academic skills, some of which also need improvement. Thomas, who's a tactile learner, requires a great deal of extra help with almost all school work.

Whatever your child's learning skills and problems may be, you will be able to offer the most emotional support and practical assistance if you remain informed about his life at school. Biannual conferences and quarterly report cards are enlightening, of course, but they don't always provide enough information on a sufficiently frequent basis to keep parents abreast of important situations, such as peer problems, changes in work habits, or a particular unit of study that just won't "sink in." Depending on the teacher's communicativeness and the size of the class, additional contact with him or her can take the form of behavior or school-preparedness checklists, regularly scheduled notes, or even brief lunch-hour phone calls. To avoid overlooking important points, make it a practice to prepare yourself by jotting down notes ahead of time. It is also a good idea to encourage a sense of participation and responsibility in your child by sharing his teacher's input with him.

Regardless of your means of communicating with your child's teacher, you'll want to create an atmosphere of give-and-take in which each of you apprises the other of important facts regarding your child's academic and social well-being. The list below suggests information that you might wish to impart to your child's teacher. Following this are eight key questions that you can ask your child's teacher.

Eight Facts to Reveal to Your Child's Teacher

- *Your child's degree of personal organization.* The teacher should be made aware of the fact that your child has a strong need for order and routine; that he functions best in an open, cluttered work space; or that he requires ongoing assistance with the organization of materials.

- *Your child's mastery of basic facts.* If your child struggles with addition or subtraction, or if he has special strategies that he uses to memorize subject material, advise his teacher.

- *The employment of a tutor.* Let your child's teacher know whether you have used or are now using a tutor to provide your child with extra help. Chances are, the teacher and tutor will want to keep their approaches and expectations uniform. It's equally important to advise the teacher if *you* have been providing this sort of help to your child on a regular basis.

- *Health-related information.* The school nurse will undoubtedly have your child's health records on file, but your child's teacher also should be made aware of any allergies or medical conditions for which medication is taken on an ongoing basis. Include any pertinent information about hearing or vision problems.

- *Past evaluations and screenings.* If your child's past school performance resulted in educational or psychological testing of any sort, his teacher should be informed of the test dates and outcomes. The teacher will certainly be aware of any diagnosed disabilities, but he or she should also know about testing that resulted in a no-change recommendation.

- *At-home situations.* You'll be doing your child a favor by apprising the teacher of the existence of household upheaval, therapy, or substance-abuse treatment by a family member. Major changes such as these can greatly affect a child's ability to function in the classroom.

- *A second language.* If another language is spoken in your home as either a primary or a secondary means of communication among family members, your child's teacher should know about it. This will help the teacher understand any discomfort your child might exhibit when faced with colloquial or slang expressions or complex oral directions.

- *Prior recommendations.* It's important to relay to your child's teacher the suggestions made by previous teachers and professionals. By candidly asking for preferential seating, leniency with regard to timed assignments, help from a peer tutor, reduced workloads, or a quiet place for your child to "decompress," you may spare your child weeks of frustration.

Eight Questions to Ask Your Child's Teacher

- *Is your child's homework completed and turned in on time?* If not, find out what the classroom procedure is for noting assignments and packing materials to take home. Ask the teacher how you and your child can work together to eliminate homework problems.

- *Does your child complete the bulk of his class work?* If not, what factors seem to stand in his way? Ask the teacher if a seating change would help, or if there are ways to temporarily modify your child's work-load so that he can experience some classroom success and develop a more positive attitude toward his school work.

- *Does your child pay attention in class?* If there is a problem, what does the teacher feel is the cause? Ask what he or she has done to rectify the problem, and describe strategies that you have employed at home to keep your child's attention on the task at hand.

- *What are your child's current reading and math levels?* Even if your child has not taken standardized reading and math tests, the teacher should be able to estimate reading and math levels based on classroom performance. Ask whether the teacher feels that your child's progress accurately reflects his abilities.

- *Does the teacher recommend any sort of professional intervention?* Based on your child's classroom performance, does the teacher feel that a tutor, a psychological evaluation, or learning disability testing is necessary? If so, ask the teacher to explain the reasons for such a recommendation.

- *On what level does your child participate in class discussions?* Does your child volunteer information, or does he offer answers only when called upon? Can he verbalize satisfactorily when he has an idea to express? Is he a good listener when others have the floor? If not, ask the teacher what is being done to help the situation, and, if necessary, discuss other possible solutions.

- *How does your child get along socially?* Ask the teacher who your child's friends are, and if there is anyone who might make a particularly good weekend or after-school playmate. Find out whether your child is at the center of things, on the fringes, or more of a loner, and discuss your child's feelings about this standing. Also ask how your child treats his classmates.

- *What can you do at home to help your child?* Your child's teacher may have specific ideas about emotional or academic support that could hasten your child's growth or rectify an existing problem. Indicate your willingness to work together with the teacher for the benefit of your child.

LEARNING STYLE AND EXTRACURRICULAR ACTIVITIES

As important as homework is, it utilizes only a small portion of a child's after-school time. Extracurricular activities and informal play times are also very important to first graders. Whereas homework develops study skills and reinforces material taught in school, sports, clubs, and at-home amusements encourage a child's social development and allow him to pursue interests at whatever pace, in whatever form, and to whatever degree he chooses. It is this freedom of choice that so delights most children. After the regimentation of the school day and the routine of homework, several hours of free time are quite a luxury!

Young children are usually drawn to after-school activities because their friends are involved or because the club or sport holds visual appeal. Most would-be ballerinas entertain visions of themselves in sequined tutus, just as the majority of first-year Little Leaguers wait breathlessly for their team shirts and caps. Scout uniforms and karate garb hold a similar attraction.

Chances are, your child will eventually lose interest in many of the activities that don't appeal strongly to his favored sense. Looker Christopher, for instance, would probably delight in an art class, but might give up fairly quickly on ice skating. Brownies would be a good "fit" for Listener Angela, and a tumbling class would be well suited to Mover Thomas, but both children would be likely to abandon piano lessons. However, even when the club or sport to which your first grader aspires seems an odd choice because it focuses on a skill he does not naturally possess, there's no harm in allowing your child to experiment—time and budget permitting, of course. After all, extracurricular pursuits of any kind will help your child develop his interests and social skills. Even quickly forsaken activities serve a purpose, in that they make the child aware of those pursuits that bring out his best.

No matter how sports-minded or socially inclined your first grader might be, it's never a good idea to allow an overscheduling of his free time with club meetings, classes, and team sports. Family-oriented activities, chosen for their broader appeal, for the purpose of exercise, or just to get the family out of the house for an afternoon, are equally important. Bike rides, picnics, drives, visits to friends, and outings to museums or historical sites all give parents and children the chance to "connect"—to talk, to laugh, and to focus on one another away from household distractions and the demands of meetings and practices. Time alone is important to your child, as well. A first grader needs ample opportunity to read, watch television, see his friends, daydream, and play with family members.

Remember, though: It's not unusual for a first grader to cheerfully leave the planning of his extracurricular activities to his parents. To be sure, some children voice a strong wish to learn karate, for example, or to become a Boy Scout. But an equal number of children give their free time little thought and, left to their own devices, would happily spend it playing in the house. Fortunately, most six- and seven-year-olds are still quite amenable to their parents' ideas and still young enough to benefit not just from those activities that appeal to their sensory preference, but also from those that challenge their weaker areas. So, if your first grader is in need of some extracurricular direction, you will be able to gently coax him toward a balance of activities—some, perhaps, with which he'll feel immediately comfortable, and one or two that will help him strengthen a less-developed skill. The following suggestions, grouped according to the sensory area each activity most often involves, should prove helpful.

Visual Activities for First Graders

An ideal first-grade visual activity provides the chance to first observe and then memorize or imitate, often by coordinating the use of the eyes and hands. The following list may contain the perfect idea for your child.

- Badminton or ping-pong
- Computer
- Crafts
- Drawing or painting
- Magic Class
- Models or building sets
- Museum programs
- Piano, recorder, clarinet, or other musical instruments
- Stamp, sports card, or coin collecting
- Typing

Auditory and Language Activities for First Graders

In order to appeal to the auditory and language skill areas, an activity should provide a child with the opportunity to socialize, lead a group, listen and learn, or display verbal talents. Here are some Listener activities that are perfect for a first grader.

- Backyard shows and plays
- Brownies, Cub Scouts, 4-H Club, or a similar organization
- Bumper Bowling League
- Ceramics class
- Children's concerts
- Chorus or choir
- Day camp or recreation programs
- Drama class
- Library story time
- Religious instruction

Gross Motor Activities for First Graders

A perfect gross motor activity for first graders is one that has few rules to get in the way of the action, involves touch or motion, encourages the use of a child's large muscles, or enables the child to spend time outdoors. Here are a a few suggestions.

- Aerobics or fitness classes
- Bicycling
- Hiking and camping
- Horseback riding
- Ice Skating
- Nature programs
- Skiing
- Swimming
- Tap, jazz, or ballet dancing
- Tumbling

When exploring extracurricular options with your first grader, please bear in mind that every child, regardless of learning style, needs physical activity for reasons of fitness and general good health. It isn't necessary that your child's physical exercise take the form of a competitive sport or a highly structured class—either of which might make some first graders uncomfortable. But, it *is* important to expose your child to one or two gross motor activities that suit him, whether they take the form of organized games or noncompetitive, individual pursuits.

HOMEWORK STRATEGIES FOR LOOKERS, LISTENERS AND MOVERS

From infancy through the kindergarten year, the purpose of identifying a child's learning style is to provide him with a more balanced approach to learning by developing his Listener, Looker, or Mover skills as needed. The parent's task changes somewhat during the first-grade year, as it now becomes important for the child to master specific academic information. You can help your first grader do this by teaching him to apply his dominant way of learning to the reading, writing, spelling, and math work he does at school and at home.

The first-grade year is the perfect time to explain to your child what learning style is, how *he* learns best, and how he can use his strong suit to master new material. The learning strategies parents employ will, of course, differ according to whether a child is by nature a Looker, a Listener, or a Mover. Here are some at-home tactics that will make learning and homework more appealing to your first grader.

Strategies for Lookers

A Looker child requires a neat, organized work space, with all of his materials in plain sight. Provide colorful, neatly labeled trays and bins in which he can store pencils, crayons, paper, and other supplies. Post a chart showing your child's various school subjects, and have him note each completed assignment. Use a variety of stickers, stars, and happy faces as rewards for staying with taxing language arts assignments.

Teach your child some visual strategies to help him remember letter sounds. Remind him that *T* looks like "Tree," *F* looks like "Flag," and *S* looks like "Snake." You can also color-code vowels to help him remember short and long sounds. Short *a*'s can be colored black; long *a*'s, gray; short *e*'s, red; and long *e*'s, green.

Encourage your Looker to draw pictures of troubling math problems—groups of balls or blocks, perhaps, to represent the numbers he wishes to add or subtract. You can provide highlighter pens, and suggest that your child use them to color important words or names in his reading (excluding textbooks, of course). And, finally, the classic flash card is an excellent tool for Lookers, who excel at memorization. Try using different-colored index cards as cues for various subjects.

Strategies for Listeners

A Listener child seldom needs reminders to do his homework. Academic work comes so easily to him that many of his assignments are fun, rather than a chore. Although he may not need much encouragement at the outset, the Listener thrives on verbal reinforcement of jobs well done. It's a good idea to be generous with phrases like "Good job!" and "What beautiful work!" On those occasions when a Listener's attention strays from a long writing assignment or a mostly visual task such as solving row after row of math problems, you might wish to offer an appealing incentive: "You may call Shawn after you've practiced your spelling words," or "Finish this page, and then you can choose a game for us to play."

It's helpful for a Listener child to learn to talk himself through difficult tasks. Remind your first grader to do this when he prints. For the letter *q*, for example, he can say, "Go around to the left, close the circle, go straight down, and put on a tail." The same strategy comes in handy when tackling other fine motor tasks, like shoe tying and belt buckling, as well as during gross motor activities. For instance, a hesitant gymnast might reassure himself with, "Bend over, tuck the head, and roll," when learning to somersault.

Finally, encourage your Listener to use a tape recorder. When he is faced with remembering something new, like math facts or the words to a song, he can record the information and play the tape back again and again, until he has it memorized.

Strategies for Movers

Mover children need the most support when it comes to academics. It's a good idea to keep the Mover's homework periods short, ending on a positive note whenever possible. Your physical presence will help keep him focused on his task, as will the elimination of household noise and other distractions. Turn off the television, unplug the phone, put the cat in another room, and occupy younger children elsewhere when it's homework time.

Your Mover will need help staying organized. No doubt, he tends to misplace things, so provide a backpack in which he can carry homework, notes, his lunch, and library books. Designate a special coat hook as the place his bag is to be hung at home. If you arrange several trays or wire baskets on his desk or the kitchen counter, your child will be able to separate his math, spelling, and workbook papers. When you explain the instructions for a particular assignment, ask for a repetition before your child goes to work.

Hugs, back pats, and "high fives" are very motivating to a Mover child. You can also offer such appealing incentives as walking the dog, playing outdoors, or helping make pizza when his homework is done. Since Movers often respond well to food rewards, periodic offerings of cheese, nuts, popcorn, or a frozen juice bar will make homework time more palatable.

It's a good idea to provide the Mover first grader with a chalkboard for printing practice. This way, he can practice his letter shapes without the added pressure of conforming to lines and margins. Suggest that he lie on his bed or a beanbag chair while reading. This will allow him to stretch and squirm to his heart's content! Try to add action to whatever your child is trying to learn. Write addition facts on cards, for example, and have your child jump over each card as he reads it aloud. Or, tape his spelling words to a wall in a darkened room, and have him move a flashlight from word to word, reading as he goes.

As you can see, knowledge of your child's learning style provides an excellent perspective for working with him at home. The right environment and appropriate homework strategies can make a big difference in your first grader's receptiveness to new material. Read on for more specific tactics!

TECHNIQUES FOR AFFIRMING
AND DEVELOPING LEARNING SKILLS

By following the progress of Christopher, Angela, and Thomas, we've seen how different learning skills result in different academic strengths and weaknesses. We've also looked at ways in which various learning strategies can be used to help a child apply his inborn strengths to the mastery of new material—even when that material is in one of his weaker subject areas.

The following sections, each devoted to one of the three learning styles, highlight the need to develop those skills that are inborn in some children but have to be cultivated in others. Each section contains two lists of toys, techniques, and learning aids. The first list offers suggestions for affirming the inborn skills of children who favor this style. These items have been included because they stimulate a preferred sense—a Listener's natural penchant for language and sounds, for example. Toys and activities on the second list are intended to develop this skill in children with a different learning style. These items also tap inborn strengths, but because they are multisensory in nature, they simultaneously tax the weaker skill, as well. Approaching skill development in this manner—from the standpoint of a child's inborn learning style—makes the exploration of a less-preferred sensory area a more enjoyable experience. By selecting those ideas that seem most suitable and most fun, you will add an interesting new dimension to the time your first grader spends at home, and will most certainly help your child meet the challenges of the school environment.

Building Looker Skills

Looker skills enable a child to observe his surroundings, remember what he sees, visualize concepts, and coordinate his eyes with his hands. Therefore, you can expect a first grader with below-average Looker skills to have difficulty with reading and writing, addition and subtraction, story problems, and artwork—all of which require skills that the child doesn't yet possess.

No matter what his ability level, however, a first grader's Looker skills can be enhanced or improved through the use of specially chosen playthings and activities. Children who are Lookers by nature will welcome their parents' efforts to provide more of the visual experiences they adore; Listeners and Movers may need a bit more convincing in the form of activities that incorporate *their* favored stimuli, be they auditory or tactile. But, whatever your first grader's inborn style, the following ideas will help you develop his Looker skills—and have fun in the process.

ENHANCING A FIRST GRADER'S EXISTING LOOKER SKILLS

Join your child in the classic game of pick-up sticks.

Treat your child to a visit to an art gallery. Allow plenty of time for him to study, compare, and return to those works of art he finds most appealing.

Play a game of jacks. Teach your child to bounce the ball and scoop first one, then two, then three, then four jacks before catching the ball in the same hand.

Study maps with your child. He will enjoy this graphic bird's-eye view of his town, city, or state. You can also play with a puzzle version of the United States map.

Buy a children's computer. *Whiz Kid* and *Learning Window*, both by Video Technology, are designed for first graders.

Encourage your child to assemble model cars and planes from kits.

Have your child look at picture books about stars and constellations, and then help him to gaze at the real thing by providing a backyard telescope.

Find the nearest planetarium or observatory, and plan a trip there with your child.

Encourage your child's artistic expression with a plentiful selection of materials—markers, glitter, paint pens, neon-colored paper, and the like.

Hide a small treasure in your house or yard. Then draw a treasure map with visual clues your child can use to find the hiding spot.

Hand-held video games, like Tiger Electronics' *Electronic Soccer*, are great for the kind of individual play a Looker loves.

Quick and Easy Origami—published by Japan Publications, USA (1988), and distributed by Kodansha International (New York, NY)—comes with ninety sheets of brightly colored origami paper and instructions for twenty-eight different paper-folding projects.

The pot-holder loom, popular during the 1950s and 1960s, is making a comeback. A seven-and-a-half-inch square model, complete with colored cotton loops, is available in the crafts aisle of most toy stores.

Label home furnishings—a bed, a lamp, a table—with cards that spell out the objects' names.

Purchase or borrow a child-sized typewriter, and take turns typing notes and stories.

ENCOURAGING THE DEVELOPMENT OF LOOKER SKILLS IN LISTENER AND MOVER FIRST GRADERS

Help your child design an aquarium or draw up a plan for a vegetable garden. Then guide him in completing the project.

Seek out a hands-on science museum or an adult museum with a children's section, and take your child there for a multisensory treat.

Teach your child to play checkers or Chinese checkers.

Play video games with your child to help improve his ability to concentrate visually.

Assemble an easy jigsaw puzzle with your child. Encourage him to match the pieces using the picture, rather than the various shapes, as clues.

Encourage your child to build with PlaySkool's *Lincoln Logs*.

Teach your child to focus on visual detail by providing binoculars for outdoor use or a toy microscope for use indoors.

Play Milton Bradley's *Win, Lose, or Draw* with your child and one or two of his friends. This will encourage him to draw.

Read your child a story in a darkened room, and ask him to picture the action. You can help by posing questions that will stimulate visual imagery, like, "What is Cinderella wearing to the ball?" and "What does her carriage look like?"

Memory by Milton Bradley is a picture-matching game that will help your child recall what he has seen.

Lego makes *Mini-Models*, which are easy-to-assemble cars, boats, helicopters, and the like.

Provide books of simple mazes, connect-the-dot pictures, and puzzles for use in the car.

Playing "Bingo" will improve your child's letter and number recognition.

Draw pictures in the squares of a calendar to indicate important events—birthdays, the first snow, and school trips, for instance—and hang the calendar in your child's room.

Teach your child to play *Battleship* by Milton Bradley. This game will encourage visual imagery and improve number and letter recognition.

Building Listener Skills

The ability to converse, express oneself, and socialize is invaluable to students of any age, but particularly important during the primary grades, when a child's self-confidence and attitude toward school are still being shaped. And, of course, Listener skills are also needed for reading, music, and certain aspects of math. Whether your first grader is a Looker, a Listener, or a Mover, he stands to benefit from the development of keen auditory and language skills.

As always, Listeners themselves will be most receptive to any Listener experience a parent provides. But even a Looker or Mover can improve his verbal and auditory skills by using toys and techniques that employ both his inborn learning skill and the skill you are hoping to spark. Here are some suggestions to get you started.

ENHANCING A FIRST GRADER'S EXISTING LISTENER SKILLS

Play *Password*, a game in which one player tries to get the second player to guess a certain word by offering synonyms and other one-word clues.

Permit your child to place phone calls to relatives and friends.

When you read together, read two books: one that your child will enjoy listening to, and a simpler one that he can read to you. If time permits only a single book, choose one that your child can manage, and take turns reading alternate pages.

Get in the habit of reading the "About the Author" information contained in most books. This may help your child view the story in a different light and stimulate his interest in the process of writing.

Suggest that your child start a diary or journal in which he can make notes about special events in his life. Encourage the use of inventive spelling so that your child can experiment with more sophisticated words.

Choose a "word of the day" from the dictionary, and spell it out on the refrigerator with magnetic letters. Read the definition to your child, and try to use the word several times in conversation.

Choose a time of day to talk about any news stories that you feel are appropriate for a first grader. Show your child the headlines and newspaper photos that relate to each story.

Suggest that your child write his own storybook. Spend time with him talking about the story, encourage him to add illustrations, and, when the work is complete, bind the finished product with ribbon or yarn.

Read poetry to your child, and encourage him to write simple poems of his own. Help him out by suggesting possible themes.

Teach your child phrases in a foreign language, borrowing from books, when necessary. Books like *Arroz Con Leche*, distributed by The Heritage Key (through catalogue only) and containing text in two languages, will prove helpful.

You and your child can take turns adding parts to a story. Record your efforts, listen to your voices, and then tell the story again, adding more detail and different voices.

Get your child a library card of his own. Familiarize him with the layout of your local library so that he'll feel comfortable selecting books from different sections, and encourage relatives to give him books as gifts.

Try to schedule one meal per day that the family can eat together, and use this time to take turns telling about the day's events.

Indulge your child's social side by having him invite a friend to stay for lunch or sleep overnight.

Browse through the week's TV listings and find a narrative show on a topic that you think would interest your child. (Dinosaurs, hurricanes, and people from other lands are a few possible topics.) Watch the program with your child, and use the commercial breaks to explain and discuss what you've seen.

ENCOURAGING THE DEVELOPMENT OF LISTENER SKILLS IN LOOKER AND MOVER FIRST GRADERS

Build your child's vocabulary by using a picture dictionary. *The Photo Dictionary*, distributed by Lakeshore (through catalogue only), contains photographs and definitions of more than 2,000 animals, people, places, and things.

To improve your child's auditory memory, play Milton Bradley's *Simon*. This game, which comes in both pocket- and full-sized versions, requires players to remember sound and light patterns of varying lengths and speeds.

Provide a child-sized stage microphone with a battery-powered amplifier. Encourage your child to use it to tell a joke, sing, or make announcements.

Keep a box of cassette tapes in the car, and play and sing the words to favorite songs on trips around town.

Subscribe to a children's magazine. Read the stories aloud to your child, and encourage him to talk about the stories by asking him questions about the pictures.

Ask your child to draw a picture of something he likes—Grandma's house, a baseball diamond, or an animal, for instance—and help him make up a story about whatever he draws.

Help your child pronounce and spell long words by teaching him to clap once for each syllable. For example, "a-quar-i-um" has four syllables, so your child would clap four times.

Teach your child a new word every day with the help of Workman Publishing's *Shoelace Calendar*. This calendar provides pictures that will help your child recall the various words.

Post a magnetic "letter of the week" on the refrigerator. Surround the letter with original or magazine pictures of things that begin with that letter sound.

Make a story board using mounted pictures cut from a magazine. You and your child can take turns telling a story about the pictures he has chosen.

Read aloud to your child daily. Concentrate on stories that involve action, or focus on his favorite subjects.

Make a game of naming synonyms. Say, "What's another word for large? . . . upset? . . . automobile?" and so on.

Encourage your child to use the pictures in a familiar book as clues to the action as he retells the story in his own words.

Texas Instruments' *Words . . . To Go!* is a hand-held computer that teaches a child to follow directions, recognize letters and sounds, define words, and create rhymes. Encourage your child to talk about what he sees on the screen.

Go for a walk with your child, and use the time to practice rhyming words and naming words with opposite meanings.

Building Mover Skills

Your child may not call upon his Mover skills when he reads, writes, or memorizes math facts, but that doesn't mean that Mover skills should be ignored. A child who possesses a Mover's speed and coordination also possesses a sense of self-confidence that will stand him in good stead in all his endeavors. It pays, then, to develop your child's gross motor skills, regardless of his natural learning preference.

Children who are Movers by nature can never get enough tactile stimulation, and so will delight in any gross motor activity you plan. Listeners and Lookers, who are less certain of their own agility and much less enamored of full-body play, will be most amenable to Mover activities that also draw upon their favored skills, whether visual or auditory. A Listener, for example, might enjoy a game of "Red Rover" much more than a foot race, while a Looker might prefer a bicycle ride through the country. The following ideas will help you build your first grader's Mover skills.

ENHANCING A FIRST GRADER'S EXISTING MOVER SKILLS

Worlds of Wonder's *SkipStick* is a jump rope with a pole attached to each end to make jumping easy.

Child-sized tool sets are available in most toy stores. Work together with your child to build a bird feeder, a balance beam, or—for experts—a playhouse.

Invest in or arrange to use a neighbor's height-adjustable basketball net. The real thing is much more challenging than a four-foot toy version, and can be lowered from regulation height to allow basket-shooting success.

Introduce your child to the joys of horseback riding.

String up a net or rope in your backyard, and use it for a game of badminton or beach-ball volleyball.

On the next breezy day, teach your child how to fly a kite.

First Sports makes an inflatable pool game called *Splash-Dunk Water Basketball*.

Wham-O's *Dragonfire* is a four-wheel scooter, complete with a foot-controlled steering mechanism. The classic two-wheel scooter is great fun for Movers, too.

Enroll your child in a dance or martial arts class.

Encourage your child to participate in an organized sport, such as softball, baseball, or soccer.

Mattel has a line of *Hot Wheels* car and truck miniatures that change color when exposed to heat and cold.

Introduce your child to skiing or ice skating.

Find the nearest amusement park that features bumper cars, and treat your child to a ride in one.

String two dozen rubber bands together to make a Chinese jump rope. You and a third person can stretch the rope into an elongated oval by looping it around the backs of your legs. Your child can then jump over, in, and out on one or both feet.

Seek out new and different playgrounds at which your child can play. Check parks, school yards, and neighboring towns to see what's available.

ENCOURAGING THE DEVELOPMENT OF MOVER SKILLS IN LOOKER AND LISTENER FIRST GRADERS

Involve your child in a backyard throwing and catching game, like "Spud" or "War."

Plan mini-adventures with your child, such as trips to a beach, an art festival, a greenhouse, or a marina.

Enlist your child's help with the planting and tending of a vegetable or flower garden. Designate one section in which he can experiment and be creative.

Suggest that your child invite some neighborhood children over for kickball or some other team sport.

■ Pitch a tent—or design a makeshift version from blankets—and camp out with your child.

Call a local college or art center to find out about acting classes for children.

Sign your child up for Cub Scouts, Blue Birds, Brownies, or the 4-H Club. Offer to help out at meetings as often as possible.

Introduce your child to the game of miniature golf.

Milton Bradley's *Twister* has a spinner that determines where players must position their hands and feet on a large mat. The game progresses until one player loses his balance.

Plan a family hike, even if it's through city streets. Pack a blanket and bag lunch for a picnic.

Contact your child's school for information about local hands-on science museums.

Take your child to a local video arcade and introduce him to a few of the games. (To avoid crowds of older children, try to be there when the arcade opens.)

Draw a three-foot by three-foot square with chalk, and divide it into three rows of three squares each. Randomly assign each square a number from one to nine; then write a ten in a semicircle at the top of your game board. The object of this game, "Chinese Potsy," is to jump from square to square in numerical sequence, reaching number ten without stepping on any lines.

Invest in a bicycle rack that mounts on your car. Transport your bicycles, and your child, to a novel location for a ride through new and different surroundings.

Draw 3 four-foot parallel lines, approximately four feet apart. Place a two-foot branch or broomstick on the center line, then stand behind one of the other lines with your child doing the same thing directly opposite you. Bounce a ball to your child, attempting to hit the stick so that it rolls in his direction. Your child will then try to "bounce" the stick back your way. The person who forces the stick across his opponent's line first is the winner.

As you review the suggestions provided above, you'll no doubt think of other skill-building activities for your child's play times. My lists are intended to serve only as guidelines. Some of your own ideas may be even better suited to your schedule; your tolerance for noise, clutter, and activity; and your child's own tastes. Feel free to experiment!

Please be patient as you watch for results. Your child's current skill levels were six to seven years in the making, and improvement may take weeks or months. Meanwhile, your efforts will no doubt grant your child a bit more of your attention, allowing him to derive maximum enjoyment—and plenty of learning-skill enhancement—from the time he spends at home.

Learning Style QuickCheck for First Graders, Ages Six to Seven

Directions: Check each of the statements below that best describes your child. Then, total the check marks in each column and compare results. You're likely to find your responses concentrated in one or two columns. This is a clear indication of the learning style possessed by your first grader.

Looker	Listener	Mover

1. Communication: When my first grader wishes to express himself . . .

Looker	Listener	Mover
☐ He uses simple language.	☐ He uses the correct verb tense.	☐ He speaks in short, direct sentences.
☐ He mispronounces some sounds and words.	☐ He enjoys conversing with adults.	☐ He mumbles some speech sounds.
☐ He is quiet, and rarely volunteers an answer.	☐ He likes to create and tell pretend stories.	☐ He may relate stories out of sequence.

2. Favorite Toys and Pastimes: When my first grader plays . . .

Looker	Listener	Mover
☐ He likes calculators and computers.	☐ He likes the TV, radio, and tapes.	☐ He likes sports and outdoor play.
☐ He enjoys crafts and models.	☐ He enjoys reading aloud and having others read to him.	☐ He enjoys bicycling, hiking, and camping.
☐ He likes to read and observe others at play.	☐ He likes to invent scenarios for pretend play.	☐ He loves to feed, clean, brush, exercise, and otherwise care for pets.

3. Fine Motor Skills: When my first grader uses his hands . . .

Looker	Listener	Mover
☐ He is precise about forming letters and staying within the lines.	☐ His printing is fairly neat.	☐ He has trouble writing on lined paper.
☐ He produces neat, complete work sheets.	☐ He instructs or reads to himself while working.	☐ He confuses the order of letters in words.
☐ He is particular about coloring and art projects.	☐ He frequently asks for assistance with art projects.	☐ He presses hard with pencils, paint brushes, and crayons.

4. Gross Motor Skills: When my first grader moves about . . .

☐ He enjoys board games more than races or tag.

☐ He uses playground equipment to perform and pretend.

☐ He swings and climbs faster and higher than his friends.

☐ He would rather draw in the sand than use playground equipment.

☐ He likes talking games, like "Mother, May I?"

☐ He loves being outdoors.

☐ He climbs mainly to get a better look around.

☐ He has average coordination.

☐ He has excellent coordination.

5. Social Skills: When my first grader mixes with other children . . .

☐ He is a loner within a group of children.

☐ He is very verbal.

☐ He is most sociable on the playground.

☐ He rarely initiates conversation, but answers when spoken to.

☐ He initiates most conversations.

☐ He expresses himself through movement rather than words.

☐ He prefers individual projects to group activities.

☐ He is sometimes reprimanded for talking too much during class.

☐ He is a leader on the playground.

6. Emotions: When it comes to my first grader's feelings . . .

☐ He rarely expresses his feelings in words.

☐ He doesn't hesitate to verbalize his feelings.

☐ He uses his whole body to express his feelings.

☐ His facial expressions reflect his feelings.

☐ He is high-strung, but calms down quickly.

☐ He blushes and cries easily.

7. Memory: When my first grader learns . . .

☐ He remembers what he sees.

☐ He learns math facts easily.

☐ He has problems recalling what he has seen and heard.

☐ He reads words by memorizing them.

☐ He reads words by sounding them out.

☐ He needs extra help to learn to read.

8. At School: When my first grader is in the classroom . . .

☐ He dresses neatly.

☐ His appearance is not messy, but not overly neat.

☐ He usually looks somewhat rumpled.

☐ He is distracted by the sight of colors or movement.

☐ He is easily distracted by sounds and voices.

☐ He is overly active and distracted by sights and sounds.

☐ He insists on keeping his work area neat.

☐ He leads discussions and volunteers answers often.

☐ He is constantly out of his seat.

Totals:_____Looker   _____Listener   _____Mover

Chapter Seven

Learning Styles in Fourth Grade

Today's fourth graders are a sophisticated lot. During the course of a single school year, a nine-year-old, for whom parental approval has long been the driving force behind nearly every word and deed, develops greater allegiance to peers. At the same time, much of the attention previously lavished on dolls, toy cars, or soccer begins to be refocused on clothing trends, friends, the opposite sex, and the social acceptability of everything from hobbies and possessions to taste in music and TV viewing habits. And, along with all this budding social awareness, nine- and ten-year-olds must cope with new academic demands. Foreign languages and musical instruments are often introduced in the fourth grade, as is the class changing required by departmentalized instruction.

Naturally, some children grow up faster than others. Sociability varies as much from child to child as does academic and physical ability. All three traits, in fact, are direct results of the same learning patterns a child has employed since infancy. For example, an early talker usually evolves into an extremely verbal child, and this language prowess makes strong social skills almost a certainty. Similarly, the baby who sleeps only seven hours a night and walks by nine months of age will, in many cases, maintain this activity level for many years. This virtually assures difficulty with tasks that require sitting still and paying attention.

This chapter describes the effects of learning style on a child's classroom and after-school life by introducing three learners—a Looker, a Listener, and a Mover—and following their progress from September to June. A Learning Style QuickCheck for Fourth Graders (see page 191) is included to help you pinpoint your own child's learning preference.

Naturally, learning style exerts a great influence on a fourth grader's academic experience. This chapter examines the different school subjects that appeal to each learner, and takes a look at typical report cards for Lookers, Listeners, and Movers. And, since conference time is so often in short supply, suggestions are also provided for improving communication between you and your child's teachers.

A nine- or ten-year-old's after-school time is a precious commodity. The activities she chooses, the people with whom she associates, and even the degree of personal organization she brings to household tasks and homework assignments are all functions of her innate learning style. This chapter includes tips on helping your child choose extracurricular activities that will best suit her learning style, and guides you in creating the best possible at-home learning environment.

While striving for well-roundedness is still a worthwhile goal for a fourth grader, as time passes, it becomes more important and more realistic to shift parental emphasis to a child's need to master academic material. To begin with, it has been shown that the development of a child's visual, auditory, and motor skills does not automatically translate into improved class work. Many children need the additional support of special learning strategies before achieving better grades. Second, as a child matures, she is likely to become less receptive to parental attempts to introduce activities that target weak skills. Third, and perhaps most to the point, parents' time is limited. It makes sense, therefore, to focus skill-enhancement energy where it will best benefit nine- and ten-year-olds; that is, on academic achievement. With this in mind, you will find suggestions at the chapter's end to help improve performance in each of your child's school subjects.

When both parent and child acknowledge and appreciate how that child learns, the expectations of both become realistic, and the parent-child relationship is marked by understanding rather than tension. Your fourth grader is, without a doubt, on the brink of a host of social and personal changes. Help your child make the most of this exciting year.

A LOOK AT THREE LEARNERS

Daniel, Ana, and Beth are fourth-grade classmates. Each child had a birthday in the late spring. Daniel and Ana are nine years and four months of age at the start of the school year. Beth, who repeated kindergarten when it was decided that she needed an extra year to mature, is a year older.

All three children have concerned, involved parents and have been exposed to similar teachers, nearly identical curriculums, and comparable after-school activities. Yet the children are as different as can be. Ana's academic strengths, as you'll soon see, are Daniel's and Beth's shortcomings. Daniel is strongest in the subject areas that puzzle Ana. Beth enjoys success only in physical education, the area in which Ana and Daniel struggle most.

It's the children's learning styles—their inborn preferences for absorbing information by visual, auditory, or tactile means—that have had such a dramatic influence on their school and home lives. Although all children do not exhibit the traits of a single learning style in this manner and may, in fact, be Looker-Listeners or Looker-Movers, each of our case-study children possesses a "pure" style. This has been done to accent the features of each sensory preference. You'll see the difference learning style can make as we meet each child at the start of the fourth-grade year.

Nine Years of Age

Meet Daniel. Daniel, a Looker, is a logical, confident, soft-spoken child. He has two friends with whom he socializes outside of school, though he usually plans an activity with just one pal at a time. Daniel's outside time is very structured; instead of inviting his friend over to "hang out," he issues carefully considered invitations for an afternoon of creating cartoons or competing at video games. Daniel's other favorite activities include throwing darts, reading about sports records, studying astronomy, and organizing his stamp collection. As you can see, Daniel is quite comfortable with solo pursuits. He'd choose drawing over a kickball game any day!

Daniel's written work is colorful, neat, and painstakingly done. It's not unusual for him to rewrite an entire paper rather than cross out or erase an error. Daniel's artwork also reflects his fine motor skills. His projects are well planned, precisely executed, and always attractive. Most include some creative variation of the geometric shapes he finds so fascinating. He also loves to design mazes and video games of his own. Daniel's abilities don't extend to the large muscles, however. He doesn't care for gym class or team sports; in fact, he long ago traded his Little League uniform for a job as score keeper. When he does spend time outdoors, you'll usually find Daniel seated at a picnic table with a comic book, a pad and pencil, or a hand-held video game.

Quiet Daniel rarely volunteers to speak in class, even though he usually knows the answer being sought. He is proud of his academic ability, but does not care for the limelight. Daniel is frustrated by the disorganization of most group projects. At school, as at home, he enjoys being by himself. Daniel is methodical about completing assignments, adores visual tasks like diagramming sentences, and excels at work involving maps, tables, graphs, and charts. Last year, his favorite math unit dealt with Roman numerals.

When reading, Daniel uses sentence context and educated guesswork to help him decode printed text into spoken words, for he is weak in the phonics skills that would enable him to "sound out." His reliance on visual memory also means that he remains a strong speller, while his Listener classmates are finding themselves less and less able to apply phonics rules to their fourth-grade vocabulary words. Daniel's written work is brief and to the point. He is a child of few words, anyway, and the simpler his written language, the less chance of error. It will come as no surprise that Daniel is having trouble with first-year Spanish. He is able to memorize the vocabulary, but stumbles time and again over pronunciation. It's clear that Daniel's orientation as a Looker helps him to excel in certain subject areas, but actually slows his progress in others.

Meet Ana. Friendly, talkative Ana—a Listener—has dozens of friends. She's always the first to welcome a new child into the neighborhood, and is as well accepted by adults and older children as by her peers. In fact, Ana carefully imitates the speech, mannerisms, and dress of her teen-aged baby-sitter, and is admired by her classmates for her sophisticated social behavior.

Ana loves to be the center of attention. She's always telling jokes and stories, and at home is a veritable fountain of information about her school day. Ana is active in the Girl Scouts, takes a Saturday-morning drama class, and has already played several small parts in her community theater. During her free time, Ana steers clear of crafts, drawing, and other fine motor hobbies, but can usually be found entertaining friends or chitchatting on the phone.

Although Ana likes the social contact that comes along with physical education and art, these two classes are still the low point of her week. She is not particularly strong or agile, and mildly resents the back-seat position she must take in gym class. In fact, Ana is bothered by her lack of gross motor ability. When the results of a recent presidential physical fitness test were posted, Ana was nowhere to be found. Ana's lack of ability in art is not quite as obvious, but her efforts are not particularly neat or creative, and she has trouble with assignments involving shapes and perspective.

In school, Ana memorizes new material easily. She loves oral presentations, and her journal writings are imaginative and peppered with descriptive phrases. Ana's book reports are long, complex, and well-organized, but her shaky proofreading skills prevent her from getting the A+ she otherwise deserves. Ana also has quite a bit of trouble with other visual assignments, like those involving charts, graphs, maps, and keyboard memorization. Frequently, she loses her place, and has trouble integrating all the details to form the "big picture." In fact, because Ana lacks the visual skills so necessary in fourth-grade math, her parents have arranged weekly sessions with a math tutor. But, in music, French, science, and social studies, Ana can rely on her strong auditory skills to master most of the information she needs to learn. Overall, her grades have always been very good, and fourth grade promises to elicit the same strong academic performance.

Ten Years of Age

Meet Beth. Mover Beth is an athletic, highly coordinated child whose physical prowess is a function of her learning style, rather than the fact that she's a year older than most of her classmates. Beth is also an emotional soul, quick to cry in anger or frustration. It's for this reason that Beth's attempts to join in the games of neighborhood children fall flat. She is well matched physically, but is reduced to tears with a frequency that quickly becomes tiresome. In fact, the social and emotional immaturity that led Beth to repeat kindergarten is still a problem. In class, her history of academic difficulties and frequent outbursts have made her something of an outcast. In the long run, Beth's rather limited social skills result in her getting along best with children who are physically competent, but a year or two younger than she.

Beth often uses her hands to help express herself. Her vocabulary, you see, is rather small, so gestures and coined terms—"measurer" for "ruler," or "plussing and timesing" for "addition and multiplication"—are quite useful. Beth also mispronounces many multisyllabic words; "pasgetti" and "ephelant" are two examples. She simply doesn't hear the difference between her version and that which is correct.

Beth often "plays rough," but her agility guarantees her winning almost every athletic contest. She adores skateboarding, swimming, softball, soccer—all active sports, in fact. Beth sticks to gross motor play even when no opponent is available. Shooting baskets in the driveway and practicing her tennis strokes against the garage wall are two of her favorite pastimes. Since Beth is slow to coordinate her eyes and fingers, she rarely attempts fine motor activities by choice. Her penmanship is sloppy, and she is often asked to rewrite assignments to make them more legible. Last year, she attempted to master the piano keyboard and recorder with the rest of her third-grade class, but soon gave up in frustration. Only in art, where messiness can be interpreted as creativity, does she feel comfortable with her finished products.

At school, Beth tries hard to pay attention to her lessons rather than the goings on around her. But it is difficult for her to keep her hands away from the science projects on a nearby table, or to resist toppling a tempting stack of books beneath her neighbor's chair. In fact, Beth's struggles with self-control are so frustrating that she eventually tunes out her surroundings altogether, preferring to amuse herself by popping the eraser off her pencil, or opening and closing the rings of her looseleaf binder. Naturally, Beth hates report-card time, for in the past, her grades have led only to withdrawn privileges.

Because Beth struggles with reading and spelling, no academic subjects come easily to her. She can barely manage a second-grade reader, yet her class textbooks are written on a fourth-grade level! Even with simpler material, Beth's reading comprehension is poor. You see, because she has to work so hard at the process of decoding, she absorbs very little of the text. Fortunately, since first grade, Beth has visited her school's Resource Lab for some individualized extra help, and this support has helped her keep abreast of written assignments and new subject matter. This year, Beth will continue to visit the Resource Lab for spelling and reading assistance.

Timed tests and long-term assignments are torture for Beth, because she cannot plan ahead or organize her work without assistance. To give Beth the best chance of completing her school work, her teachers have begun shortening the child's assignments and have moved her desk closer to theirs. On a positive note, Beth likes the experimentation and hands-on aspect of science, and is the first to bring in items from home that relate to her social studies units. Beth's parents encourage any interests related to school and learning. They keep her well supplied with magazine and newspaper articles about pollution, they've helped her set up a recycling center in the garage, and they've provided her with a telescope.

There's no question that among our case-study children, it is Beth whose learning style creates the greatest need for support. But, with the combined efforts of her parents and teachers, Beth will enjoy both academic progress and social growth during her fourth-grade year.

Which learning style does your fourth grader possess? Is she a neat, organized student, who learns by mostly visual means? If so, she's a

Looker, like Daniel. Or, is she a Listener, like Ana—very social and unusually good at following directions and mastering new material? Or, like our Mover, Beth, is she weak in most academic subjects, remaining attentive only when an assignment involves her active participation? The Learning Style QuickCheck for Fourth Graders, located on page 191, will help you find out for sure. As you read the statements contained in the QuickCheck, mark those that best describe your child. You're likely to see a heavy concentration of checks in one or two columns—a clear indication of your child's sensory preference.

HOW LOOKER, LISTENER, AND MOVER FOURTH GRADERS DEVELOP

Daniel, Ana, and Beth are clearly different students, with their striking dissimilarities also reflected in the nature of their friendships and outside interests. Listener Ana, for example, impatiently awaits recess one day because she wants to display the sophisticated braid her mother wove for her that morning. Mover Beth is equally impatient, but the cause of her restlessness is the forbidden game of handball she has planned with one of her buddies. And Looker Daniel would be perfectly happy to skip recess altogether, so engrossed is he in the product map he's making for social studies class.

While each child experiences some growth during fourth grade, that growth isn't necessarily a balanced affair. The academic differences between our three learners—and between real-life fourth graders who share their learning styles—remain intact. This is due to the fact that each school subject utilizes particular skills—skills that are one learner's strength, but another's shortcoming. Fourth-grade math, for example, covers Roman numerals, place value, fractions, and other concepts best suited to a visual learner. Science, at this level, is primarily a hands-on subject, and therefore is understood best by Lookers and Movers. And the language arts—grammar, foreign language, and literature—involve many auditory exercises, making this field a natural arena for Listeners. To see how Daniel, Ana, and Beth handled fourth grade's academic and social challenges, let's look at each child at the school year's end.

Ten Years of Age

Daniel. As he reaches his tenth birthday, Looker Daniel continues to keep to himself and seek out his own personal "space" in which to work and play. Daniel has always been accepted by his peers, but lately, despite his reserve, he is becoming more popular. You see, his fourth-grade classmates now place greater value on one another's achievements. So, Daniel's unmatchable Nintendo skills, the gold medal he earned in the school spelling bee, and his prize-winning artistic creations have won his classmates' ongoing admiration. Lately, the girls in Daniel's class have also begun noticing his impeccable manners and flawless appearance.

At school, Daniel excels in penmanship, spelling, and math, due to his innate fine motor ability and well-developed visual memory. A lack of sounding-out skills has caused Daniel to progress rather slowly in reading and in textbook-based subjects such as science and social studies. However, he leads the class when it comes to map assignments, charts, and other projects that tap his artistic skills.

The older Daniel gets, the more frustrated he becomes with the classroom antics and academic shortcomings of some of his peers. He keeps his impatience to himself, however, lest a sigh or comment lead to some ugly confrontation. Daniel continues to steer clear of activities and children with the potential for trouble, for he enjoys a pleasant relationship with his teachers and wants nothing to change that.

Daniel's current ambition is to be an architect like his uncle. Blueprints fascinate him, as does the idea of dressing up for work each day and performing a job in relative privacy. Daniel and his father frequently stop by his uncle's firm to look around. Visits to his uncle's house are a treat, as well, because Daniel gets to sit and draw at a drafting table in the family's home office.

At school conference time, Daniel's teachers suggest that he pay closer attention during lectures, since he sometimes misses an important point or a verbal direction. Aware of Daniel's tendency to tune out when involved in a game or faced with a long-winded speaker, the boy's parents agree. In addition, because Daniel would very much like to improve his reading skills, the family has asked his language arts teacher to suggest several high-interest, low-level books that the boy can tackle during the summer months. Daniel's work habits and perseverance helped him greatly during fourth grade, and on the whole, his academic performance was quite satisfactory. School remains a positive experience for him, and he looks forward to entering next year's art contest and to enjoying the fifth-grade privilege of working on the school newsletter.

Ana. By the end of fourth grade, Listener Ana has become the social hub around which all the activities and get-togethers of her friends revolve. Ana is seen as an authority on style and social behavior, and her friends make it a practice to run their ideas and comments by her for approval before trying them on anyone else. Like the older girls she so admires, Ana herself has helped make boy-girl pairings among her classmates something desirable by organizing outings involving classmates of both sexes and by openly declaring her "boyfriend" of the moment.

Ana thinks she would enjoy being a teacher or an actress, but is not as serious as Daniel about looking ahead. When pressed by a well-meaning adult about her plans for the future, Ana usually casts a friendly look of amazement and responds, "I'm much too young to think about any of that." Gregarious, fun-loving Ana worries only about the here and now, and tries to wrest the maximum enjoyment from activities that showcase her verbal talents.

Ana's classroom efforts are consistently reinforced by high grades. Her superior reading skills enable her to take the lead in many classes, because textbooks and works of literature pose no problem at all. Ana's fine motor skills are a bit weak, however, so she doesn't fare quite as well with creative projects, and continues to need a tutor's help with math computations. Fortunately, the fourth grader's verbal skills and positive attitude do much to offset her academic shortcomings. At year's end, in fact, Ana's teachers commend her for her leadership qualities and her willingness to seek assistance, and put together a packet of school work to help the child keep her skills sharp during the summer months. Ana, always eager for new privileges and higher social status within her school, can't wait to attend fifth grade. From her conversations with older friends, she is well aware of the various fifth grade-versus-sixth grade contests that will be available to her. Ana also looks forward to performing in the class talent show and trying out for the "Brainbusters," an interscholastic team whose claim to fame is a wealth of general knowledge.

Eleven Years of Age

Beth. Mover Beth is a year older and, thus, somewhat larger than most of her female classmates. Nonetheless, as she approaches age eleven, Beth exudes a sense of confidence about her body that is lacking in many fourth-grade girls. As sure-footed and agile as ever, Beth is especially proud of her accomplishments in gymnastics—a sport that she has embraced passionately from the first. Recently, Beth has also begun to assist a neighbor by amusing her two preschool sons, and this twice-weekly job has given a further boost to the fourth grader's self-image.

At the end of fourth grade, Beth's best friend is a nine-year-old girl from the neighborhood. Like Beth, the friend is very coordinated and prefers to be on the go at all times; but, as a third grader, she makes none of the uncomfortable social demands so characteristic of Beth's class-mates. You see, Beth doesn't care at all about fashion or gossip. She'd much rather shoot baskets beneath the driveway lights than don a trendy nightshirt and giggle her way through the sleep-overs that have suddenly become so popular with her peers. Yet, Beth does show signs of a budding social awareness. She has been the subject of her cattier classmates' verbal jabs for years. Lately, though, she has begun to react with shame and a hopelessly left-out feeling, rather than the spurt of hostility that was something of a trademark during the previous four years. Beth has also begun to be embarrassed by her emotional displays, and this new awareness has occasionally helped her to think before lashing out in anger, and to consider solutions before dissolving into tears.

Last fall, Beth wanted to be a professional tennis player. She was thrilled by the prospect of earning a living at athletics, and envious of the many teen-aged professionals for whom formal schooling is but a memory! However, since a recent demonstration at her school by the police department's K-9 unit, Beth has decided that a police career might be a better choice.

Beth still struggles with most aspects of her school work. Her spelling and handwriting are poor because of weak visual skills, and her math computations are disordered and sloppy. Far from memorizing the multiplication tables, Beth has yet to master addition and subtraction facts. The child is still nearly two years behind most of her classmates in reading, and this fact makes much of her social studies, science, and language arts work exercises in frustration. Beth's teachers recommend that she continue to receive shortened, untimed assignments—twenty math problems, perhaps, instead of the fifty her classmates are given—to reduce frustration and encourage more consistent effort. It is also suggested that Beth continue to be seated at the front of the classroom, and away from such high-traffic areas as the drinking fountain, the pencil sharpener, and the doorway. Beth's teachers feel these tactics have helped Beth tremendously during fourth grade. Even Beth, who looks forward to next year only because it brings two extra gym classes per week, concurs. During the summer, Beth will be taking tennis lessons, playing in a softball league, and continuing her mother's helper job, but she has agreed to see a tutor twice a week to keep her skills at their current level. (Please refer to Chapter Nine, "Learning Problems and Possibilities," for more information on learning difficulties such as Beth's.)

THE RELATIONSHIP OF LEARNING STYLE TO A FOURTH GRADER'S SCHOOL PERFORMANCE

Just like the curriculums of earlier grades, the fourth-grade curriculum includes only one Mover subject—physical education. The rest of your child's course material can be divided into Looker and Listener subjects. What follows is a look at the visual and auditory aspects of the fourth-grade curriculum. First, each subject is categorized according to its corresponding learning style. To further illustrate the degree of challenge posed by each subject to a given learner—math to a Looker child, for instance—sample first- and last-quarter report cards have been provided, along with a subject-by-subject look at each learner's overall academic experience.

Looker Subjects

The typical fourth-grade classroom is alive with color and detail. Chalkboards, bulletin boards, and walls are decorated with posters, charts, maps, and displays of students' work. It comes as no surprise, then, that Looker skills are quite valuable.

Looker fourth graders usually excel at the spelling, capitalization, and punctuation components of *language arts*, each of these facets being a visual exercise. You see, a Looker's ability to memorize and envision spellings is much more reliable than a Listener's use of phonics. And Lookers rarely overlook the need for a punctuation mark or an upper-case letter, because they are able to view entire sentences both as single units and as combinations of independent phrases.

The need for sharp visual skills makes fourth-grade *math* a Looker subject. Listeners may be the first in their class to memorize math vocabulary and grasp newly explained concepts. However, as computations become increasingly complex and multiple-digit long division, fractions, and decimals are added to the picture, a Looker's fine motor skills and ability to form mental images are likely to boost her to the top of her class.

Art is another subject that calls upon a Looker's skills. Similarly, *handwriting*, which was discussed in Chapter Six (please see page 130), continues to be a Looker subject because it draws upon visual and fine motor abilities. These same skills enable Lookers to excel at *computers*, because their innate finger dexterity, eye-hand coordination, and instant recall of the keyboard make assignments seem more like play than work.

Listener Subjects

Every fourth-grade subject requires that a child "tune in" to a certain degree and then process the information she hears. However, there are particular areas of study whose strong auditory slant makes them perfectly suited to Listeners.

Reading is perhaps the most important fourth-grade Listener subject, because books, texts, and periodicals are now used in every academic class. With their sophisticated verbal and auditory skills, Listeners are the learners best equipped to sound out unfamiliar words, remember difficult pronunciations, comprehend what is read, and recall details after the fact.

Listeners' auditory strengths also put them at an advantage in *science* and *social studies*. It's true that Lookers have the easiest time with visual aids, such as charts and maps, but Listeners excel at reading and remembering textbook information. They also have little trouble remaining attentive during the lectures, projects, and note-taking that make up the bulk of their class time, and can easily recall what they've heard.

Fourth-grade *foreign language* consists mainly of the memorization of simple dialogue and basic vocabulary terms. As such, much of the class work is oral in nature, with the teacher explaining, pronouncing, and then requesting recitations of each day's lesson. A Listener, with her sharp ear, quickly memorizes the new alphabet, and has little trouble mimicking pronunciations and memorizing word lists.

The grammar portion of fourth-grade *language arts* is easy for most Listeners. A child with well-developed auditory skills quickly spots errors of tense, subject-predicate agreement, or sentence structure, and offers corrections that are instinctive—that is, based on what sounds right, rather than on a particular rule of grammar. For example, a Listener might correctly begin a sentence, "If I were a . . . ," even though she knows that "I was" is the usual pairing, and the reason behind the use of "were" has never been explained to her. Listeners also have the edge when it comes to composition, since their writing efforts are often as detailed and imaginative as their everyday speech.

Vocal music is another Listener subject. In music class, a fourth grader deals simultaneously with rhythm, tone, lyrics, and instrumentation, and is expected to understand and remember the historical background of each new composition. This calls for a discriminating ear, the ability to listen for extended periods of time, and a knack for rote memorization—-in other words, Listener skills. As was explained in Chapter Six (see page 131), it is possible for a Listener to be tone-deaf. Even so, children with this sensory preference usually learn a song and comprehend its significance more quickly than their Looker or Mover peers.

Typical Report Cards for Lookers, Listeners, and Movers

Having matched each fourth-grade subject with the type of learner who finds it most appealing, let's take another look at the classroom performances of Daniel, Ana, and Beth. As you would expect of three children with different learning styles, their report cards are not at all alike. In fact, a look at each child's first- and last-quarter grades clearly shows Daniel's preference for visually oriented subjects, and Ana's affinity for the auditory. Mover Beth, on the other hand, is hard pressed to find any appeal at all in the fourth-grade curriculum.

FOURTH-GRADE REPORT CARDS FOR LOOKER DANIEL

First-Quarter Report		*End-of-Year Report*	
Language Arts	B+	Language Arts	B
Social Studies	B	Social Studies	B
Science	B	Science	B+
Math	A+	Math	A
Spanish	B-	Spanish	B
Computers	A	Computers	A+
Art	A+	Art	A+
Music	B	Music	B
Physical Education	B	Physical Education	B
Handwriting	A+	Handwriting	A+
Conduct	A+	Conduct	A+

Daniel's grades are well above average. His lowest grade, a B- in first-quarter Spanish, reflects his pronunciation difficulties, rather than a lack of effort. Since neither gross motor nor auditory skills are

Daniel's strong suit, he also receives B's in courses like physical education, music, and even the last quarter of language arts, which focused heavily on composition. Daniel's auditory skills also hold him back a bit in social studies and science, where his ability to envision helps him enjoy the classes' historical and categorical aspects, but his less-than-perfect grades attest to his trouble with the memorization of facts. Daniel's grades are so consistent that there is no more than a half-grade variation in any subject between September and June. This is a tribute to his self-discipline and excellent work habits.

FOURTH-GRADE REPORT CARDS FOR LISTENER ANA

First-Quarter Report		*End-of-Year Report*	
Language Arts	A	Language Arts	A+
Social Studies	A	Social Studies	A
Science	A	Science	A
Math	B-	Math	B
French	A	French	A
Computers	B	Computers	B+
Art	B	Art	B-
Music	A	Music	A
Physical Education	B	Physical Education	B
Handwriting	B	Handwriting	B
Conduct	B	Conduct	B-

Ana's facility with language and listening activities is clearly reflected in her grades. Her strongest performances are in subjects with an auditory slant, like music, French, and the reading portion of language arts. Ana listens so well in class that she often masters much of the subject matter long before she reads her textbook. However, because of the visual orientation needed to grasp such concepts as place value, fractions, patterns, and perspective, both math and art pose a problem for Ana. In fact, weekly meetings with a tutor are all that has enabled Ana to keep her math grade above a C. In art, she manages by "borrowing" project ideas she remembers from past years.

The B's Ana earns in computers, art, physical education, and handwriting are direct reflections of motor skills that are, in her case, just average. Ana continues to labor over the computer keyboard, but puts in the extra effort needed to earn a B.

FOURTH-GRADE REPORT CARDS FOR MOVER BETH

First-Quarter Report		*End-of-Year Report*	
Language Arts	C-	Language Arts	C-
Social Studies	C-	Social Studies	C-
Science	B-	Science	C
Math	C-	Math	C-
French	—	French	—
Computers	C-	Computers	D
Art	C+	Art	B-
Physical Education	A	Physical Education	A
Handwriting	C-	Handwriting	C-
Conduct	C	Conduct	C

Beth's love of physical activity and difficulty with all but the hands-on aspects of learning are clearly reflected in her grades. Her strongest performances are in classes that encourage active participation and movement about the room: physical education, art, and science. Conversely, her lowest grades are in subjects that depend on sitting and listening, or, worse, written assignments. Beth's work in language arts, social studies, math, computers, and handwriting is actually worse than her grades indicate. Aware that she's been studying with a Resource Lab teacher, Beth's classroom teachers hesitated to defeat her by assigning a D. Similarly, Beth's C in conduct was intended as reinforcement for her progress in the area of self-control. You see, with Resource Lab support, Beth brought her reading level up a full grade, and, as she gained confidence, her classroom behavior also became more acceptable. Only in French, where she was completely frustrated, did Beth revert to her former attention-getting antics. Her teachers, recognizing that foreign language is not a priority for Beth right now, scheduled her for extra Resource Lab time in place of French class.

WORKING WITH YOUR CHILD'S TEACHER

Each of the fourth graders you met in this chapter learns by a different means. Like many visually oriented children, Daniel is organized and self-directed. Ana, who is most responsive to sound and language, is also a good student. However, both children have found that their innate skills alone cannot guarantee school success. And Beth, who's attuned to touch and movement, needs even more support than her Looker and Listener classmates.

Unfortunately, school conferences and report cards cannot always paint a complete picture of your child's school life. However, you can keep abreast of changes in your fourth grader's social and academic standings by initiating more frequent contact with her teacher. Depending on your child's needs, a behavior or school-preparedness checklist, regularly scheduled notes, or brief lunch-hour phone calls to her teacher can be most informative. To avoid the omission of important points during these communications, jot down thoughts and questions ahead of time. Also consider sharing the teacher's input with your child.

The following lists have been designed to guide you in achieving more effective parent-teacher communication. Each topic relates to your child's academic or social well-being. The list directly below suggests information that you may wish to disclose to your child's teacher. The second list suggests questions that you may wish to ask of your child's teacher.

Eight Facts to Reveal to Your Child's Teacher

- *Your child's degree of personal organization.* Tell the teacher whether your child is orderly or haphazard in her approach to school materials and personal belongings. Mention any effect your child's organizational level has had on her school work. You may also wish to suggest organizational strategies that have proven helpful in the past.

- *Your child's mastery of basic facts.* Let the teacher know whether your child now uses or seems to be in need of special strategies to help her memorize subject material.

- *The employment of a tutor.* Tell the teacher if you have used or are now using a tutor, so that the teacher and tutor can coordinate their methods and goals.

- *Health-related information.* Make both the teacher and school nurse aware of any physical conditions that might affect your child's classroom performance.

- *Past evaluations and screenings.* Alert the teacher to the possibility of recurrent school-work problems by telling him or her of any educational or psychological testing that your child underwent in past years.

- *At-home situations.* Since even temporary upheaval can greatly affect a youngster's school performance, be sure to advise your child's teacher of any major changes in your home life.

- *A second language.* Make the teacher aware of your fourth grader's at-home use of a second language. The use of another language often affects a child's acquisition of English grammar and vocabulary skills.

- *Prior recommendations.* Advise your child's teacher of any seating or class-work modifications used by previous teachers to improve your child's school performance.

Eight Questions to Ask Your Child's Teacher

- *Is your child's homework completed and turned in on time?* Find out how you, your child, and the teacher can work together to eliminate homework problems.

- *Does your child complete the bulk of her class work?* Ask the teacher whether modifications, temporary or permanent, are needed to improve your child's attitude toward her school work.

- *Does your child pay attention in class?* Discuss strategies that might improve your child's ability to apply herself to tasks and assignments at school and at home.

- *What are your child's current reading and math levels?* Ask if the teacher feels that your child's progress accurately reflects her abilities.

- *Does the teacher recommend any sort of professional intervention?* Find out if your child might benefit from professional evaluation or remedial services.

- *On what level does your child participate in class discussions?* Ask if your child voluntarily contributes to group lessons, if she expresses herself satisfactorily, and if she remains attentive when others are speaking.

- *How does your child get along socially?* Ask the teacher whether your child seems at ease among her peers, and whether her social skills seem appropriate for a fourth grader. If your child seems to be a loner, ask the teacher to recommend a youngster or two who might be appropriate playmates.

- *What can you do at home to help your child?* Find out if your child might benefit from improvement in one or more skill areas, and if there are techniques you can use at home to boost your child's growth in those areas.

LEARNING STYLE AND EXTRACURRICULAR ACTIVITIES

It should come as no surprise that a fourth grader's learning style greatly influences her selection of extracurricular pursuits. Certainly, the interests of the three children discussed in this chapter—Daniel's love of video games, Ana's fascination with the theater, and Beth's enthusiasm for sports—are all offshoots of the children's sensory preferences. And, just like the special qualities of our three learners, your own child's sociability, athleticism, or creativity will be reflected in the pastimes she chooses to pursue.

By fourth grade, your child may well have tried her hand at a long list of clubs, sports, and hobbies. Or, she may only be starting to display an interest in extracurricular activities. Whatever the case, don't be surprised if her interests seem to change with great frequency. By now, you see, most children need to be rewarded on some level for their participation in an activity. Those who instead are bored or discouraged by their own poor performance gradually leave the ranks of each organization. In fact, most nine- and ten-year-olds are well aware of what they can and cannot do successfully, and tend to make extracurricular choices accordingly. Movers gravitate toward sports; Lookers, toward artistic and, often, solitary pursuits; and Listeners, toward the clubs and activities that provide the social stimulation they adore.

As a rule, you should allow your fourth grader to take the lead in choosing outside activities. Since extracurricular pursuits exist so that children can spend their free time doing what they like and developing their hobbies, it's pointless to coerce a child into an activity in which she has no interest—no matter how great the potential benefits may be. Art club, for instance, may demand too much sitting still, or music lessons, too much practice time, to hold some children's interest for long. Other fourth graders may be inclined to follow the lead of their friends, rather than the wishes of their parents, when selecting after-school activities. In either case, it's wise to allow your child to experiment with clubs, teams, or lessons that she thinks she'll enjoy and that your budget will permit. Try not to express your disappointment in your fourth grader's choice of activity, your longing for her to exhibit the talents possessed by another family member, or your determination that she enjoy social or athletic opportunities that were lacking in your own childhood. Your child will be much better served by your unconditional acceptance of her own selections and by any practical help you can offer. For instance, if your fourth grader appears to be intrigued by a particular club, class, or sport, but seems hesitant about taking the first step, you can best help her by providing as much information as possible. Similarly, if your child wants to try an activity that you don't believe will hold her interest—if your Listener likes the idea of stamp collecting, for instance—you should nevertheless encourage her experimentation.

In most cases, a fourth grader will stay with those activities that best fit her learning style. If after several weeks' trial she's not enjoying herself, there will be no harm in letting her drop out. After all, children have a right to enjoy their leisure time, and since it's sometimes difficult to anticipate whether a new activity will be a good "fit," experimentation may be unavoidable.

Although it's generally not advisable to persuade a fourth grader to try an activity that seems foreign to her, for reasons of health and fitness, every child, regardless of learning style, needs to develop herself physically. Competitive sports aren't a necessity, particularly for Listeners and Lookers, who are often uncomfortable with their gross motor skills. But there are plenty of noncompetitive pursuits— horseback riding, hiking, swimming, and tae kwon do, to name a few—that will help Lookers develop more physical confidence. And you'll find just as many group-oriented activities—camping, skating, and jazz dancing, for example—that will provide exercise for a Listener. Just be sure not to permit an overscheduling of your child's free time. Family activities, solitary pursuits, and unstructured visits with friends will improve your child's relationships with others and help her develop a strong sense of self.

Of course, there are times when a child seems bored and has trouble filling her after-school hours. If your fourth grader has experienced little success in choosing extracurricular pursuits, you can't go wrong by suggesting activities that fit her learning style. Following are a few ideas for each type of learner.

Activities for Fourth-Grade Lookers

Visually oriented nine- and ten-year-olds usually excel at fine motor pursuits, as well as activities that call forth their ability to envision and recall. Most Lookers also love creating and organizing attractive displays. Here are some ideas that may appeal to your child.

- Astronomy
- Beginning carpentry
- Collecting stamps, coins, or shells
- Cooking and baking
- Creation of a homemade newspaper or book
- Drawing, painting, or other crafts
- Model construction
- Photography
- Sewing or weaving
- Video games

Activities for Fourth-Grade Listeners

As a rule, Listeners are good conversationalists who are at ease around children and adults alike. Most Listeners exude self-confidence born of repeated social success, and are well suited to group activities and any pursuit with an auditory slant. The following list may contain some good ideas for your fourth-grade Listener.

- Acting classes
- Bowling league
- Chorus or choir
- Corresponding with a pen pal
- Day camp or recreation programs
- Girl Scouts, Boy Scouts, or a similar organization
- Interviewing for the school paper
- Participating in peer tutoring
- Roller skating
- Writing and staging plays

Activities for Fourth-Grade Movers

Most Movers find sports very appealing, and love to spend time outdoors. At nine or ten years of age, Movers often delight in new and different pursuits, as long as the rules are simple and physical activity is a component. These ideas may interest your young Mover.

- Aerobics or fitness classes
- Archery
- Bicycling
- Girl Scouts, Boy Scouts, or a similar organization
- Gymnastics
- Hiking and camping
- Ice skating
- Karate, tae kwon do, or another martial arts class
- Long-distance running
- Volleyball

HOMEWORK STRATEGIES FOR LOOKERS, LISTENERS, AND MOVERS

By the fourth grade, most of the responsibility for completing school work should fall on the child. However, parents can greatly lighten the load and increase their child's chances for success by preparing a work space appropriate to the child's learning style, providing needed resources and materials, lending support when problems arise, and assisting in the formulation of a daily "plan of attack" that better organizes the child's assignments. The following are some specific ideas for helping your fourth-grade learner get the most from class and homework.

Strategies for Lookers

A Looker's preference for organization and order serves her well when school work is concerned. No doubt, your child's written work has always been neat. By the fourth grade, she may have taken to personalizing it, as well, by using different-colored inks, or by adding illustrations, a chart or graph, or an attractive cover. A Looker enjoys the process of writing as much as the end result, so don't be concerned if your child devotes more than the prescribed amount of time to written work. Her standards of acceptability are very high!

Lookers like to keep their desks and other work spaces as well organized as everything else in their lives. It's certainly a good idea to furnish your child with an array of art and stationery supplies, but it's better not to disrupt her sense of order by surprising her with a cleaned desk or rearranged shelves. You see, the layout of a Looker's supplies is never a random affair. Items are sorted and displayed according to their owner's carefully thought-out system.

Fourth-grade Lookers work well with flash cards. You can encourage your child to use this technique with multiplication tables, spelling words, dates of historical events, or science vocabulary. You might also suggest that your child color-code her notes. Boxing new terms and circling important names helps separate the most significant material from the surrounding text, and also provides Lookers with pleasingly attractive notebooks. If feasible, encourage your child to use a highlighting marker in her textbook to denote key names and terms. Many schools will not permit the marking of school property, but you may be able to secure an old copy from a company that specializes in used textbooks (check your Yellow Pages), or to buy a new copy directly from the publisher. Just make sure to get the correct edition! Finally, to help with long reading assignments, offer to read some of the material to your child, and teach her to note important facts on index cards.

Strategies for Listeners

Most Listeners have enjoyed so much academic success by fourth grade that their school work is completed with little prodding. However, your help may be needed in selecting and enforcing the best time of day for homework. Listeners are very busy children!

Because Listeners are not visually attuned to such problems as misspellings and missing punctuation, they often need assistance with the proofreading of written work. Provide your child with guidance and help her focus on the problem area; then allow her to find the error herself.

Your child may also need you to clarify instructions. Encourage her to read directions aloud. If this doesn't help, you might wish to offer a verbal explanation: "These math problems will all be done the same way. To figure averages, first you add the scores, then divide."

Permit your Listener to do her homework with soft music playing, but insist that the television and rock music be turned off. It's too distracting! It's a good idea to affirm your child's learning style in other ways, too. For instance, you might encourage her to make use of verbal repetition, to organize important facts into a song, or to record material on a cassette for playback at bedtime.

Strategies for Movers

A fourth-grade Mover needs a great deal of help at home; yet, she is the most likely to sabotage your efforts through her natural haphazardness. Homework assignments may not be recorded, the proper materials may be left at school, notes from the teacher may be lost in transit, and the teacher's verbal directions may be missed altogether. You can help your Mover organize by encouraging her to pause before leaving the classroom or house to review a specially prepared subject checklist. This practice will jog her memory about assignments and remind her to pack the proper items. You might even ask your child's teacher to initial each day's checklist to ensure that nothing is overlooked.

At home, a Mover needs a special place to work, away from noise, family distractions, and favorite toys. The Mover's work space may have to be set up daily, since pencils will break, paper will disappear, and workbooks may slip, unnoticed, between the desk and the wall. It's a good idea to provide a different-colored folder for each subject's assignments so that all work pertaining to your child's weekly spelling list, for example, is kept in one place, while her dittos pertaining to Indian tribes remain together, as well. Ask your child to bring her folders home each day so that you can review the contents together. This will be a big help when it's time to study for a test.

Your physical presence will encourage your child to persevere with reading assignments or written work, but it's equally important to avoid getting visibly frazzled. Saying, "Learning fractions is hard work. Let's find a new way to practice them," is much more helpful than, "We've been over these fractions a jillion times! I can't believe you don't know them yet!"

You can incorporate a Mover's preference for action into many homework assignments. When studying social studies dates, for instance, try writing each of the decades or centuries, as appropriate, on an index card and attaching the card to a shoe box. Then, as your child correctly recalls each date, she gets to toss a checker or coin into the box bearing the corresponding answer. When practicing multiplication tables, you can encourage your child to sway to the left when saying, "two times two," and to the right when responding, "four." You can also practice math and spelling with sets of magnetic numbers and letters.

Homework time can be greatly improved when your child's learning style is a factor in the selection of her work space and the formulation of study strategies. Assignments become more appealing, retention of facts becomes easier, and the entire homework process becomes less stressful for both of you. The next section presents additional ideas for learning-skill development.

TECHNIQUES FOR IMPROVING A FOURTH GRADER'S ACADEMIC PERFORMANCE

Our case studies have shown us that by fourth grade, a child's academic strengths and weaknesses are quite obvious—just as much to the child as to her teachers and peers. Listener children, as a rule, continue their strong performance in reading and language arts, and take to foreign languages with ease. Lookers demonstrate a continued aptitude for spelling, math, the fine arts, and computers. Without intervention,

Movers tend to fall further behind in academics. Even subjects like science, with its pleasing hands-on aspect, pose a problem because Movers have trouble reading the textbook.

When both parent and child appreciate the impact of learning style on the child's academic performance, it becomes easier for parents to offer understanding and support. Because academics loom so large in fourth grade—and because parents and their children are apart for so many hours each school day—it pays to place priority on the affirmation of inborn learning style rather than the attainment of balanced skills. By encouraging your child to use her preferred sense when absorbing and processing class material, you will help her improve her school perform-ance even when she has no natural affinity with the subject being studied. This can best be achieved through the development of special learning strategies that capitalize on a child's strongest skills, and through the use of multisensory activities and materials—activities and materials that draw upon both a child's preferred sense *and* the sense needed for mastery of that subject matter.

In the previous pages, you learned some general learning-style-based homework strategies. The following seven sections provide more spe-cific learning strategies, as well as a wide range of multisensory tech-niques and materials. Each of these sections focuses on one of the various skills demanded of a fourth grader: reading, language arts, penmanship, computers, science, social studies, and math. Each one opens with a discussion of the components of the subject area, and continues with a list of tools, tactics, and learning aids that tap a child's Listener, Looker, or Mover traits, thereby improving her performance. Some strategies can be employed in the classroom, others will help with homework, and still others are intended to broaden a child's interest in the subject matter. Read through the lists carefully, and try out those suggestions that seem most appropriate for your child. You are both likely to profit from the time you spend together implementing and fine-tuning your fourth grader's newest learning tactics.

Building Reading Skills

There are several skills involved in the reading process. First, a child must learn to recognize or decode words, which involves sounding out or otherwise transforming a printed word into one that is spoken. Next, the child must possess a vocabulary sufficient to define the words she reads, whether from memory, sentence context, or the structure of the word itself.

And, finally, a child must be able to read smoothly enough to focus on the whole product rather than just the reading process itself so that she can comprehend and recall the sequence and content of printed material.

It may well be that only one or two of these skills causes your fourth grader difficulty. You might wish to ask your child and her teacher exactly where they feel the trouble lies. Once you've pinpointed a skill that needs improving, the following suggestions may prove helpful.

TECHNIQUES TO IMPROVE WORD RECOGNITION SKILLS

Continue—or resume—the practice of reading to your child. Select a mystery, an adventure, or a story about children that your fourth grader can identify with, and read a chapter every day.

Classic tales in video form enable a child to "see" a story before reading it. Decoding new words is often easier when the story's setting and sequence of events seem familiar.

Make regular trips to the library, allowing enough time for your child to browse in the juvenile section. Guide your child in selecting books with enough appeal to guarantee her sticking with long or difficult text.

If your child struggles to sound out words, consider hiring a tutor. One-to-one work can often clarify basic elements of phonics.

Investigate the possibility of purchasing used textbooks for home use. Your child would be free to write in these, which could prove helpful when rereading at test time.

Encourage your child to highlight important words in her notebooks with a marker such as the PENTECH *Trilighter*. This marker contains three fluorescent colors in a triangular shape meant to fit in the student's palm.

TECHNIQUES TO IMPROVE READING VOCABULARY

Workman Publishing's *Shoelace Calendar* introduces a new word for every day of the year. Most terms are accompanied by pictures to clarify meaning.

Purchase a dictionary, such as the *Macmillan Dictionary for Children* (New York, 1977). In addition to explaining word meanings and usage, this volume contains a pronunciation key and a pictorial history of language.

Provide a children's thesaurus in which students are treated to synonyms, antonyms, and homonyms for each alphabetically listed word. Some versions, like Andrew Schiller's *In Other Words: A Beginning Thesaurus*, published by Lothrop, Lee, and Shepard Books (New York, 1977), contain illustrations to clarify word meanings.

Oxford's *The Facts on File Junior Visual Dictionary* (New York, 1989) emphasizes visual detail and expands vocabulary through pictures of skin-diving gear, an automobile dashboard, and other terms.

Workman Publishing's *365 Things Every Kid Should Know!* is a calendar that builds vocabulary related to American culture with terms like "Rose Bowl" and "fossil fuel."

TECHNIQUES TO IMPROVE READING COMPREHENSION

Locate a classic that you think will interest your child. Then, borrow the book and its video version simultaneously. Your child's reading efforts will be encouraged and rewarded when she sees the story come to life.

If your child's reading comprehension skills are very poor, consider borrowing some books on audio tape from your school or local library. Your child can follow along in the book as the text is read aloud to her.

Encourage your child to close her eyes after reading a passage and imagine a picture of what she has just read. With practice, the art of creating mental images will become automatic.

If your child likes to draw, suggest that she sketch a picture of the action in each story or chapter.

Enlist your librarian's help in locating high-interest, low-reading-level books published especially for children with reading difficulties. By fourth grade, most struggling readers are offended by the idea of reading material intended for children two or more years younger.

Building Language Arts Skills

Language arts is a broad term that encompasses the skills a child needs to communicate through spoken or written language. On the elementary school level, most language arts programs include lessons in grammar, spelling, capitalization, punctuation, and sentence and paragraph structure. Once the basic rules are learned, language arts skills provide a foundation not only for the introduction of foreign language, but for a lifetime of proper use of the mother tongue!

Your fourth grader may have difficulty with only one or two language arts skills, and a glance at her most recent composition may be enough to tell you where her problem lies. Are her sentences complete and properly punctuated? Are her grammar and spelling correct? If you're not sure, don't hesitate to ask her teacher which of your child's language arts skills needs strengthening. Here are some skill-development ideas that will help.

TECHNIQUES TO IMPROVE SPELLING SKILLS

■ If your own phonics background is strong, show your child how to break her spelling words into sound units, e.g., "black" into "b-l-a-ck," and "thing" into "th-i-ng." Then, urge her to break the words into syllables, e.g., "vacation" into "va-ca-tion." The ability to spell words by sound and syllable will increase her chance of including all the required letters.

■ Franklin's *Elementary Spelling Ace*, a hand-held computer that stores 50,000 words, can help to build spelling and language skills. Once entered into the computer's memory, spelling words can be used in games like "Hangman."

■ Encourage your child to picture a chalkboard in her mind. Then spell aloud each of her spelling words, and urge her to picture the words on the chalkboard. Ask about such visual details as the color of the chalk being used and the color of the chalkboard itself. Attention to such details will enhance your child's ability to recall the correct spellings.

■ Examine your child's spelling words to see whether any visual or verbal strategies might help. For example, the word "together" can be envisioned as three smaller words—"to," "get," and "her"—combined. Or, the saying "*I* before *E*, except after *C*" might apply.

■ Provide a copy of Barron's *A Pocket Guide to Correct Spelling* (New York, 1990) for your child to use at home and at school. This book is particularly helpful for written work because words are listed without pronunciations or definitions and can be located much more quickly than they can in a regular dictionary.

TECHNIQUES TO IMPROVE GRAMMAR, SENTENCE STRUCTURE, AND PUNCTUATION

■ Encourage your child to color-code the parts of speech in various sentences. Nouns can be highlighted in yellow, adjectives in green, verbs in blue, and so on. The same technique can be used to familiarize your child with sentence parts—subjects, predicates, prepositional phrases, and the like.

■ If your child uses grammatically incorrect speech, try rephrasing her statements as grammatically correct questions, as though you were echoing her thoughts. For example, if your child says, "My class don't have no homework," you can follow with, "Your class doesn't have any homework? That's great!" If this is done in a nonjudgmental tone, you will subtly reinforce proper grammar.

■ To improve your child's punctuation skills, write a few sample sentences on a large piece of paper using two-inch upper-case letters and one-inch lower-case letters. Have your child dye elbow macaroni and glue it in the appropriate places to serve as apostrophes, quotation marks, and commas. She can hang the finished product on her wall as a model for future compositions.

■ To encourage writing, buy a brightly colored notebook to serve as your child's diary or journal. Assure your child that she can share her thoughts or not, as she wishes, but explain that she is to make an entry every day.

■ Try referring to parts of speech and sentence parts by other names— names that *define* the different terms. Instead of "noun," say "person, place, or thing." Rather than "adjective" and "adverb," try "describing words." In place of "verb," say "action word." With enough repetition, your child will soon associate these definitions with the standard terms.

TECHNIQUES TO IMPROVE FOREIGN LANGUAGE SKILLS

■ Barron's *Beginner's Bilingual Dictionary* (New York, 1989) is available in French, Italian, and Spanish, and accompanies words with pictures.

■ Encourage your child to use newly learned foreign vocabulary around the house. Label household items and furnishings with cards bearing their foreign names.

■ Check The Heritage Key catalogue for multicultural books and gifts from around the world. Places represented in the catalogue include Mexico, India, Korea, Latin America, and Jamaica.

■ Children's language tapes accompanied by picture books are available on different instructional levels. Children sing, color, and play games while learning new words and phrases.

■ Share with your child travel videos that feature countries whose inhabitants speak the language your child is learning.

Building Penmanship Skills

Some school districts place a heavier emphasis on handwriting than others. Our case-study children's report cards bore penmanship grades, but some schools cease this practice after grade three, once the cursive alphabet has been mastered. Regardless, the fourth grader who can produce legible, well-formed letters has two advantages over the student whose handwriting is poor. First, since cursive letters were originally designed so that the writer's pen strokes would flow smoothly and quickly across each line, the student with good penmanship will complete written work with less effort than will someone who's in the habit of retracing lines or lifting the pen between letters. Second, that student will be spared the aggravations a poor writer faces when she has to proofread sloppy work, justify misunderstood spelling, or rewrite an unacceptable paper. Granted, few fourth graders can produce the kind of wall-chart penmanship displayed in classrooms all across the country. But, if improved handwriting—or the development of an acceptable substitute—can make a difference in your fourth grader's school work, surely the subject deserves some attention. Here are some ideas for improving your child's penmanship.

TECHNIQUES TO IMPROVE PENMANSHIP

GripStix by PENTECH are pencils that ease the strain of writing by providing indentations for the index finger.

Pencil and pen grips—which slip over writing instruments, making them easier to hold—are available in plastic or rubber.

Provide your child with a beginner's book of calligraphy to promote writing as an art form and to stimulate your child's interest in the appearance of her everyday written work.

If your child's cursive writing is very difficult to read, consider letting her type her work. Barron's *Kids Can Type Too!*, by Christine Mountford (New York, 1987), shows how to master both typewriter and computer keyboards.

Type-right by Video Technology is a color-coded keyboard designed to teach typewriting. Lessons and progress tests are included.

Building Computer Skills

These days, it's not unusual for a child's computer knowledge to exceed that of her parents. We live in a high-tech age that's becoming increasingly complex. To prepare the next generation, most schools begin weekly computer instruction in kindergarten. Of course, many American homes contain personal computers and word processors; but whether your household is among this number or not, and regardless of your own computer knowledge, there are ways in which you can help your child feel at home with what may currently seem a most intimidating piece of equipment. Here are some ideas.

TECHNIQUES TO IMPROVE COMPUTER SKILLS

Help your child memorize the computer keyboard with *Type-right*, a color-coded keyboard by Video Technology.

Consider purchasing a secondhand electric typewriter for your child's room. Chances are, this will be used strictly for fun, but each time your child hunt-and-pecks out a note to a friend, she will become more familiar with the keyboard.

■ To give your child access to as many different video games as possible, borrow and trade games with friends and neighbors. As your child begins to feel confident with a variety of games, her ease with computers will increase, as well.

■ Video Technology offers several inexpensive computers designed just for children. Investing in one for your home and encouraging its frequent use as entertainment may do a great deal to decrease your child's keyboard anxiety.

■ If computers are used at your place of employment, arrange for your child to receive an unhurried guided tour. A "field trip" of this type may increase her interest in and understanding of the computer process.

Building Science Skills

By fourth grade, most schools' science curriculums have become quite complex. Between lectures, reports, projects, and experiments, nine- and ten-year-old students are bombarded by subject material from all angles. Naturally, your child will find some units and some methods of study much more intriguing than others. And, even though much of the responsibility for a subject's appeal lies in the teacher's approach, your child's own prior knowledge will have a lot to do with her interest in and commitment to the program offered at her school. Here are some ideas to help improve your fourth grader's performance in science.

TECHNIQUES TO IMPROVE SCIENCE SKILLS

■ Angela Wilkes' *My First Nature Book*, published by McKay (St. Croix, VA, 1990), describes fun and easy science projects from plaster casting to flower pressing.

■ Encourage your child's interest in astronomy with a backyard tele- scope and trips to a local planetarium.

■ Invest in a children's science kit for at-home experiments.

■ Encourage your child to borrow children's science magazines, like *Ranger Rick* or *National Geographic World,* from the library. If you read aloud to your child, substitute a magazine for your usual book once or twice a week. Or, your child can read the magazines on her own.

■ Seek out nearby places for outings that are fun and educational. A hands-on museum, a greenhouse, a nature preserve, a farm, and a zoo nursery are just a few ideas.

Building Social Studies Skills

Fourth-grade social studies is a course with many facets. For perhaps the first time, students grapple with history, geography, anthropology, global issues, and current events. Moreover, fourth-grade curriculum materials may be gleaned from such diverse sources as periodicals, television, videos, and visiting lecturers, while course work may include independent research, group work, and hands-on projects.

It's certainly safe to assume that your child will feel most at ease with social studies material when she has a bank of general knowledge on which to draw in class, and when the terminology used during the course of study sounds somewhat familiar. The following ideas can help your child approach fourth-grade social studies with interest rather than intimidation.

TECHNIQUES TO IMPROVE SOCIAL STUDIES SKILLS

■ Borrow or invest in a globe for your home. Many globes are available with raised terrain that will increase the globe's appeal as it improves your child's grasp of world geography.

■ Involve your child in the composition of a family history or a dated family tree.

■ Rand McNally's *Kids' Map of the United States* (Chicago, 1990) is illustrated with sketches of fun things to see and do across the country.

■ *Passport to the World* is a geography game by Texas Instruments. Each player is assigned a destination and answers questions about that region's food, clothing, climate, and famous people, among other topics.

■ If your child likes to read, she may enjoy and learn from biographies, works of fiction, and natural history books that pertain to her current social studies unit. A children's librarian can help you locate appropriate materials.

■ *The Doubleday Children's Atlas* (New York, 1987) and Rand McNally's *Children's Atlas of the United States* (Chicago, 1989) both contain maps, photos, facts, and figures that will give your child a better understanding of her country and the world.

Building Math Skills

Most fourth graders are old hands at addition, subtraction, multiplication, and division. This year, though, they are expected to put their computational skills to work on fractions, decimals, and complex equations. Students who have always enjoyed and succeeded in math will find this challenge exciting; children who have always struggled with math can quickly become lost. Yet, regardless of a fourth grader's math ability, she will be required to take the subject for several more years.

Academic concerns aside, numbers and computation are an unavoidable part of our adult lives. It stands to reason, then, that by working with your child to improve her grasp of math fundamentals, you will be doing her a tremendous favor! Following are some ideas to get you started.

TECHNIQUES TO IMPROVE MATH SKILLS

■ Milton Bradley's *Quizmo* has forty game cards on which your child can practice multiplication and division. Special markers are included.

■ Purchase a calculator with oversized keys for your child's use at home. This will encourage her to do computations for fun.

■ Suggest that your child do her math problems on graph paper, which has both horizontal and vertical lines to help in the spacing and alignment of tabulations.

■ Texas Instruments' *Speak & Math* is a computer game that provides multiplication, division, and word problems at three different levels.

■ Provide your child with her own set of carpentry tools, and encourage her to measure and build along with you. Working with tools encourages the development of those visual skills necessary for math success.

As you focus on providing those at-home experiences and learning tools that will bring about improvement in your child's school performance, I urge you to be diplomatic! Nine- and ten-year-olds are well aware of and, in many cases, quite sensitive about their academic shortcomings. An overzealous effort on your part may serve only as a blatant reminder of classroom struggles that your child would rather forget about when at home. So, instead of bombarding your learner with books, toys, and activities, try to carefully select one or two techniques that seem appropriate for her, and then *suggest* rather than *insist* that she try them out.

I also caution you not to expect overnight success. Your child's proficiency—or lack thereof—in each of her school subjects has been more than four years in the making. Given the fact that a subtle approach is most effective, it may take many weeks before either of you notices heightened interest, stronger skills, and greater confidence on your child's part. Any of these gradual changes will be proof that your efforts to help your child master academic material are, indeed, paying off!

Learning Style QuickCheck for Fourth Graders, Ages Nine to Ten

Directions: Read the statements below, and place a check next to each characteristic that seems to describe your child. Total the checks in each column, and compare your totals. You're likely to find your responses heavily concentrated in one column, or evenly divided between two. These results will provide a clear picture of your fourth grader's preferred learning style.

Looker	Listener	Mover

1. Communication: When my fourth grader wishes to express herself . . .

Looker	Listener	Mover
☐ Her sentences are short and unelaborated.	☐ She speaks in long, complex sentences.	☐ She speaks in short sentences, and mispronounces some words.
☐ She rarely volunteers answers in class.	☐ She often volunteers answers in class.	☐ She is quiet in class, but loud on the playground.
☐ Her vocabulary is about average for her age.	☐ She has a huge vocabulary.	☐ Her vocabulary is rather small.
☐ She prefers to communicate face-to-face.	☐ She likes to chat on the telephone.	☐ She avoids using the telephone whenever possible.

2. Favorite Pastimes: When my fourth grader has free time . . .

Looker	Listener	Mover
☐ She spends much of her time at the computer.	☐ She opens a library book from her favorite series.	☐ She enjoys attending sporting events like football games and rodeos.
☐ She excels at video games.	☐ She memorizes songs and dialogue from her favorite videos.	☐ She excels at soccer and softball.
☐ She assembles puzzles and kits with ease.	☐ She is often chosen for leading roles in school programs.	☐ She can act out a part in a play, but is unable to memorize her lines.
☐ She enjoys board games, but is a stickler for rules.	☐ She takes charge when playing games.	☐ She prefers outdoor play to indoor play. She tends to lose pieces to indoor games.

3. Fine Motor Skills: When my fourth grader uses her hands . . .

☐ She produces beautiful, creative art projects.

☐ She tolerates art class, but may repeat a project from one year to the next.

☐ She likes the hands-on aspect of art, but is messy in her use of materials.

☐ Her school work is neatly done.

☐ She turns in acceptable but not overly neat paperwork.

☐ She writes off the line and into the margin. Her number columns often drift.

4. Gross Motor Skills: When my fourth grader moves about . . .

☐ She is best at eye-hand games, such as horseshoes and badminton.

☐ She requires a lot of prodding to participate.

☐ She is agile and very coordinated. She is good at all gross motor activities.

☐ She prefers noncontact sports, such as running and hiking.

☐ She prefers playground games that involve word play, like jump rope.

☐ She is usually the game leader and team captain.

5. Social Skills: When my fourth grader mixes with other children . . .

☐ She tends to be a loner within the group.

☐ She is sociable, and maintains interaction by talking.

☐ She seeks out other children who enjoy noisy, active play.

☐ She prefers to work on individual, rather than group, projects.

☐ She prefers group projects to working alone.

☐ She does not work well independently or in a group. She requires frequent teacher assistance.

6. Emotions: When it comes to my fourth grader's feelings . . .

☐ She does not readily express emotion.

☐ She freely expresses her feelings by talking about them.

☐ She expresses her feelings nonverbally by shouting, hugging, jumping, or stamping her foot.

☐ Emotional displays make her uncomfortable.

☐ She is understanding and sympathetic to her friends' feelings.

☐ She tends to be moody, impatient, and easily frustrated.

7. Memory: When my fourth grader learns . . .

☐ She writes and doodles to help herself remember.

☐ She is good at memorizing poems, jingles, and facts.

☐ She has trouble remembering what she sees and hears.

☐ She has a large sight vocabulary.

☐ She remembers new vocabulary words after hearing them only once.

☐ She remembers action and movements.

8. At School: When my fourth grader is in the classroom . . .

☐ Her desk is well organized.

☐ She is fairly organized.

☐ Her work area tends to be a mess.

☐ She conscientiously follows class rules.

☐ She sometimes gets in trouble for talking and passing notes.

☐ She is often up and out of her seat.

☐ She dresses neatly, with coordinated accessories.

☐ She likes to put together her own outfits, which may or may not match.

☐ Her clothes are often rumpled and grass-stained.

☐ She excels in math and spelling.

☐ She excels in social studies and reading.

☐ She enjoys doing science projects. She may be receiving extra help in reading and math.

Totals: _____Looker _____Listener _____Mover

Chapter Eight

Learning Styles in Eighth Grade

Eighth grade can be a confusing time. There's no denying that early adolescence is stressful to both parent and child, for it's a period during which the child is torn between the pressures exerted by socially aware peers and the safe haven represented by the toys and activities of yesteryear. Many eighth graders respond by exhibiting a strange mix of childish-versus-teen behavior. Parents quickly learn that to expect one type of behavior at any given time almost guarantees their child's display of another!

Whether a thirteen-year-old is precocious or somewhat immature, eighth grade represents a turning point in his life. The eighth grader is expected to be self-reliant about class work and homework. He also sees the future beckon, for perhaps the first time, as he learns the function of guidance counselors and experiences the heady, almost frightening power that comes with choosing elective courses and selecting from among the array of extracurricular activities that are part of junior high and middle school life. On top of all this, "popularity" now becomes the ultimate social goal of almost every student, and boy-girl pairings are in such abundance that even the most socially resistant thirteen-year-old is likely to find himself taking a second glance in the mirror and worrying over clothing and hair styles.

An eighth grader's social inclinations, his classroom conduct and study skills, and even his physical abilities can all be traced to his learning style. Since birth, the adolescent has been attuned to particular environmental stimuli, be they visual, auditory, or tactile. A walk through the school cafeteria will confirm this. Looker students sit off to the side, perhaps with a friend, eating quietly and absorbing every· detail of what's taking place around them. Listeners see lunch time as a social hour, and are likely to be at the head of a table full of admiring friends. Movers find reason to leave their seat ten times in twenty minutes, for a drink of water, another straw, a redder apple, and so on.

This chapter tells the stories of three eighth-grade learners: a Looker, a Listener, and a Mover. As you follow the children's progress and development from September to June, you'll enjoy a unique view of each child's social life, classroom performance, physical abilities, and relationships with family. No doubt, you'll see your own child reflected in one of our three learners. A Learning Style QuickCheck for Eighth Graders (see page 233) is included to confirm your observations.

It comes as no surprise that learning style has a tremendous influence on a fourth grader's academic experience. This chapter describes the academic performance that typically accompanies each learning style, and looks at different ways in which you can establish positive communication with your child's teachers. Because a child's sensory preference affects his actions and choices outside the classroom as well as in, this chapter also examines the almost inevitable social results of learning styles, and provides suggestions for parents who are approached for or choose to offer advice aimed at helping their child become more at ease socially. A host of extracurricular activity ideas are provided, as well.

By eighth grade, parents should have formed realistic expectations about a child's classroom performance. And, given the limited amount of time most parents have with their teen-agers—not to mention the dwindling patience many thirteen- and fourteen-year-olds have with parental assistance—it's wise to focus on academic improvement rather than the general well-roundedness that is a goal during a child's early years. To that end, this chapter discusses materials, techniques, and strategies that will stimulate your child's intellectual curiosity, help him with homework assignments, and improve his study skills.

Eighth grade is not too late to effect change. With patience and restraint, parents *can* help their teen-ager achieve. This chapter will help you understand your child's learning strengths and weaknesses, enabling you to set reasonable academic standards and realistic goals for the future.

A LOOK AT THREE LEARNERS

Kim-Lee, Mark, and Shawn have just begun eighth grade at a suburban middle school. The children have been classmates since kindergarten, and they all celebrated their thirteenth birthdays during the preceding spring.

Because these three teen-agers possess different learning styles, each is drawn to different elements of his or her surroundings and responds to these surroundings in different ways. Kim-Lee has always been visually oriented; Mark is attuned to language and sounds; and Shawn learns best through movement and touch. As a result, despite our learners' similarly supportive home environments, their frequent sharing of teachers, and some twelve years of exposure to identical resources within the community, the children have interests, talents, and work habits that are amazingly dissimilar. Not all children display the characteristics of a single learning style in this manner. Some are combination learners—Looker-Movers, say, or Looker-Listeners—and exhibit traits from two sensory areas. However, for the sake of clarity and to highlight the features of each individual learning style, I've chosen to portray Kim-Lee, Mark, and Shawn as possessing "pure" styles. Let's visit our learners at the start of the eighth-grade year and see how sensory preference has shaped each child.

Thirteen Years of Age

Meet Kim-Lee. At first glance, Looker Kim-Lee seems quite unflappable. Quiet and serene, she has never revealed much of herself even to her family and lifelong friends. But, a closer look reveals a very driven thirteen-year-old who is often tense, ill at ease in social situations, and unwavering in her motivation to achieve. Every teen needs a means of self-expression. For some, it's sports; for others, it may be a club presidency. For Kim-Lee, her good grades and reputation as a hard worker are their own rewards.

Kim-Lee has three close friends, only one of whom she met through school. The other two girls are neighbors whom Kim-Lee has known for many years. All three friends are as reserved as Kim-Lee, and the time she spends with each of them is usually scheduled ahead of time for a specific purpose—completing a school project, for example—rather than being a spontaneous affair. Kim-Lee and her friends find the prospect of dating to be quite appalling, for none of them possesses the gift of small talk or the wherewithal to enjoy herself at a party, much less on a date! At the moment, Kim-Lee happens to admire a certain boy, but she is much too embarrassed to admit this to her friends, and would rather die than act on her feelings. Instead, in her usual from-the-sidelines fashion, Kim-Lee becomes emotionally, if not actively, involved in the social lives and problems of her classmates. Her long-time habit of quietly watching interactions and goings on makes Kim-Lee privy to some fascinating details. Although she is as uncomfortable as ever with displays and declarations of emotion, and though she's far from ready to test the waters herself, her careful observations have actually taught her a great deal about social behavior.

Naturally, Kim-Lee is a teen of few words. People enjoy talking to her, though, because her intent gaze is quite flattering to any speaker, and she never forgets a face! In her spare time, Kim-Lee enjoys practicing calligraphy, writing and illustrating children's stories, and playing Nintendo. She has become an extremely popular baby-sitter because she is vigilant, neat, and reliable. In true Looker fashion, Kim-Lee always comes prepared with a baby-sitter kit that includes crayons and paper, snap-together blocks, puzzles, and a board game or two. It's a tossup as to who enjoys the kit's contents more—Kim-Lee or her young charges.

Kim-Lee is fairly well coordinated, although in gym class, she much prefers solitary activities, like archery or the broad jump, to team sports. You see, Kim-Lee is bothered by the loose organization and unpredictability that is part of such group games as field hockey, volleyball, softball, and the like. She was approached as a candidate for eighth-grade kickline, but hastily declined such a high-profile position. Except for walks and an occasional bike ride, Kim-Lee avoids most gross motor activity at home.

Quite the opposite is true of Kim-Lee and fine motor pursuits. Always artistic, she does most of the cartoons for her school newspaper. At school and at home, she doodles and draws constantly, and has begun personalizing book covers and decorating T-shirts for her girlfriends. Kim-Lee is also quite adept at the computer, whether playing a game, creating graphics and headings for the newspaper, or composing a term paper of her own. Her parents encourage her to borrow or rent as many computer games as she likes, but strongly urge her to develop her gross motor side, as well. Recently, they asked her to consider taking lessons in baton-twirling or skating.

Kim-Lee has long been aware that her attention wanders during lectures, and that she frequently forgets verbal instructions. To compensate, she carries a special homework assignment book, and does thumbnail sketches pertaining to the day's lesson in the margins of her notebooks. She reviews her notes daily, recopying, outlining, and highlighting the material to help herself absorb it. Naturally, Looker Kim-Lee does well in visual subjects like math, computers, and art. Proud of her attractive, creative work, she attacks science and social studies projects with relish, but falters in auditory efforts, like the retention of material discussed in class and the taking of notes during films and videos. Kim-Lee is quite good at the memorization of foreign language vocabulary and spelling, but doesn't do nearly as well with English, where no study lists are provided!

At thirteen, this Looker is well aware of her learning strengths and weaknesses. Since good grades and the opinions of her teachers are very important to her, she will, no doubt, continue to apply her visual strategies to her school work. Although Kim-Lee may feel increasing social pressure as she moves through the school year, eighth grade should pose no new academic challenges for her.

Meet Mark. Socially, Listener Mark is Kim-Lee's polar opposite. Mark shows no signs of discomfort in groups or with the opposite sex; in fact, he's a great conversationalist who always seems to know the right thing to say. Introductions, apologies, advice, and even terms of endearment come easily to Mark. His teachers and parents often joke that he possesses the social graces of a cosmopolitan forty-year-old!

Mark is very much influenced by the views of older teens and by the opinions of his peers. In fact, very little that Mark buys, wears, or attempts is ever spontaneous. Rather, most of Mark's moves are calculated for their effect on his social status, and rehearsed for maximum appeal. This way, he can be assured of a place among the most stylish and most popular boys in the school. Inevitably for a teen-ager held in such high regard, Mark has developed quite a following of his own. But, Mark so enjoys talking that he really doesn't listen to idle chatter, and frequently interrupts his friends in mid-sentence. Luckily, Mark's own views carry so much weight that his classmates are willing to overlook this habit.

Naturally, Mark does a great deal of socializing in his free time, as well. Joking and laughing with a group of friends and chatting on the phone are two of his favorite pastimes. When alone, Mark reads voraciously, often to the accompaniment of music. Mark enjoys the series of plays and concerts his town sponsors each summer, and can't wait until his parents allow him to attend rock concerts. It's no surprise that Mark was voted this year's Student Council homeroom representative. Although only one meeting has been held so far, Mark finds the concept of student government quite fascinating, and is glad to be a part of it. His other school interests are the Drama Club and the French Club— both perfect showcases for his talents!

Mark tends to shy away from cooking, crafts, and other fine motor activities, because he has long known that his eye-hand coordination is not the best. It is for the same reason that earlier attempts at the piano and saxophone met with failure, despite his love of music. Mark also accepts that his handwriting and school projects will never have the visual appeal of some of his classmates' efforts; it's taken years of hard work just to get his paperwork to its present acceptable level. Mark's full-body coordination is average. Unhappy about giving less than a stellar performance, but unable to produce one, Mark avoids team sports both at home and at school. He does, however, enjoy those aspects of gym class that emphasize cooperation instead of perform-ance—spotting his classmates during tumbling, for example, or serving as row captain during the taking of attendance.

Mark has always been a good student. His auditory skills enable him to easily take notes, read textbooks, and glean important information from movies, lectures, and assemblies. His projects and experiments may be somewhat lacking, but Mark more than makes up for this with creative, dynamic oral presentations and nonstop class participation. He loves learning the vocabulary and historical aspects of foreign language, and is easily the best conversationalist in this year's French class. Mark has chosen to drop art and computers—classes in which he lacks the skills needed to excel—in favor of speech and vocal music. He has coped with his ongoing math struggles by enrolling in a basic math class, rather than beginning the algebra-geometry-trigonometry sequence chosen by the better students. Even with less-involved work and the slower pace adopted by his math teacher, Mark assumes he'll be needing regular help from a tutor.

Like Kim-Lee, Mark has learned to make the most of his learning strengths to compensate for any weaker skills. He studies and reads out loud, makes frequent use of a tape recorder, and tries to use verbal strategies to remember visual material. To recall the order of the planets in the solar system, for example, Mark recites the following sentence, in which each word begins with the corresponding planet's first letter: *My Very Efficient Mother Just Sent Us New Potatoes."* To flourish in the eighth grade, Mark need only continue to study and interact according to the learning style he appears to understand so well.

Meet Shawn. Mover Shawn is not a particularly sociable teen-ager. In fact, he says little, seems ill at ease around strangers and in crowds, and does whatever he can to avoid "connecting," be it by eye contact or phone. Because he is most comfortable around physical boys like him-self, Shawn's chief social outlet is sports. As captain of the football and lacrosse teams, and as a participant in a community baseball league and various intramural sports, Shawn's after-school hours are quite full. Team sports are ideal for someone of Shawn's athleticism and social reserve. They afford a showcase for his talents, ample opportunity to interact with peers, and even, although through no particular intent of Shawn's, a sort of hero status that attracts the admiration of boys and girls alike. Shawn's penchant for physical contact—hugs, back slaps, and hair ruffling, for example—and his inclination to dress for comfort, rather than style, combine to lend him an air of maturity that he doesn't really possess.

Shawn has neither time for nor interest in the clubs and service organizations that figure in the lives of many adolescents. As far as casual "hanging out" goes, Shawn would rather do his at the handball courts than in a mall or someone's basement. This Mover has always loved the outdoors, and, even at thirteen, routinely ignores books, games, and the telephone in favor of backyard and street play. His passion for action carries over to foul-weather pursuits, as well. When forced to remain indoors, Shawn watches police and war movies or wrestles with his German shepherd.

Shawn's fine motor skills don't approach the level of his gross motor ability. His handwriting has always been marginal; he's never been good at video games; and his difficulty understanding design and measurement and following directions has kept him away from wood-working and other crafts. As a way of improving his written work, Shawn is trying hard to learn to type. For now, the hunt-and-peck method is all he can manage, so Shawn types his short assignments and relies on his older brother for longer papers.

Seeking help with school work is nothing new to Shawn. For years, he needed the same sort of support at home that he received in his school's Resource Lab, and did his homework side by side with one of his parents. Lately, though, he seems to resent his parents' hovering and has requested that they reserve their efforts for occasions when he's really stumped and asks for help. Naturally, his homework isn't as well done—or, for that matter, as frequently done—as before, but Shawn really *is* trying. Nowadays, Shawn is likely to appeal to his older brother or his friends for assistance with reports or big assignments; alone, he can't manage to pull a long-term project together.

At his parents' urging, Shawn has signed up for an elective computer course, and has opted for study hall instead of a second elective. His family feels that keyboard and computer knowledge is a "must" for Shawn, and that he can use his study hall time for unfinished work or, when necessary, for Resource Lab. Shawn takes a remedial reading class, rather than a foreign language. His science, social studies, and English classes provide him with more than enough exercise in vocabulary and spelling!

Last year, with his teachers' permission, Shawn began carrying a pocket calculator for math computations and a small tape recorder for taping lectures. At first, he worried about the social ramifications of making his need for help so obvious, but Shawn is so admired that no one dares to tease him. Like Kim-Lee and Mark, Shawn has learned, over the years, to work around his learning weaknesses. The new availability of interscholastic teams brought by Shawn's eighth-grade status, combined with the teen's increasing popularity and freedom to hand-pick certain courses, has created a potential for enjoyment that, until now, was missing from Shawn's school life.

Can you see your own eighth grader in any of our learners? It may be that Looker Kim-Lee's reticence and self-direction reminds you of your own son or daughter. Or, maybe Listener Mark's social and academic competence sounds more than a little familiar. If not, perhaps Shawn's athletic ability and classroom struggles strike a familiar chord. On page 233, you will find a Learning Style QuickCheck for Eighth Graders that will erase any doubts. By marking the behaviors that are most characteristic of your child, and then totaling the marks in each column, you will get a vivid picture of the methods your thirteen-year-old uses to interact and learn.

HOW LOOKER, LISTENER, AND MOVER EIGHTH GRADERS DEVELOP

Looker Kim-Lee, Listener Mark, and Mover Shawn all follow the dictates of an inborn sensory preference when learning from and reacting to surroundings. As a result, these three adolescents have developed unique sets of social, physical, and academic skills.

As our three learners progress through their eighth-grade year, their development continues on course, influencing their grades, their friendships, their hobbies, and their overall attitude toward school and home. While the highlight of Mark's week might be social dancing in Friday's gym class, for example, his long-time classmates Shawn and Kim-Lee dread the week's end for that very reason. And while grades and homework have long been a source of tension between Shawn and his parents, Mark and Kim-Lee receive only positive feedback at conference and report-card time.

As the school year draws to a close, let's return to our three learners to see how each teen handles life as an eighth grader.

Fourteen Years of Age

Kim-Lee. For the first time in her life, Kim-Lee is concerned about being overlooked by her peers. Mind you, she isn't interested in being the center of attention, but it rankles a bit when her classmates garner praise and admiration for scholastic efforts that Kim-Lee easily duplicates but chooses to keep to herself. At fourteen, Kim-Lee has begun to place some value on the opinions of her peers—a sure sign of social growth.

During eighth grade, Kim-Lee became active in the Art Club. The club's handful of members are mostly loners like Kim-Lee, and she happily participated in the formation of a school gallery, feeling no social pressure whatsoever.

Kim-Lee recently sketched a collection of fashion designs, some of which she'd like to transform into the real thing. Her parents have signed Kim-Lee up for a summer sewing class, which should help her realize this dream.

Kim-Lee has already been selected Art Editor of the school paper for her freshman year. Her parents, in an effort to help their daughter branch out a bit, have also convinced her to play intramural tennis and volunteer at her church's Sunday School program next fall.

At school, Kim-Lee's neatness and precision help her to continue her strong performances in math, computers, and art. She also remains a highly organized, self-directed student who takes great pride in her work. At year's end, Kim-Lee's lagging auditory skills still hold her back in language arts, foreign language, science, and social studies classes, all of which require a good deal of reading and note-taking. However, our Looker's beautifully executed projects and reports continue to have a positive effect on all of her grades.

Kim-Lee's teachers agree that she is a pleasure to have in class. Certainly, she is an "easy" student to teach, for she usually produces high-quality work on demand and requires almost no attention in the process. Despite her current yearning to become a fashion or interior designer, Kim-Lee's guidance counselor has urged the teen to continue Spanish, computers, and the course of study recommended for college-bound students. Academically, high school is sure to pose few problems, and even holds some social promise now that Kim-Lee has begun to involve herself with her peers.

Mark. Now approaching the end of eighth grade, talkative, affable Mark has already had five "girlfriends." He and his female pal of the moment do not date, per se, but declare their devotion by holding hands, sitting together at lunch, passing notes, and talking on the phone at least twice each evening. But Mark manages to have plenty of time for his male friends, as well as for the long list of activities in which he's involved. In fact, Mark tends to spread himself too thin, and became so busy early in the year that keeping up with school work posed a bit of a problem. However, a disappointing first-quarter report card provided quite a jolt, and Mark has since devoted more time and attention to course work.

Between Student Council meetings and functions, the French Club, the Drama Club, and the Chorus, Mark stays after school nearly every day, and is busy many evenings, as well. He did such a fine job in a supporting role in the Drama Club's annual production that he has a shot at next year's lead. Finding himself with some free time once the play was done, Mark recently began serving as a reporter for the school paper. He enjoys this so much that, during the summer, he plans to put together a proposal for a teen column and submit it to the editor of his town's weekly paper. This summer also looks socially promising, for, as incoming freshmen, Mark and his friends are finally old enough to attend the parking-lot dances held each Friday night at the high school. And, even though it's only June, Mark has already received four invitations to summer parties, and has signed up as a junior counselor at a local recreation program.

Mark's command of language continues to be evident in his high-quality essays, his self-assurance during class discussions, and his ease with conversational French. Our Listener also remains a strong reader, and has such good recall of the material discussed in his classes that he rarely uses his notes or study sheets. However, at year's end, Mark's less-developed visual and fine motor skills still hold him back in math and such creative pursuits as report illustration and map making.

Mark's teachers have complimented him on his ability to put his natural outspokenness to work for him. He has always managed to spice up even the dullest lecture with intelligent questions, witty comments, and well-thought-out arguments. But, where Mark's interjections and asides used to get him into frequent trouble, maturity has taught him to use restraint and a respectful tone. Nowadays, he's an asset to every class.

With the proper support and guidance, Mark is almost assured of maintaining his current academic standing, and is certain to thoroughly enjoy the host of new extracurricular activities to which he'll be exposed as a freshman. He has already been elected Vice President of next year's French Club, and plans to continue his involvement with the Drama Club and the school paper. There's no doubt that high school will be an exciting time for a student with Mark's social and academic capabilities.

Shawn. During the school year, Mover Shawn became part of a clique of athletic boys and girls. His new friends gather regularly at sporting events, in the school yard, and in front of one another's television sets, each one comfortable with peers who share a love of sports. While one of Shawn's friends might occasionally be enamored of another, none has yet achieved the social confidence necessary to express this by spending time alone with a member of the opposite sex! Actually, though, the clique's very existence will eventually help each member reach that point. You see, Shawn and his friends inadvertently feed one another's egos by focusing on athletic talent, rather than classroom performance.

Besides his involvement in sports, Shawn has become active in the school's Safety Patrol, a small group of students who monitor their fellow classmates' hallway behavior during class changes and before and after school. Shawn is also proud of having been selected from the Monday study hall group to make deliveries for the main office. Shawn was recently approached by some classmates about running for freshman class treasurer, but, finding the prospect of such responsibility somewhat alarming, he firmly vetoed the idea. Instead, he looks forward to applying for membership in the Boys' Leaders' Club, and trying out for junior varsity sports teams. Shawn has also heard some interesting talk about the existence of several paying jobs for freshmen, not unlike the work he did for the main office. In this case, though, Shawn would be part of the high school's custodial, kitchen, or nursing staff.

At the moment, Shawn believes he would be perfectly suited to an elementary physical education teaching position. He'd very much like to coach, as well, but doesn't see how he could combine the latter with elementary schools' later dismissal times. Shawn lacks the academic confidence to consider the obvious solution—teaching in a high school—believing, like so many youngsters, that the brighter a teacher, the higher his or her grade assignment. Sooner or later, Shawn will have to face the fact that college, required of every teacher, will be no small feat for him.

You see, Shawn's school work remains average, at best, even with the help of classroom modifications and remedial instruction. As he matures, our Mover's lagging visual and auditory skills still lead to problems with reading, writing, spelling, and math. These days, however, Shawn has an easier time compensating for some academic limitations and resigning himself to others.

This year, Shawn's teachers have seen him progress from a disorganized, mildly disruptive classroom influence to someone who has begun to take responsibility for his school work and behavior. With an eye toward the future, Shawn's guidance counselor has suggested that the boy add a technology class to next year's high school course load and that he continue with computer class. In fact, Shawn can reap many social and vocational benefits from high school as long as he continues his involvement in sports, accepts the support of his parents and teachers, and maintains a realistic view of his academic capabilities. Much more so than the course of study found in grade school, or even middle school, high school curriculums are rich and varied enough to hold something for every type of student.

THE RELATIONSHIP OF LEARNING STYLE TO AN EIGHTH GRADER'S SCHOOL PERFORMANCE

Most junior high and middle schools offer a wide variety of courses, allowing students and their families a measure of control over the formulation of class schedules. Of course, much of eighth-grade academics continues to be required work, but in many cases there is flexibility about the level and focus of even such curriculum staples as math and language arts. In addition, the existence of elective courses enables students to pursue individual interests within the framework of an ordinary school day.

Just like elementary school subjects, eighth-grade subjects can be categorized according to the different learning skills called into play by each discipline. Mover skills—body awareness and agility—are drawn upon only during physical education. But the visual and auditory skills possessed by Lookers and Listeners are exercised time and again during the school day. In the two sections that follow, typical eighth-grade courses are separated into Looker and Listener subjects. To further highlight visual and auditory aspects of the eighth-grade curriculum, sample first- and last-quarter report cards are presented for each of our case-study teens, along with a subject-by-subject look at each learner's academic experience.

Looker Subjects

In the course of a school day, most eighth graders encounter posters and bulletin boards, a variety of hallway displays, and an array of visual aids wherever they go. Lookers, naturally, are most attuned to the visual appeal of their surroundings, and are the most enamored of certain curriculum components, as well.

Math, in any form, is a visual subject. Whether performing long division or working with intricate algebraic equations tackled by top students, a Looker's ability to envision, memorize, and compute is a tremendous asset. For the same reason, spelling, capitalization, and punctuation—the visual components of *language arts* described on page 167—continue to appeal to Looker students.

Computer and *art* classes are often no longer requirements in junior high and middle school, so it's likely that many of the students in these classes are Lookers. After all, it's the sight-oriented teens who possess the eye-hand coordination, fine motor dexterity, and visual skills needed to earn top grades. *Handwriting,* although no longer a graded subject, remains a similarly pleasurable exercise for Looker teens. *Technology,* a course that blends and expands upon the teachings of yesteryear's "shop" classes, demands these skills, as well. And, of course, technology also requires knowledge of measurement techniques and an ability to follow written directions—two more Looker strengths.

Listener Subjects

Eighth-grade students utilize their auditory skills in every one of their classes. Certain subjects, however, have a focus on language and sound that makes them particularly appealing to those who possess the Listener learning style. An eighth-grade Listener, for instance, can be expected to shine in *reading,* due to the strong phonics skills that enable him to breeze through increasingly complex printed material, as well as his excellent comprehension and recall of text. Further, a Listener continues to have the edge in *social studies* and *science,* and now also enjoys an advantage in such courses as *health* and *home/career skills.* As mentioned in Chapter Seven (see page 168), social studies and science also have certain Looker elements. However, oral presentations, class discussions, and group projects are an even larger part of each class, and are most easily handled by those with strong auditory skills. In addition, Listeners are the most comfortable with eighth-grade textbook material and are usually the best at note-taking, a process that requires a careful ongoing screening of what is heard in class.

Chapter Seven described *foreign language* class as an auditory exercise—a Listener subject. This continues to be the case in eighth grade, with Listeners applying their inborn verbal and phonics skills to the memorization and mastery of the vocabulary, culture, and history of another land.

Eighth-grade *language arts* encompasses the study of literature, grammar, composition, and spelling. Listeners retain an advantage in all but the last area of study because they are at ease with reading, have an almost-instinctive grasp of word usage and sentence structure, and can express their thoughts clearly and accurately.

By eighth grade, *vocal and instrumental* music have usually been designated as elective courses, or, in some cases, have been reduced to extracurricular activities. Listener skills are very much in demand in these classes, as chorus members memorize the rhythm and lyrics of each new song, and musicians fine-tune the individual parts of each piece of music and then blend those parts into a melodious whole. However, as eighth graders are introduced to increasingly sophisticated musical selections, the reading of complex written scores and the dexterity required to transform them into music becomes more and more a task for Lookers.

Typical Report Cards for Lookers, Listeners, and Movers

Now that we've grouped eighth-grade subjects according to the learning skills each commands, let's look back and assess some of the grades earned by our three learners. The report cards that follow highlight the academic strengths and weaknesses that usually result from a child's inborn preference for particular types of stimulation. You'll see that subjects with a strong visual component are Kim-Lee's best, while Mark shines in classes that employ his auditory and verbal talents. Shawn gets a taste of school success, as well, by relying on outside support and by selecting his courses with care.

EIGHTH-GRADE REPORT CARDS FOR LOOKER KIM-LEE

First-Quarter Report		*End-of-Year Report*	
Language Arts	B	Language Arts	B+
Math	A+	Math	A
Social Studies	B+	Social Studies	B
Science	B	Science	B
Spanish	B	Spanish	B+
Computers	A+	Computers	A+
Physical Education	B	Physical Education	B
Art	A+	Art	A+

As has always been the case, Kim-Lee's report cards are something of which she can be proud. It's almost a shame that, despite her consistent effort and methodical approach to school work, she receives an occasional B, but Kim-Lee labors over the reading of eighth-grade textbook material and has a bit of trouble with such Listener-oriented tasks as remembering new vocabulary. Fortunately, Kim-Lee's maps, time lines, charts, graphs, and other projects are so superior to those of her classmates that they offset any less-than-satisfactory test performances. And, there are no troublesome texts to hinder Kim-Lee's work in art, math, and computer classes.

Despite her difficulty with pronunciation, Kim-Lee loves her Spanish class. The beautifully decorated room makes Spanish history come alive, and Kim-Lee delights in her grasp of tricky Spanish vocabulary. Her visual skills stand our Looker in good stead when it comes to English spelling, capitalization, and punctuation, as well. As Kim-Lee gradually gains control over her class schedule during the coming years, she will most certainly select those elective courses that draw upon these same excellent Looker skills. In the meantime, Kim-Lee continues to expend such consistent effort in *all* classes that her beginning and end-of-year grades are very similar, and most of her grades are quite good.

EIGHTH-GRADE REPORT CARDS FOR LISTENER MARK

First-Quarter Report		*End-of-Year Report*	
Language Arts	B+	Language Arts	A
Math	C	Math	C+
Social Studies	A-	Social Studies	A+
Science	B	Science	A
French	B+	French	A
Speech	B+	Speech	A
Physical Education	B	Physical Education	B
Vocal Music	A-	Vocal Music	B+

As in Kim-Lee's case, Mark's steady grades are a reflection of his consistently high-quality school work. He was somewhat disappointed with his first-quarter grades, but devoted more time to school work thereafter. This year, Mark elected to take vocal music and a speech course in place of art and computers. Both of his choices reflect his enjoyment of sound and language, and both replaced classes that highlighted one of his weaknesses—fine motor coordination. As always,

Mark earned B's in physical education. He's not extraordinarily agile, but his leadership skills are good, and he obviously enjoys the class so much that he receives above-average grades.

Mark still sees a math tutor on Sunday evenings, and more often when the need arises. The tutor, in turn, is in weekly contact with Mark's teacher, and provides the perfect link between Mark's rather shaky skills and any puzzling new class material. Mark was fascinated by this year's American history curriculum, and his interest is reflected in his high social studies grades. In fact, Mark became so interested in whaling that he made it the subject of a sophisticated twenty-page term paper, which his father typed and Mark "illustrated" with sketches photocopied from various books. Because his parents decline to do more than assist with research and typing, Mark didn't do quite as well on his science project, a homemade anemometer. Once the projects were out of the way, however, Mark went right back to earning his usual A's in science.

EIGHTH-GRADE REPORT CARDS FOR MOVER SHAWN

First-Quarter Report		*End-of-Year Report*	
Language Arts	C-	Language Arts	C
Math	C	Math	C
Social Studies	C	Social Studies	C-
Science	C+	Science	B-
Remedial Reading	C+	Remedial Reading	C
Computers	B-	Computers	B
Physical Education	A	Physical Education	A

As always, Shawn achieves his best grades in subjects that require his active participation. Physical education, naturally, poses no problem at all. And, with the benefits of at-home practice and a teacher who doesn't push him beyond the most basic programs, Shawn also does well in his computer class. For years, the experimentation aspect of science has made this one of Shawn's best academic subjects, and eighth grade has been no different, particularly since the entry of the best students into an accelerated science program has minimized classroom competition. Earlier in the year, Shawn did find himself missing the art classes that had so long been a part of his school life, but he heard so much from fellow students about this year's addition of art history reading assignments that he now knows he made the right choice in dropping the course.

Remedial reading, enrollment in the slowest-paced classes, the extra work time afforded by study hall, and the occasional help of Shawn's older brother have combined to keep Shawn's language arts, math, and social studies grades in the "C" range. To Shawn's great relief, this has meant an end to his Resource Lab visits. Shawn had long been bothered by his need for special attention, and is now determined to make it a thing of the past.

WORKING WITH YOUR CHILD'S TEACHERS

Most parents hope to stay as informed as possible about their child's experiences away from home. Yet, even if the teen in question is among those who cheerfully share feelings and volunteer personal details, a great deal of the school experience remains unaccounted for. I don't for a moment recommend that parents try to learn every detail of their child's life. Eighth graders need their privacy! However, you will be able to help your teen through a painful social situation, a frustrating unit of study, or a prolonged lapse of effort only if you are aware of the problem's existence.

Chapters Six and Seven discussed the benefits of initiating and maintaining contact with your child's teacher, above and beyond biannual conferences and quarterly report cards. (See pages 133–136 and 171–173 for details and suggestions.) After all, grade schoolers spend many of their away-from-home hours under the watchful eye of their classroom teacher, who can often provide clues to any changes in a child's behavior, attitude, or study habits. In junior high and middle school, however, the task of staying informed is complicated by the number and variety of teachers, courses, and peer interactions to which a teen is exposed during the course of each day, as well as the increasingly social focus of extracurricular life. Gone are the days when your child and his sole teacher could understand and accept each other's quirks with an intimacy born of some twenty-five hours spent together each week. Whereas it was recommended in Chapters Six and Seven that parents volunteer information about their child's academic skills, work habits, and educational history, it is unreasonable to strive for a similar rapport with, perhaps, six or seven different teachers, each of whom your child may see for only thirty or forty minutes a day. Most secondary schools employ counselors, crisis intervention teachers, or other support personnel to monitor major problems; but unlike grade school, there is no one adult to whom parents can turn for blanket information when their child faces a problem at school. Nevertheless, there are means by which you can keep abreast of the highs and lows that befall your child during his life as an eighth grader. The following suggestions may help.

- *Attend parent organization meetings.* Regardless of your level of involvement in the parent organization at your child's school, these meetings can give you an inside track on such topics as school regulations and procedures, support services, personnel changes, new programs, and scheduled events.

- *Learn as much as you can about your child's teachers.* Most school districts host a "Meet the Teacher" night. Don't miss this opportunity to view your child's school through his eyes! Even a brief stop at each class will give you a feel for the teacher's personality, along with valuable information about books and supplies, homework policy, upcoming projects, and expectations regarding behavior and class participation. From the start, try to get your child talking in general terms about unusual or notable classroom happenings. Each time he describes a humorous conversation, reports on disciplinary tactics, or relates a story about a teacher's personal life, more light will be shed on the teacher and class under discussion. You may also wish to turn to other parents for information about teachers to whom their children were assigned in the past. To be fair, however, you should seek second and third opinions before making any negative assumptions.

- *Make your child's teachers aware of your interest.* If you're struck by a teacher's creativity or level of commitment, send a note of commendation or thanks. If your child seems particularly enthusiastic about a project or unit of study, don't hesitate to apprise the teacher of this fact. Doing so can make the teacher more aware of your child's involvement, and may even have an effect on the format of future assignments. You should feel equally free to write or call when questions or problems arise. However, it's important to be tactful and open-minded. A teacher who feels that he or she is under scrutiny may minimize interaction with the student in question so as not to create further conflict. The teen, in turn, may miss out on some valuable one-to-one instruction.

- *Be aware of the fine line between concern and control.* Most eighth graders are both flattered and reassured when parents show an interest in their school life. But, let that interest be interpreted as nosiness or interference, and the same teens are quick to bristle. As a rule, it's safe to ask your child questions that convey your interest in his friends and school work provided that your tone remains nonjudgmental, your demeanor casual, and your remarks and questions relatively impersonal. Avoid prolonged discussions of subjects that make your child uncomfortable, as well as open-ended queries that require long, drawn-out replies. For example, if your teen responds to, "So, who usually sits at your cafeteria table?" by shrugging and turning his back, or greets, "What are you doing in social studies?" with a martyred sigh, it's probably best to change the subject. Communication may be easier when your questions focus on your child's friends, rather than your child, and when you relate stories from your own school days that parallel what you suspect your eighth grader is facing.

If your child seems to be struggling in a particular class—if his grade in the subject shows a significant decline, for instance, or if he voices an ongoing dislike of the teacher or the class—it's time to contact the teacher for a conference. It's a good idea to prepare your questions in advance so that you'll be sure to come away from this meeting with the clearest possible picture of your child's work and behavior. The following are some good topics for discussion.

- *What is the policy regarding homework?* Find out what the teacher's expectations are and whether your child completes assignments and turns them in on time.

- *What sort of class work can your child expect?* Ask about the usual format of each class and whether your teen pays attention during lectures. You may also wish to inquire about your child's participation in discussions, and to ask whether he takes notes when needed and prepares sufficiently for tests.

- *What sort of relationships does your child have with his classmates?* Find out how your child gets along with his peers. Ask whether he assumes the role of leader, observer, or antagonist, and whether there is anyone with whom he has a particularly close relationship. If so, find out whether his peer interactions seem to be affecting his school work.

- *Does your child work up to his academic potential?* Ask the teacher whether your child's classroom performance corresponds to his level of ability. You might also inquire about the consistency of your teen's effort and interest level. Find out whether your child might feel more challenged—or less overwhelmed—in a faster- or slower-paced class.

- *How can you help at home?* Find out if there is anything you can do to make this particular class a more positive experience for your teen. Request specific ideas that might help your child improve his grades, and ask if the teacher recommends any sort of professional intervention.

LEARNING STYLE AND EXTRACURRICULAR ACTIVITIES

Eighth graders have had several years in which to try their hand at any available artistic, organizational, athletic, and recreational pursuits. Most are fully cognizant of their creative, physical, and social abilities. Simply put, they've discovered which activities work for them and which do not!

By the time a child reaches thirteen or fourteen, he can be spoken to honestly, albeit tactfully, about his immediate and long-term goals. With luck, your child will involve himself in the activities that will best help him to achieve those goals. If not, it isn't too late to intervene.

First, it's a good idea to limit the number of after-school organizations to which your child belongs. All too often, either an adolescent's desire to belong or his parents' goals for his future result in a jam-packed weekly schedule that is quickly coupled with irritability, stomachaches, headaches, depression, or fatigue—all signals of possible "overload." Explain to your child the value of unstructured time, and help him decide which activities are most important and which should be dropped.

Second, help your child avoid disillusionment by diplomatically suggesting that he steer clear of pursuits in which he's not likely to meet with success. Guide him in examining the activity's appeal. If, for example, he has limited vocal talent, but nevertheless yearns to be chosen for county-wide chorus, help him see that he's really being motivated by the group's elite status, his desire to follow the lead of a friend, or the potential for missing classes on practice days, as the case may be. Of course, if your child is realistic about his lack of talent, there's no harm in his pursuing the activity on another level—joining the school chorus, say—simply for the fun of it. On the flip side, you can guarantee a boost to your child's self-esteem by convincing him to stick with those activities he has enjoyed in the past. Remind him that even the most beloved pursuits can occasionally become boring, but that this is often only temporary. Even if your teen questions the activity's social acceptability—if he is embarrassed about carrying his saxophone around the school on lesson days, for example, or if he refuses to align himself with the Theater Club's current in-group—there may be ways he can pursue his interest outside of school.

And, finally, even the most competent teen can benefit from a challenge. Depending on the nature of your relationship with your eighth grader, you may be able to encourage him to venture into previously untried areas. Provide all the information you can find and all the behind-the-scenes support you can muster, and stand behind any decisions to bring along a friend for moral support.

Naturally, different after-school pursuits work best for different learners. Although your teen may not always be amenable to your ideas about his free time, and will probably gravitate on his own towards pursuits that reflect his learning style, you *may* be able to help him vary his extracurricular diet. Some of the following suggestions may prove useful.

Activities for Eighth-Grade Lookers

Lookers are usually among the most confirmed homebodies. But, by eighth grade, even the most reticent teens yearn to be more popular and confident. You'll have the greatest success helping your child reach this goal if the activities you suggest tap his areas of interest. For Lookers, it's wise to focus on pursuits that do not require strong people skills, but guarantee a modicum of success to the visually oriented. One of the following ideas may be right for your child.

- Art shows and programs
- Astronomy
- Carpentry
- Collecting stamps, coins, or trading cards
- Computer activities
- Math clubs and teams
- Models and crafts
- Photography
- Science exhibits
- Video and board games

Activities for Eighth Grade Listeners

Since Listeners devote much of their attention to the development of an active social life, they gravitate toward group activities. But individuality is a desirable quality, as well, so you may wish to encourage your teen to also consider hobbies and activities separate from those of his school friends. Here are some suggestions.

- Acting class
- Baby-sitting
- Bowling league
- Church youth group
- Community theater subscription
- Family outings
- Service clubs
- Skating lessons
- Storytelling and essay contests
- Student government

Activities for Eighth-Grade Movers

Because of their constant involvement in sports, most teen Movers are relatively at ease with same-sex peers. They may not be brilliant conversationalists, but their friendships with teammates are often comfortable. Most athletic pursuits, therefore, are good choices for Movers. You might also suggest nonsport activities that your child can enjoy without feeling academic or social pressure. The following list contains some ideas for Mover teens.

- After-school recreation program
- Bowling league
- Decorating and cleanup committees
- Ecology groups
- Group tennis lessons
- Hiking, fishing, and camping
- Ski club
- Town pool membership
- Track and field events
- Volleyball

THE SOCIAL IMPLICATIONS OF LEARNING STYLE

During the adolescent years, a child is hard at work carving out an identity and forming friendships with peers who either share his interests or reflect the values, behavior, and social wherewithal he'd like to possess, himself. At thirteen and fourteen, a child's opinion of himself is largely based on what others think of him, and so is quite fragile. The lofty air he exhibits one minute—"I really belted that softball! Now, everyone will want me on their team!"—can just as quickly be erased—"Sara sat by Paul at lunch today. I guess she doesn't like me, after all."

Both in school and out of school, an adolescent's experiences, achievements, and sense of confidence have tremendous social implications. And, as you might suspect, these experiences—whatever their outcome—are largely based on learning style.

Most Lookers won't actively seek feedback from friends or family, but are nonetheless well aware of others' opinions. A raised eyebrow here or a scornful glance there is all the proof a Looker needs that peer judgment is being passed. At thirteen, the Looker is as self-motivated and goal-oriented as ever, but the fruits of his labors are not held in as high regard as they were a few years back. Let's face it, good grades and manners just don't impress teens as much as friendliness, a sense of humor, athletic ability, or stylish clothes—none of which is likely to be among a Looker's strong points! Adolescent Lookers tend to have one or two close friends, though they don't share much personal information with them. And, while they may appear outwardly serene, Lookers' reticence and inability to make small talk usually combine to make these teens downright uncomfortable at group social events.

Friends' opinions are a veritable driving force for adolescent Listeners. The average Listener is so group-focused that his sociability often prevents him from developing any personal interest beyond reading. The Listener will join a team or club if accompanied by his friends, but is more interested in monitoring the words and actions of its older members and having a good time than in achieving a group goal. Because Listeners are so friendly and outgoing, "fitting in" is not a problem, but in the classroom, a Listener's talkativeness and love of the limelight earn as much teacher disapproval as they do classmate admiration. At thirteen, however, school performance is of lower priority than social status. Lookers may be lauded by the adults in their life, but Listeners are popular with the group that really counts—their peers!

By eighth grade, Movers are finally able to taste the hard-won respect of their classmates. The Mover's tendency to cut up in class is suddenly seen in a new light. Although his antics probably annoyed his grade-school classmates, adolescent peers are likely to find his behavior amusing, and may secretly wish to act the same way. Moreover, the thirteen- or fourteen-year-old Mover's athletic prowess and muscular physique are often the envy of his male peers, while females are thrilled by his playing performances and by the remote air that is, in actuality, a result of social unease. At this age, female Movers are often worlds apart from their same-sex peers in terms of interests and skills, but are readily accepted as "pals" by boys. Movers have spent years scrambling to match the accomplishments of their Looker and Listener classmates.

Suddenly—effortlessly—it is their *natural* ability that earns them peer admiration. Adolescent Movers never lack for friends, for everyone now wants to be one!

Tips for Encouraging Social Growth

Given the social implications of learning style, parents may wish to lend a discreet hand in the preservation of their teen-ager's sense of confidence. Here are some ideas to try with your Looker, Listener, or Mover.

- Quietly investigate school course listings for classes in which your child's learning style will help him shine. For example, journalism and band are possibilities for Lookers and Listeners, respectively; and dance and home-skills classes are well suited to most Movers. Find out as much as you can about the courses that seem best, and pass this information on to your child along with your reasons for recommending the classes.

- Keep abreast of your child's social life by appearing interested, but not inquisitive; available, but not determined to pry into his problems. It often helps to voice your own excitement and frustration with daily life. Seeing and hearing a parent "vent" can convince a teen of the emotional benefits of doing so.

- If your child is sedentary, remind him of the importance of physical activity. You can plan family activities and can also suggest solo exercise. An added benefit to bike rides, walks, swimming lessons, and other "public" pursuits is that the reticent child becomes more visible to peers.

- Although the term is used loosely when applied to most young teens, opinions are still sharply divided on the appropriateness of eighth-grade "dating." If you or your child is hesitant about his readiness for ventures into the dating world, it's probably best for him to stick to boy-girl group outings or double-dates with a pal—assuming his interest in the opposite sex extends even that far! You can be sure, however, that same-sex friends are important. If need be, you can expose your teen—without pressure—to children of families with similar values by planning two-family get-togethers, or allowing him to invite another teen to join your family outings.

- Encourage your child's feelings of independence in any way you can. Allow him to manage his own money, send him shopping for his own clothes, encourage his work around the house or for hire, and allow him every possible privacy—from a separate restaurant table for him and a buddy to closed-door sessions when friends visit the house.

- When possible, focus on coeducational schools and activities. When boys and girls witness the ups and downs of one another's lives within a nonthreatening everyday environment, each develops understanding, empathy, and respect for the opposite sex. Social competence is an inevitable, if gradual, result.

- Make your teen aware of his best features, be they academic or physical. At thirteen, even the most gifted or attractive child may doubt his worth. Compliments, if genuine, can provide a much-needed lift.

- If your teen has expressed doubts about his ability to handle social situations, encourage him to anticipate awkward or embarrassing turns of events. It often helps to practice responses through role-playing. A ready answer to an intimidating bully, thoughtless friend, or teasing adult can be a real lifesaver to a momentarily panicked adolescent!

HOMEWORK STRATEGIES FOR LOOKERS, LISTENERS, AND MOVERS

By eighth grade, noting, preparing for, and completing school assignments should primarily be the responsibility of the student. You can support your teen's efforts by suggesting work strategies that capitalize on his learning strengths, and by working behind the scenes to maintain a home environment conducive to study and learning. This can be accomplished by insisting on nutritious meals and reasonable bedtimes; by creating a quiet, organized work space; by supplying reference materials and stationery supplies; by making yourself available for assistance or advice; and—perhaps most difficult—by readily providing transportation to music lessons, cultural events, study group meetings, and the library. Here are some strategies that will make homework and learning more appealing to your eighth-grade learner.

Strategies for Lookers

From the time they can first grasp a pencil, most Looker children enjoy seat work, and this preference generally remains strong throughout the school years. Your eighth-grade Looker will appreciate a desk or other private work space in which he can store his supplies without fear of other household members making a mess of things. You can encourage your Looker teen's creative side by supplementing ordinary desk-top items with neon markers, colored chalk, stencils, oil crayons, and glitter pens. Your neat, methodical Looker will also benefit from a bulletin board and chalkboard near his work area.

As a rule, eighth-grade Lookers are quite self-reliant when it comes to recording, organizing, and completing school work. You may wish to encourage your child's use of different-colored inks, thumbnail sketches, and highlighting to make note-taking more interesting. The idea of using separate notebooks and folders for each subject may be quite appealing, and, at test time, you can also suggest that your child condense his notes into outline form—a technique that simplifies the memorization of facts. Although most Lookers like to study alone, your child may welcome your offer of a last-minute oral quiz. If your teen seems bogged down by a particular unit of study or a difficult piece of literature, you might search out a video or generously illustrated book that can provide missing background information.

Strategies for Listeners

Most Listener teens have little difficulty with homework. A parent's biggest problem is convincing the Listener to find time to get the work done. It is often helpful to mandate a homework time at the start of the school year. However, the Listener's extracurricular schedule often is so full that you may have to be flexible. If this is the case, frequent reminders about homework's priority status are probably in order. Fortunately, once they get started, most Listeners are responsible enough to see their assignments through, though they are likely to appreciate an offer of proofreading or typing assistance.

The presence of a friend often makes study time more palatable to the Listener. You may also wish to suggest that your child tape-record material, and that he read instructions and notes aloud. As an auditory learner, your teen will remember facts and terms better if he hears them. Therefore, if your Listener is stumped by a certain mathematical process or science procedure, remind him to talk himself through the work, step by step. It may also help to furnish books or videos that relate to, and generate further interest in, any units of study that your Listener finds troublesome.

Strategies for Movers

Eighth-grade Movers are often unmotivated students, particularly when it comes to reading and written assignments. At home, it's not unusual for assignments to go undone because the Mover teen either has forgotten what the specific task was or has left the necessary books and papers at school. You can suggest that your child carry an index card in his pocket, and that he use it to note the homework assigned in each class. He can then refer to the card before leaving school to make sure he's taking home all that he needs. You may also wish to steer your child toward the use of a single five-subject notebook, complete with pockets for loose papers. This, coupled with a backpack, will help him keep track of his work.

At home, the teen-aged Mover needs a quiet work space with plenty of room to spread out his assignments. If your child is disorganized, as many Movers are, or if he has trouble deciding where to start, it's a good idea to prepare his work area ahead of time by setting out the paper, pens, and pencils he will need for his work. Then, with your child's permission, you can review his assignment list and help him set out the needed books and work sheets. It also helps to remain nearby but involved in a task of your own, so that you can answer questions and offer encouragement while still leaving the responsibility for homework completion to your child. You may well find that the sight of you, deep in concentration, will motivate your Mover to focus on his own work.

If your child has a great deal of homework, encourage him to take breaks between assignments. Ultimately, only he can control how long it takes to finish everything, but you can lend a hand by establishing set times for homework—even using before-school hours if your child seems to be at his best in the morning. When your Mover has to study for a test, he may need you to select the most important information from his text- and notebooks. You can offer to assist your child with reviews, but he may find that the presence of a classmate makes the task of studying more enjoyable. For long-term projects, show your teen-ager how to map out a work schedule that divides assignments into small, manageable segments, but ensures that the project will be finished on time. Your Mover may also appreciate the provision of background information. Videos and magazine photographs, for example, can improve his grasp of social studies and science material. And, to help your child through literature assignments, you might wish to check bookstores for an abbreviated version of the book in question. Since handwriting is rarely a Mover's strong suit, you can also provide your child with a typewriter and the offer of your assistance with the typing of long assignments.

TECHNIQUES FOR IMPROVING AN EIGHTH GRADER'S ACADEMIC PERFORMANCE

By the age of thirteen, students are somewhat set in their classroom performance levels and their attitudes toward school. Lookers, for example, find school fairly rewarding. They particularly enjoy the process of designing and executing solo projects like reports, maps, inventions, and visual aids. Class participation and group projects, on the other hand, present uncomfortable social demands that most Lookers would rather avoid.

Listeners, who have logged in years of academic and social success, have reason to look forward to each and every school day. Many Listeners see class work as a necessary means to an end—social opportunity. So, even if their immediate goal is only chatting with a certain someone outside of English class or meeting with the eighth-grade dance committee, Listeners see school as a positive force in their lives.

Movers struggle as much with eighth-grade academics as they did with the course work of earlier grades, but the introduction of elective classes finally enables them to steer clear of language, art, music, and anything with a heavy reading requirement. With support, Movers can pass most or all of their required subjects; and, though they may frequently feel discouraged, they can redeem themselves in their own eyes and the eyes of their peers once they exit the classroom. Because of their physical talents, eighth-grade Movers are often popular teens despite their social reticence.

Can an adolescent's parents play a role in their child's academic life? Will their teen accept their help—and can it really make a difference? In most cases, it's simply not realistic to expect much progress when parents and teens try to tackle homework or remedial work together. Adolescents are usually too fractious, their self-esteem too fragile, and their relationship with parents too emotion-charged for parent and child to accomplish much as a team! Even the most nonjudgmental and diplomatic mom or dad is likely to meet with failure in this regard. Nevertheless, you need not stand idly by, watching your child struggle with course work. Instead, you can help by making sure your teen understands the concept of learning style and knows how his style can be tapped to assist his academic efforts. You can also lend a hand with the selection of a course of study that best reflects your child's interests and abilities. School guidance counselors should be able to give you the background information you need to offer informed advice.

In the previous pages, you learned some general learning-style-based homework strategies. The following five sections, which cover the courses required of most eighth graders, suggest more specific learning strategies, as well as a number of multisensory techniques and materials, which draw upon both the sense needed for mastery of the subject matter and another sense—preferably, your child's favored sense. Review these suggestions with an eye towards selecting those that you feel would work best with your child's sensory preference. You're certain to find that use of appropriate strategies improves both your child's classroom performance and his overall confidence. As an added bonus, your child's behavior at home may also be more positive and productive once you and he begin working in harmony toward a common goal.

Building Reading and Literature-Appreciation Skills

Depending on where your child attends school and the level at which he reads, he may, as an eighth grader, find himself exposed to anything from remedial techniques to literary classics. Some schools offer a single course encompassing poetry, biography, short stories, and the like; others offer a different course for each genre; and still others make literature a part of the language arts curriculum.

The skills involved in reading are no different in eighth grade than in first. The level of a student's ability to decode, or translate the printed word into one that is spoken; the size of his vocabulary; and the degree to which he comprehends what he reads are what determine his overall reading performance. Whether your eighth grader needs help with phonics or with the deciphering of Homer's *Odyssey*, you, the parent, can help. Here are some ideas.

TECHNIQUES TO IMPROVE READING SKILLS

■ Put your child in charge of reading aloud to a younger sibling.

■ Encourage the use of a bookmark so that your teen can either rest his eyes while reading or close his eyes to visualize the action—without losing his place.

As a visual strategy for keeping track of characters and events, teach your teen to compose a scrap-paper time line when reading longer stories.

To allow your eighth grader to enjoy a story without pronouncing every word himself, treat him to a book on tape. The Mind's Eye catalogue contains mysteries, westerns, and adventures from which you can choose.

Encourage your teen to determine the meaning of new vocabulary words—asking you, if he's not inclined to use the dictionary. This way, he'll be better able to follow a story line than he would if he simply skipped over the unknown.

Rent a classic movie, such as *To Kill a Mockingbird*. Then, after your teen-ager has enjoyed the film, provide him with the book.

A phonics review can improve your teen's reading skills. Look for a tutor who can present beginning phonics at an interest level appropriate to teens.

Share the joy of literature by reading stories, poems, and novels along with your teen. Discuss the material from time to time, asking questions designed to make your child think: "Why do you suppose the heroine returned to high school?" or "What did you think of the story's ending?"

To build vocabulary, buy a book of crossword puzzles, and work them together during car trips or on rainy weekend afternoons.

Purchase Putnam's *The Clear and Simple Thesaurus Dictionary* (New York, 1978) for your home. This easy-to-use book identifies slang terms and lists words with both synonyms and antonyms.

Building Language Arts Skills

Most eighth-grade curriculums include some form of language arts— the study of spelling, grammar, research skills, and writing techniques. The presentation of language arts material varies from district to district, as does the tendency to group students according to ability levels, but the purpose of the program is the same across the country. In the long run, the goal is the improvement of a student's written and spoken usage of English. A more immediate benefit, however, is better research papers—and, as a result, better grades!

By eighth grade, a teen has written and received grades on many compositions and reports, and so should have no difficulty determining his weakest language arts skills. However, if your child is unable to pinpoint areas that need improvement, you can review samples of his work and make that determination together. Of course, his language arts teacher should also be a good source of information.

Because strong language arts skills result in better written work, the expertise your teen acquires in this class will serve him well in all of his studies throughout his academic career. The following are some suggestions for helping your teen get the most from his language arts course work.

TECHNIQUES TO IMPROVE LANGUAGE ARTS SKILLS

■ If your child's spelling is very poor, he may need the support of a dictionary or spelling guide at his desk at home. Consult your child's teachers about the possibility of his using one in class, as well.

■ Suggest that your Looker try to picture a word in his mind, or that your Listener pronounce it carefully to himself before putting the word on paper. Either method will help avoid careless misspellings.

■ After your teen has composed a rough draft of a theme or report, ask him to read it aloud to you. Doing so will make him aware of most grammatical or structural errors without your saying a word.

■ Explain to your child that a first draft is *expected* to contain mistakes. Suggest that he make corrections in blue pencil before beginning his final copy.

■ Keep on hand a reference book like Margaret D. Shertzer's *The Elements of Grammar* by Macmillan Publishing (New York, 1986). Such a book will help both you and your teen clarify issues of capitalization, punctuation, and parts of speech.

■ To improve your teen's enjoyment of composition, suggest that he enroll in a creative writing class. There, ideas and feelings will carry much more weight than grammar and punctuation.

■ If your child has trouble getting started on creative writing assignments, suggest that he record his story or essay on a cassette as he makes it up. Then, he can revise and edit as he transfers his thoughts from tape to paper.

■ Show your teen how to "map," rather than outline, a planned theme. By organizing his material in graphic form, he will be able to see the interplay among his various ideas. One way to map is to place a main idea in the center of a sheet of paper, circle it, and then write secondary points on lines that branch out from the center.

■ For teens with access to a word processor or computer, the ability to type can cut paper-writing time in half! If your child's school doesn't offer a typing class for eighth graders, check local vocational or technical schools for the availability of a summer or weekend program.

■ Give your child a Franklin *Spellmaster*—a small computer that verifies and corrects the spelling of over 80,000 words.

■ To improve your teen's grasp of foreign-language vocabulary and usage, rent a foreign film with English subtitles. Or, plan a family excursion to an ethnic neighborhood or city in which the language spoken is the one your child is studying.

Building Science Skills

The study of weather, rocks and minerals, matter, elements and compounds, gravity, and the solar system are all typical components of an eighth-grade science curriculum. As in language arts and math, many school districts offer similar course work on various ability levels. Others, however, use eighth-grade science to begin separate courses of study for college-bound versus vocationally oriented students.

Whatever their assigned titles, middle school and junior high science classes are pretty evenly divided in terms of visual and auditory stimuli. Course work includes a great deal of reading and note-taking, as well as the memorization of complex vocabulary, the absorption of lecture and film material, and the utilization of lab equipment. Obviously, the eighth grader with a bit of science background will be more interested in and more adept at science assignments and experiments. Here are some suggestions for improving your child's science knowledge and ability.

TECHNIQUES TO IMPROVE SCIENCE SKILLS

Surprise your teen with well-illustrated, easy-to-read books on any science topic in which he shows interest. Ecology, astronomy, and oceanography are a few possibilities.

Dale Seymour Publications offers colorful and informative science posters (through catalogue only) that work as well as room decor as they do as science resources.

At gift-giving time, choose a science game like Aristoplay's *Pollution/Solution: The Game of Environmental Impact* (through catalogue only). This particular game requires each player to battle pollution in his or her section of a township.

Invest in a backyard telescope to stimulate the entire family's interest in the solar system.

Make it a point to include a bit of eighth-grade science in family trips. Work in a visit to a cavern, a quarry, a recycling facility, or a planetarium.

If you live near a zoo, find out if it offers a weekend or summer program that trains teens to work with animals.

Encourage your teen to make his own sketches of science terms and experiments. Besides making his science notebook more visually appealing, this habit will help develop your child's skills of observation.

Offer to help your child study for tests. As you quiz him on various topics, call the Listener's attention to his "inner voice" and the Looker's attention to his "mind's eye."

Only a very motivated teen will tackle *National Geographic* or other adult science magazines. However, there are several children's magazines with enough pizzazz to both enlighten and hold the attention of the average thirteen-year-old. *3-2-1 Contact, Ranger Rick,* and *National Geographic World* are three good examples.

■ Encourage your teen's interest in nature by giving him hiking gear, the materials needed to start a vegetable garden, or the components of another science-oriented activity.

■ Be on the lookout for PBS television specials on topics that might interest your teen—tornadoes, for example, or archaeological digs. A thirteen-year-old may not be too eager to watch such shows during prime time, but your creation of a tailor-made videotape will help fill those rainy weekends.

Building Social Studies Skills

Eighth-grade social studies can take many forms. Some districts emphasize civics, or the study of government. Others offer a separate course in American history. Still others combine the two and add a healthy sprinkling of geography. But, regardless of the content of your eighth grader's social studies course, he'll be making daily use of his reading, note-taking, and class-participation skills.

Just as with science, the social studies student who finds his course work appealing is likely to listen harder, read longer, and put more of himself into papers and projects. Happily, it's not too late to spark this kind of interest in your eighth grader. The following are some ideas to help you make social studies facts and figures more palatable—and related resources more available—to your resident teen-ager.

TECHNIQUES TO IMPROVE SOCIAL STUDIES SKILLS

■ Post Barnes & Noble's *The Junior Wallchart of History* in your family room. This colorful chart enables a student to view simultaneous events in history.

■ An excellent reference book is Simon & Schuster's *The Timetables of History: A Horizontal Linkage of People and Events* (New York, 1982). This book traces major events in politics, philosophy, the arts, science, and technology from 5,000 B.C. to the present.

Help bring the past to life by renting videos whose stories center on famous periods of history. *Cleopatra, Ben-Hur,* and *Gone With the Wind* are a few examples. If your child likes to read, he may find historical novels equally helpful. While novels and films may not always be factually correct, they provide a colorful and informative look at the moods and customs of the times.

Your teen's room may be decorated with pop-star posters, but you can claim equal time by adorning the basement walls with Dale Seymour Publications' posters of past presidents, state flags, and famous United States documents (through catalogue only).

Provide your child with a small tape recorder to ease the listening demands of lectures and films. This device can also be used for constant playback of important facts and dates.

To stimulate your teen's interest in geography and culture, pick up one of Fodor's many guidebooks to other countries. Some of the more exotic titles are *Hawaii, Australia,* and *Cruises and Ports of Call,* all by Random House (New York).

Educational Insights' battery-operated *Geo-Safari* will help your teen sharpen his geography skills. Players select maps of various parts of the world, and press keys to identify countries, states, capitals, landmarks, oceans, and the like. A correct answer brings a musical salute.

Check out photo-essay books from your library. Many of these "coffee-table" books contain beautiful photographs of various peoples and places.

Stimulate your teen's interest in other cultures by planning a family outing to an ethnic neighborhood in a nearby city—New York's China-town, for example. After shopping, dining, and seeing the sights afforded by such a cultural center, you can rent a corresponding travel video to teach your teen even more about your "hosts'" heritage.

While a globe may be difficult to store in your home, an atlas serves the same purpose, and, in fact, provides much more detail. Atlases such as the *Rand McNally Road Atlas: United States, Canada, and Mexico* (New York, 1991) contain a host of fascinating facts and figures.

Building Math Skills

The content of the eighth-grade math curriculum varies greatly from city to city. In some parts of the country, advanced eighth graders begin a sequential course of study that encompasses all areas of math and continues throughout high school. Meanwhile, students with lesser math skills can take another year of general math before beginning the sequence as ninth graders, while the weakest students need not begin the sequence at all! But, elsewhere in the country, eighth graders are assigned by ability level to different tracks of a single math course. This course covers geometric shapes, classification and measurement of angles, powers, bases, and square roots. A student's performance during the course of the year determines his math track for the following year.

Whatever your child's curriculum and level of study, math courses will probably be part of his school life for at least several more years. Here are some techniques that will improve your teen's ability to understand and apply math concepts.

TECHNIQUES TO IMPROVE MATH SKILLS

■ If your teen still struggles with multiplication tables, he should probably be allowed to use a calculator in class. The Canon *Mini Desktop Calculator*, with its large keys and angled display, would be perfect. As early in the year as possible, speak to the teacher about using this—or a comparable model. You may save your child many weeks of frustration.

■ *Cuisenaire Rods*, by Cuisenaire Company of America (through catalogue only), are colored rods of different lengths that stand for number values. These can be used throughout middle school to teach the decimal system, powers, roots, fractions, and introductory algebra.

■ Dale Seymour Publications' *Googolplex* (through catalogue only) is another hands-on math device. These colorful plastic shapes and connectors can be used to make up to ninety-two geometric configurations, both simple and complex.

■ Keep on hand a mathematical reference book, like *Webster's New World Dictionary of Math* by Prentice Hall (New York, 1989) or *The Silver Burdett Mathematical Dictionary* by Simon & Schuster (Englewood Cliffs,

NJ, 1989). Both of these reference works define, graphically illustrate, and give working examples of the terms used in math class.

Geo D-Stix, from Dale Seymour Publications (through catalogue only), are color-coded sticks of varying lengths. Students use the sticks to create mathematical configurations and geometric shapes.

Liven up math by hanging a poster that deals with the subject's historical aspect. For instance, Isaac Asimov's "The History of Mathematics," distributed by Dale Seymour Publications (through catalogue only), traces events in math history.

■ *S'Math,* by Pressman, is a board game that provides practice with mathematical tables and equations. Players build onto existing equations, Scrabble-fashion, using one of the four math operations: addition, subtraction, multiplication, or division.

■ Enlist your teen's help with elaborate cooking projects, and leave most of the measuring to him. As you work, make a game of determining what each measurement, and the recipe's overall yield, would be if you were to halve, double, or triple it.

Texas Instruments' *Super Speak & Math* displays math problems on three different challenge levels. Although *Super Speak & Math* is recommended for ages six to twelve, it's perfect for the middle-school student who still has trouble with math facts.

Whether by instituting an allowance system or by sending him shopping with a flexible list and a fixed amount of cash, help your teen learn to budget money.

Naturally, not all of the techniques listed above will be right for every student. In some cases, my suggestions may duplicate a technique or resource that you've already introduced to your teen; in others, you may read the tip and instinctively know that it would not work. But, if the above-mentioned ideas make you more aware of the kinds of home support and enrichment so beneficial to every teen learner, my lists will have served their purpose!

Please remember that, despite your best efforts, it's simply not realistic to expect your thirteen-year-old's C- in science to improve to an A within the span of the next marking period. But, when working with your child, you should be as concerned with personal growth as you are with academic achievement. An improved grade-point average may well be one of the results of your learning-style-based efforts to help your teen. Much more important, though, are the realistic planning of his future course of study, his heightened interest and greater pride in class work and projects, and a parent-child relationship that's free from the kinds of tension that arise when the former has too-lofty expectations, and the latter chooses not to strive for what he knows to be impossible. In the end, you see, the knowledge of how your teen learns best will benefit you both!

Learning Style QuickCheck for Eighth Graders, Ages Thirteen to Fourteen

Directions: Read the statements below, and mark each one that seems characteristic of your child. When finished, total the checks for a clear picture of your teen's preferred learning style.

Looker	Listener	Mover

1. Communication: When my eighth grader wishes to express himself . . .

Looker	Listener	Mover
☐ He carefully watches his audience.	☐ He listens and speaks easily and effortlessly.	☐ He often feels tongue-tied.
☐ He participates in discussions when called upon, but rarely volunteers.	☐ He is uninhibited about speaking in class.	☐ He avoids eye contact with the teacher so as not to be called upon.
☐ He has an average-sized vocabulary.	☐ He has a very large vocabulary.	☐ He has a small vocabulary.

2. Favorite Pastimes: When my eighth grader has free time . . .

Looker	Listener	Mover
☐ He loves to use the computer.	☐ He reads a great deal, and often follows the works of a single author.	☐ He enjoys outdoor activities, like running, camping, and fishing.
☐ He likes video games and TV sports.	☐ He loves to visit with friends and talk on the phone.	☐ He plays a different sport each season.

3. Fine Motor Skills: When my eighth grader uses his hands . . .

Looker	Listener	Mover
☐ He shows great dexterity, and coordinates his eyes and hands quite easily.	☐ He shies away from fine motor tasks like typing and assembling models.	☐ He feels clumsy using his hands, except when his large muscles come into play, as in sports.
☐ He has excellent handwriting and does precise artwork.	☐ His penmanship and artistic efforts are average.	☐ His penmanship and artwork are often quite sloppy.

4. Gross Motor Skills: When my eighth grader moves about . . .

☐ He prefers noncontact activities, like hiking and bicycling.

☐ He prefers group activities to individual pursuits.

☐ He gravitates toward contact and competitive sports, like lacrosse and soccer.

☐ He has average coordination, and is very aware of his athletic shortcomings.

☐ He avoids games and activities that might make him look foolish.

☐ He excels at every sport he attempts.

5. Social Skills: When my eighth grader mixes with other teens . . .

☐ He tends to pair off with one or two close friends.

☐ He is very sociable and thrives on group activities.

☐ He likes physical closeness and often touches the person to whom he's speaking.

☐ He is self-, rather than socially, motivated.

☐ He is very motivated by the opinions of friends.

☐ He is more sociable on the playing field than at social gatherings.

6. Emotions: When it comes to my eighth grader's feelings . . .

☐ He keeps his feelings in check.

☐ He doesn't hesitate to express his feelings.

☐ He tends to express his feelings with actions rather than words.

☐ He is made uncomfortable by displays of emotion.

☐ He is sympathetic and understanding when it comes to his friends' feelings.

☐ He tends to be impatient, moody, and easily frustrated.

7. Memory: When my eighth grader learns . . .

☐ He doodles and jots down notes to aid his memory.

☐ He works well with a tape recorder.

☐ He remembers actions better than spoken or written words.

☐ He makes frequent use of mental pictures when remembering.

☐ He talks to himself and listens to an inner voice for answers.

☐ He is aware that he has trouble memorizing, and seeks helpful strategies.

8. At School: When my eighth grader is in the classroom . . .

☐ His best subjects are art, math, science, and computers.

☐ His best subjects are English, foreign language, and social studies.

☐ All academic work is a challenge. He excels only in physical education.

☐ He is happiest working alone.

☐ He does his best work in groups.

☐ He learns best when he is an active participant in the lesson.

☐ His work and study habits are excellent.

☐ His socializing sometimes gets in the way of his school work.

☐ He requires a lot of support when studying and doing assignments.

Totals: _____Looker   _____Listener   _____Mover

Chapter Nine

Learning Problems and Possibilities

From infancy on, each child clearly displays her sensory preference—that is, an affinity for visual, auditory, or tactile information—and can be categorized as a Looker, Listener, or Mover, with skills particular to her learning style. Indeed, throughout the preceding chapters, all of our case-study learners' development and academic achievements have been very much a function of the ways in which they absorb and respond to the vast array of information that surrounds them.

Sometimes, a child shows such a decided preference for one kind of sensory input—one learning style—over another that she blocks out information coming in from other channels and actually gets "stuck" in one way of perceiving environmental stimuli. Because the world of academics taxes the senses of sight and hearing equally, a single-channel Looker or Listener, or a Mover who has failed to adequately develop either of the academically oriented channels, is bound to experience frustration in the classroom. And so, quite often, these children wind up being labeled "learning disabled."

In some cases, of course, a child's history reveals a possible organic origin of the learning disability, such as prenatal problems, a head injury, or a family history of learning problems. Happily, the course of educational therapy is the same whether a child's classroom difficulties are primarily learning-style related or organic in nature, so parents needn't despair if a specific diagnosis can't be agreed upon.

This chapter examines learning preferences that can become learning disabilities, and also provides a look at other conditions that can disrupt the academic process. Since so many learning problems surface during the elementary school years, the relationship between learning problems and the onset of academic work is clarified.

Academic problems usually result in a child's being referred for evaluation. Therefore, this chapter offers some valuable information about the nature of educational and diagnostic testing. Included are descriptions of commonly used tests, suggestions for making sense of your child's test results, tips for highlighting strengths instead of weaknesses, and definitions of some frequently encountered diagnostic terms. In addition, since there has been much debate about the fallibility of various diagnostic tests, you'll find within this chapter a hard look at the validity of a typical testing situation.

Besides classroom modifications and such school services as individualized reading instruction, speech and language therapy, and daily time in a resource room, additional outside support is available to struggling learners. This chapter describes various treatments and therapies, and looks at the pros and cons of delayed school entry and grade repetition. Finally, for parents of children whose self-esteem is battered by the daily challenges posed by learning problems, a list of guidelines is included to help you offer the maximum at-home support.

A generation ago, most parents bowed to the authority of school personnel when it came to the fate of the challenged learner. But times have changed! If you wish to become actively involved in educational decisions that will have a direct bearing on your child's future, you've come to the right place.

THE LEARNING DISABILITY PUZZLE

No hard-and-fast relationship exists between learning preferences and learning disabilities. In fact, educational professionals disagree about what constitutes a learning disability in the first place. Partly because there is no universally accepted test battery to confirm such a condition's existence, the definition of "learning disability" can differ not only from state to state, but even between neighboring school systems. Some districts, for example, consider a thirty-point discrepancy between a child's scores on the visual-motor and language segments of an IQ test to be a reliable indicator of learning disability. Others hold that even a ten-point difference reveals a decided and potentially problematic preference for one sensory modality over another.

The employment of the learning-disabilities label itself is subject to debate. Many authorities subscribe to the idea that *all* learning problems, regardless of severity, are physiological and representative of varying degrees of brain dysfunction. Other experts believe that the

majority of learning problems are learning-style related; that is, inci-
dences of near-exclusive adherence to one sensory mode. The learning-
disabilities cause-and-effect war has, in fact, already spanned many
years, and as it rages on, I find it helpful for my clients and their families
to focus on the positive—the fact that a great many learning problems,
regardless of cause, can be minimized through a specific course of
learning-style-modification techniques such as those described
throughout this book. How much more inspiring is this belief than the
suspicion that a quirk of genetics or an injury in babyhood has made a
child's academic performance a foregone conclusion, and that it may
therefore be resistant to anyone's efforts at remediation!

In my experiences with a vast array of academic stumbling blocks in
clients of all ages, however, I never lose sight of the fact that the issue of
learning disabilities is complex and controversial, and that research can be
cited to support almost any view of the subject. The definition of learning
disability is constantly in flux, and there is no definitive measure of a
disability's existence or the severity of a given problem. A so-called "se-
verely reading disabled" grade schooler may respond beautifully to therapy focused on improving her Listener skills. Or, a child whose neurological tests show negative results for organic causes may nevertheless fail to
progress when learning-style modification is attempted, seeming to defy
her own test results. It is sometimes necessary to change approaches
midstream, working over time to determine what helps and what does not.

Meeting a particular child's needs by effecting change in her learning
skills is my top priority. However, if a child's history suggests that her
school struggles may have an organic cause—if she was born after an
abnormally long labor, for instance, or if she has suffered a head injury—
I refer that child to a pediatric neurologist for evaluation. I make similar
referrals for children who achieve little or no academic headway despite
a course of therapy involving multisensory materials and tailor-made
strategies aimed at effecting learning balance. Conversely, family doc-
tors, pediatricians, and neurologists refer patients to me when it is
evident that a child's learning skills—amassed over a lifetime of reliance
upon a favored sense—are holding her back in the classroom.

How does a learning style become so extreme that it leads to a
learning disability? Let's look at Amanda, a seventh grader who came
to me for evaluation because of difficulty with reading assignments.
Amanda has trouble pronouncing and remembering the meanings of
multisyllabic words, and cannot seem to pinpoint a passage's main idea
or recall facts related in the text. IQ testing reveals a twenty-five-point
spread between Amanda's verbal and performance abilities—a spread

indicative of a learning disability. (See page 238 for details.) Amanda, it turns out, is a Looker who has failed to develop the auditory skills critical to classroom success.

. The same nearly exclusive reliance on a single sense can develop in Listeners and Movers, as well. Nine-year-old Peter, for example, wrestles with spelling and math, and has very poor handwriting. In contrast, his language skills are excellent. Peter's testing shows a discrepancy between verbal and performance scores that is ten points greater than Amanda's, suggesting a Listener who has thus far failed to develop essential visual perception and eye-hand skills.

Then there's Evan, an extremely active preschooler who cannot seem to follow directions, has little success with coloring and cutting, avoids sit-down activities at all costs, and has nearly unintelligible speech. Since the diagnosis of "learning disabled" is seldom used until mastery of academics poses a problem, Evan will not be labeled as such until he is of school age. However, it is immediately evident that this little boy is a Mover with significant language and visual-motor delays.

As with all my clients, I treat Amanda's, Peter's, and Evan's learning problems with educational remedies. As you've seen in earlier chapters, there are a host of strategies that children and their parents can apply to make difficult school work more palatable by involving a favored sense in an academic task that taxes a weak area. And, most of the children in my practice show significant improvement in their skill levels in a surprisingly short time, while enjoying a corresponding and much-needed boost to their self-esteem in the bargain. In my experience, the positive approach almost always yields equally positive results.

WHEN THE INTRODUCTION OF ACADEMIC WORK REVEALS A PROBLEM

Why do so many learning problems escape notice until the grade-school years? A tremendous amount of learning certainly takes place beforehand, but at the child's own pace and usually with a loving and unfailingly attentive parent to hand-pick the experiences that the child will like best. Even in preschool and kindergarten, though there may be some study of letters and numbers, the chief emphasis is usually on socialization. Preacademic work is introduced only through experimentation and play.

Suddenly, with the advent of first grade, there exists standardized testing and a curriculum jam-packed with materials to memorize, concepts to grasp, and tasks to perform on command. No matter how creative the teacher and how child-centered the classroom, children sense the pressure to adjust to a stranger's routine and to then meet her expectations, to match the performance of classmates, and—at report card time—to emerge shining from a subject-by-subject evaluation.

All of this is unfamiliar and stressful territory to a child, and some children are better equipped to conform than others. Chapters Six and Seven showed that school-related responsibilities as simple as sitting through a music class can be torture for as many children as are delighted by the activity. Similarly, certain children pick up new reading vocabulary on the first try, while others are still wrestling with letter sounds or last year's material at Christmas time. In the long run, many children will breeze through academic subjects on the strength of their learning skills. More than a few others, though, will find their paths slowed by a learning disability; an inability to focus their attention on the work at hand; or a hearing, vision, or language problem.

If your child is having problems with class work, this book should help you identify her learning-style strengths and weaknesses, and suggest plenty of ways in which you can develop her weaker skills while helping her apply her strengths to specific course work. However, if, even with your help, your child struggles with academics, you should by all means seek assistance from your child's school. This does not mean that you should discontinue working with your child at home. Your support, encouragement, and learning-style-based suggestions will be of tremendous help to your child, both emotionally and practically. However, in many cases, a child stands to benefit greatly from the diagnostic testing and remedial services available in schools or from outside professionals.

Resource labs and self-contained special education classes, designed to provide support and tutorial services to struggling learners, abound throughout the country. The exact criteria for entry into such programs vary from state to state, but to qualify in all cases, a student's academic performance must be significantly lower than that predicted by her tested intellectual ability. It's important to remember that despite poor classroom performance, some children's test results do not support the existence of a learning disability. In these cases, one must look elsewhere for the cause of learning problems and for assistance with developing strategies to minimize them.

An educational evaluation is in order any time one or more of the following statements characterize your child's classroom performance. Seek assistance if your child:

- Is in first grade and cannot grasp the names of letters or the sounds they make.

- Is in first grade and cannot write or recall numbers, forgets the sequence of numbers, or cannot recall the meaning of such math symbols as the "plus" (+) and "minus" (-) signs.

- Has great difficulty with one school subject while others come easily.

- Is not performing at grade level in one or more subjects despite average or above-average intelligence.

- Displays emotional distress through frequent crying, school avoidance, loss of self-confidence, or the onset of bed wetting.

When a child's classroom behavior or performance suggests the existence of a learning disability, the teacher refers the child to the school psychologist or psychometrist for an evaluation. (See "Who Are the Experts?" on page 252.) Should test results prove the teacher's hunch correct, goals and methods of remediation for that child are put in writing in the form of an Individualized Educational Plan (IEP). The child then receives needed help from the appropriate support personnel—a learning disabilities teacher, a speech-language pathologist, and/or a reading specialist. Consultations with outside medical professionals such as an audiologist or developmental optometrist may be recommended, as well.

THE FACTS ABOUT EDUCATIONAL AND DIAGNOSTIC TESTING

Educational and diagnostic testing are used to determine the scope and nature of a child's school-related problems, as well as the best course of treatment. Generally, the school psychologist or psychometrist undertakes an assessment of the child's abilities. Private-practice psychologists or developmental specialists affiliated with a local college, medical center, or mental health facility can provide the same service to students.

The sooner a learning problem is identified and remediation is set in motion, the better the chances that a child will be able to catch up with her classmates. Since parental observation can be as strong an indicator of classroom difficulties as are a child's grades, I routinely recommend that parents make teachers aware of changes in their child's attitude toward school and school work.

Components of Diagnostic Testing

An educational assessment covers all aspects of the referred student's background and classroom performance, and includes some variation on the following:

- The teacher's report
- A classroom observation
- A developmental history
- An IQ (intelligence) test
- An achievement test
- Learning-modality testing
- Criterion-referenced testing
- Class-work samples

The descriptions that follow will help you better understand the purpose and nature of each of these diagnostic tools.

The Teacher's Report

When a child is referred for testing, the classroom teacher is usually asked to clarify problem areas by completing a detailed checklist of classroom behaviors. In many cases, the evaluator confers with the teacher for additional details.

A Classroom Observation

By observing and noting the attentiveness, classroom performance, and peer interactions of the child in question, the evaluator can glean important information about the student's academic and social skills. This practice gives the evaluator a firsthand look at the child's classroom behavior and responses to ordinary methods of instruction.

A Developmental History

In this component of the diagnostic evaluation, the parents furnish information about the child's medical and educational history, including the ages at which physical and social milestones were met (e.g., when the child first sat up or was toilet trained). This data helps the evaluator paint an overall picture of the child's development, and in some cases pinpoints early indicators of a learning problem.

A Test of IQ (Intelligence Quotient)

The purpose of an IQ measurement is to separate a child's innate ability from environmental influences. The scoring process compares the child's responses with those of other children in her age group. The Wechsler Intelligence Scale for Children–Revised (WISC–R) is one test commonly used for measuring IQ. This test is divided into two parts—a Verbal Scale, which corresponds with Listener abilities, and a Performance Scale, which involves Looker skills. The student earns a score on each subtest, and the scores are combined to determine the child's Full Scale, or overall, IQ.

An Achievement Test

An individual achievement test such as the Wide Range Achievement Test–Revised (WRAT–R) is used to determine the grade level at which the child is performing in reading, spelling, and math. The examiner's observations of the child's approach to her work constitute an important facet of the achievement test.

Learning-Modality Testing

Testing devices such as the Zaner-Bloser Modality Kit or my own Learning Style QuickChecks identify a child's learning strengths, whether auditory, visual, kinesthetic, or a combination thereof. This information reveals the best sensory channel through which to approach a child's skill development.

Criterion-Referenced Testing

Instead of providing a statistical comparison of the child's abilities, criterion-referenced testing determines the level of the child's skills. For instance, the evaluator might note, "Bobby can multiply single-digit numbers, sound out two-syllable words, and use a table of contents." These tests can be borrowed from the regular curriculum, or made up as needed based on a checklist of skills expected to be mastered by a particular grade.

Class-Work Samples

In this segment of the diagnostic assessment, the parents provide a file of recent school work. A review of sample test papers, compositions, work sheets, artwork, and creative writing pieces tells the examiner which assignments are most difficult for the child, how much positive and negative feedback the teacher routinely provides, and which aspects of class work the child excels in.

Understanding and Responding to a Diagnostic Report

When all tests have been administered and scored, and all observations and interviews have been completed, the evaluator prepares a report that spells out his or her findings and makes recommendations for educational modifications, if needed. As a rule, diagnostic reports are quite detailed and can run as long as ten to fifteen pages in length. It's understandable that parents, stunned by the revelation of a problem and very likely baffled by educational jargon, often leave the postassessment meeting somewhat in the dark about their child's test results and the reasons for particular recommendations. But, this doesn't have to be the case! Here are some suggestions that will help you play an active role in your child's educational planning.

1. When reviewing the diagnostic report, begin at the end—the "Summary and Recommendations." The compilation of test data that precedes this section can be confusing and, by itself, meaningless.

2. Ask the examiner to define any professional jargon. Jot down his or her responses, and use these notes to refresh your memory later on.

3. Ask permission to tape the session during which test results are explained. The scope of the discussion and the unfamiliarity of the terminology and subject matter make it virtually impossible to digest everything at once.

4. Request a copy of the report to reread and absorb at a slower pace at home.

5. Once you have reread the report at home, feel free to call the examiner with additional questions or comments.

6. Guard against feeling intimidated by the professionals who are working with your child. You know your child better than anyone else, and you may feel that some components of the evaluation simply do not "fit." If so, it's important to be honest about your reaction before the test results and recommendations become a part of your child's Individualized Educational Plan and permanent record.

The "Down Side" of Educational Testing

It's important to be aware that test results can be wrong. To begin with, the validity of the entire test battery depends upon the experience and expertise of the examiner. Any child, too, can have an "off" day and fail to display her actual potential, or suffer from test anxiety that disrupts her performance. The following considerations should also be kept in mind when reviewing the diagnostic report and meeting with teachers and other professionals at your child's school.

- While intelligence testing attempts to separate innate ability from environment, most tests reward experience. This means, for example, that the child with frequent opportunities to work puzzles at home or school is likely to do better with a particular test puzzle than a child lacking this experience.

- Children from cultural and socioeconomic minority groups are prone to poor performance on individual test batteries. Intelligence tests, in particular, have been criticized as largely reflecting white middle-class values and attitudes, and, in fact, may be administered by a professional who does not understand the child's home culture and language.

- The intimidating nature of the test situation can cause an anxious child's performance to break down. The examiner's unfamiliar face, his or her no-nonsense air, the briefcase, the stopwatch, and the silence of the testing room can all be threatening to a child.

- Speed is considered a virtue in IQ testing. This means that the child who daydreams, contemplates answers carefully, or does not perform well under pressure will be penalized.

- The Verbal and Performance Scales of the WISC–R (see page 244) correspond to Listener and Looker skills, respectively. Since scores can be expected to reflect the subject's learning preference, both of these scales penalize Movers.

- By their very nature, IQ scores set up expectations in the minds of teachers, parents, and children. Too much may be demanded of high-scoring children, or too little from those who earn low scores.

Translating a Diagnostic Report
Into Positive Learning-Style Terminology

On your own, you can translate your child's diagnostic summary into more positive learning-style terminology. This technique shifts the focus away from a learner's weaknesses—"Kristin exhibits auditory perceptual difficulties," for example—to her strengths—"Kristin is a Looker, highly attuned to visual stimuli." This positive approach helps to pinpoint appropriate remedial techniques and specialists simply by identifying inborn learning style. For example, a Listener child often has lagging Looker skills that might warrant the use of books on tape or the practice of reading instructions aloud. Similarly, a Looker's or Mover's weak Listener skills might convince her parents to consult a speech-language pathologist.

On the whole, the use of learning-style terminology can help you view your child's overall educational picture—from learning problem to at-home course of action—clearly and succinctly, as in, "To improve classroom performance, Kristin needs to develop her Listener skills." To help you become more familiar with the technique of reframing standard diagnostic terminology, here is an example of a typical summary and its learning-style-focused counterpart. This report concerns Sarah, a third-grade student who is eight years four months of age.

Diagnostic Report

Verbal IQ: 92
Performance IQ: 114

Sarah's reading problem affects all academic subjects. Her auditory perceptual skills related to reading are at a beginning first-grade level; her actual reading level is second grade, second month. Sarah demonstrates problems remembering what she hears, and her ability to attend breaks down in the presence of noise. She has difficulty memorizing math facts. Her strengths include visual memory and eye-hand skills.

Learning-Style Report

Sarah is a Looker by learning style. She has average intelligence, excellent visual memory and visual-motor skills, is a good speller, and is strong in math computations. Sarah would benefit from auditory training with the school speech-language pathologist to sharpen her ability to distinguish sounds and blend them. This, in turn, should improve her reading skills. Preferential seating near the teacher may improve her ability to follow verbal instructions.

As you can see, both of Sarah's diagnostic summaries deal with the same issues—her weak auditory and reading skills. In the first report, Sarah's strengths and weaknesses are simply listed, almost as a "given," with no attempt made to tie the two together or suggest a reason for the discrepancy in her ability levels. However, the report that is reframed into learning-style terminology acknowledges the child's academic difficulties while maintaining a very positive tone. The blame, so to speak, for Sarah's academic shortcomings is placed on learning-style imbalance—auditory skills that don't measure up to the child's demonstrated visual abilities. Most parents, I'm sure, would rather their child's diagnostic summary read as the second does, if only because it states that help is available!

COMMON CONDITIONS THAT DISRUPT THE NORMAL LEARNING PROCESS

Some deterrents to academic progress are more common than others. The problems listed below, which are often cited in diagnostic reports, may at first sound ominous and unfamiliar. However, the accompanying explanations will help you better understand those obstacles that may be facing your child.

Language Disorders

A child with a language disorder usually has a limited vocabulary and difficulty expressing her thoughts in words. Auditory memory and auditory perceptual skills are weak, so she is impaired in her ability to understand language and remember what she hears. It's not surprising that children with language disorders usually have a great deal of trouble following directions.

Learning Disabilities (LD)

A learning-disabled child has average or above-average intelligence, normal hearing and vision, and no primary emotional problems to interfere with learning. Despite these facts, the LD child is unable to perform academically on par with her intellectual potential because of problems with attention, perception, memory, or thinking. As a result, she is unable to do grade-level work in reading, writing, spelling, or math.

Dyslexia

Dyslexia, one type of learning disability, is, by definition, "a disturbance in the ability to read." This diagnosis is sometimes misapplied to struggling readers who can be readily helped with therapy aimed at strengthening auditory and visual skills. A truly dyslexic child is one with average or above-average intelligence who continues to be a nonreader or progresses only slightly despite an individualized therapy program.

Attention Deficit-Hyperactivity Disorder (ADHD)

A child with ADHD is overactive and unable to control her motor behavior. As a result, she cannot focus attention sufficiently to be successful in a classroom setting. Attention Deficit Disorder (ADD) is the term applied to children whose concentration and task-completion problems exist without hyperactivity.

Developmental Vision Problems

A child can have 20/20 vision, yet still have visual-processing or visual-perceptual problems that hamper her school work. A developmental vision problem may be at fault when a child becomes quickly fatigued when reading, tends to skip words or sentences, or makes many errors when copying from chalkboard to paper.

TREATMENTS THAT CAN HELP

When the reason for a child's learning difficulties has been isolated, the parties involved in her educational-planning conference formulate a set of goals for the child and then schedule appropriate support services. Such services might include classroom modifications and such in-school support as speech-language therapy, individualized reading instruction, peer tutoring, or time spent in a learning disabilities lab. There are other treatments that can help, as well, and these fall into two categories: those that ready a child to learn, and those that teach specific skills and subject material. Some of these treatments are controversial, some work best in conjunction with others, and none can be considered right for every child. It is sometimes necessary for the professionals to recommend several different courses of action in turn before discovering which treatment or therapy is most helpful.

What follows is a look at some of the currently available treatments and the professionals who use them. The inset "Who Are the Experts?" on page 252 describes the training and role of various experts in the different child-related fields.

Treatments That Ready a Child to Learn

Nutritional Therapy

Some children who receive the label "learning disabled" or "hyperactive" have specific nutritional deficits—vitamin or mineral deficiencies, for example—that interfere with learning. Other children have food allergies that result in inattention and poor classroom performance. Still others have a diet too heavy in refined sugar, which can lead to unstable blood-sugar levels and fluctuations in activity level.

A nutritional evaluation can determine a particular child's dietary needs, and an individualized diet can eliminate food additives and other unwanted substances, and supply needed nutrients in appropriate amounts. The Feingold Diet, for example, targets hyperactivity and short attention span by removing sugar, food colors, and chemical additives from a child's diet. As is the case with all therapies, dietary modifications of this type are extremely successful with some children and ineffective with others.

The tests necessary to determine if a child is a candidate for nutritional therapy are performed by an allergist. He or she may then refer the child to a nutritionist for the development of a personalized diet.

Medication

When hyperactivity or an inability to control attention continues over a prolonged period of time and persists even after educational and clinical intervention, medication may be prescribed. Ritalin and Cylert, both of which stimulate neurotransmitters needed to process information, are most often used in these circumstances. Medication is not always an effective means of reducing activity level or improving attention span. However, when these drugs do work, a child's academic performance can improve dramatically. Only a medical doctor can prescribe and monitor a child's progress during a trial period of medication.

Vision Therapy

Vision therapy consists of special optical training exercises designed to coordinate and relax eye muscles. Vision therapy can improve a child's ability to sustain extended periods of close work—reading and writing, for instance—without tiring. These exercises can also improve a child's ability to copy work from chalkboard to paper. A developmental optometrist is the professional to consult about the feasibility of vision therapy for your child.

The Irlen Technique

The Irlen technique is a relatively new treatment that has proven helpful to some children with dyslexia and other reading problems and learning disabilities. With the Irlen method, colored lenses are prescribed to lessen the effects of full-spectrum light sensitivity, a problem that can cause a distorted perception of print. The appropriateness of Irlen therapy and the color of the lenses to be used is determined on an individual basis by a trained Irlen examiner.

Physical Therapy

Physical therapy is prescribed by a medical doctor for children with organic problems brought on by birth trauma or childhood injury. During this treatment, a physical therapist uses massage and specially designed exercises to help a child improve or regain mobility.

Occupational Therapy

This treatment, which, like physical therapy, requires a doctor's prescription, is most frequently suggested for children with fine motor and coordination problems. During treatment, the occupational therapist

Who Are the Experts?

Should you wish to consult an expert for help with a problem that may hamper your child's ability to learn, these professionals may be contacted directly, or you may be referred to them by either a diagnostician or your family physician or pediatrician.

Allergist. *This medical doctor specializes in environmental medicine—the diagnosis and treatment of allergic reactions activated by air-borne elements, foods, and other substances.*

Audiologist. *This specialist holds a master's degree in audiology. He or she tests hearing and fits and repairs hearing aids.*

Developmental optometrist. *A developmental optometrist holds a doctor of optometry degree, and is specially trained to work with children. This specialist tests vision as it relates to school performance, and prescribes corrective lenses and/or eye exercises.*

Developmental psychologist. *This specialist holds a doctorate in psychology and works specifically with children. He or she administers and interprets psychological tests with a focus on child development and learning.*

Learning disabilities teacher. *This specialist holds a bachelor's or master's degree in special education. He or she plans individualized instructional programs within the school system for students with learning difficulties.*

Nutritionist. *This health care professional specializes in nutritional sciences. Some nutritionists are registered dieticians, holding a bachelor's degree in nutrition or a related field and having passed a national examination.*

Occupational therapist. *An occupational therapist holds a bachelor's or master's degree in occupational therapy and requires a physician's referral. This specialist works with the physically and mentally challenged, teaching self-help, fine motor, and social skills to promote independence.*

Ophthalmologist. This medical doctor specializes in the diagnosis and treatment of diseases of the eye.

Pediatric neurologist. This medical doctor is trained to work with children, and specializes in the diagnosis and treatment of childhood disorders of the nervous system.

Physical therapist. A physical therapist holds a bachelor's or master's degree in physical therapy and requires a physician's referral. He or she uses massage and therapeutic exercises to help patients improve or regain physical functioning.

Psychometrist. A psychometrist holds a master's degree in psychology. This school specialist administers and interprets diagnostic tests to pinpoint learning problems.

School psychologist. A school psychologist holds a master's degree or doctorate in school psychology. He or she administers and interprets diagnostic tests to determine developmental delays, learning disabilities, or emotional problems; counsels students; and consults with classroom teachers.

Speech-language pathologist. This specialist holds a master's degree in communication disorders. He or she evaluates and provides therapy for disorders of language, speech, voice, and articulation, and also diagnoses and treats auditory disabilities.

teaches self-help, eye-hand, and social skills designed to promote a child's independence.

Treatments That Teach
Specific Academic Skills or Material

Professional Tutoring

Tutoring is usually provided after school hours and gives assistance to the child who's wrestling with the comprehension of academic material and the completion of school work. In most cases, a professional tutor is a classroom teacher, learning disabilities teacher, or reading specialist. The tutor reviews assignments and explains material in an effort to help the child stay abreast of her classmates.

Language Therapy and Auditory Training

This therapy improves a child's ability to understand language and express herself verbally. Exercises and activities are designed to build vocabulary, enhance the ability to listen, and strengthen auditory memory. Auditory training improves a child's ability to isolate sounds and sequence and blend them for reading. A speech-language pathologist is the professional to consult for language therapy.

It's important for parents to realize that in the case of non-mainstream treatments—vision training, Irlen lenses, and dietary modifications, for example—experts disagree regarding the therapies' effectiveness. I have found that each of these treatments demonstrates convincing results with certain children. Because I consider it my responsibility to make parents aware of all available treatments, I maintain a file of those that can be found in the Oklahoma City area, and make referrals on a case-by-case basis. Parents who are exploring non-mainstream therapies on their own should question other parents or consult with a reference librarian for recently published magazine and journal articles concerning the remediation of learning disabilities. Happily, research in this area is ongoing and ever-changing. Better solutions to today's learning problems may be months, or even just weeks, away.

THE BENEFITS OF DELAYED SCHOOL ENTRY AND GRADE REPETITION

Children who face the challenge of academics without sufficiently developed auditory or visual skills or, perhaps, without the necessary social maturity, almost always have a more difficult time with school work than do their classmates. When a child is younger than most of her classmates or has lagging skills that threaten to undermine her academic efforts, there certainly seems to be a case for granting her more time to mature. Yet, the subject of kindergarten readiness is controversial and emotion-charged, and the issue of grade repetition is even more so. This is largely due to the possible social repercussions of a child's being separated from her peers and placed in a class of younger children. In my experience, and particularly with five- through eight-year-olds whose delayed school entry or repetition of a grade is handled sensitively, the potential academic gains usually outweigh any social stigma attached to being "left back." The following sections examine the options of children whose school-readiness or academic skills are somewhat behind those of their classmates.

Delaying School Entry

Some school districts perform a readiness screening several months prior to the start of kindergarten to identify those four- and five-year-olds who may not yet be able to hold their own in the classroom. A typical screening might require a child to stack blocks, copy shapes, draw a person, walk a straight line, identify colors, and count to ten. Difficulty with such tasks can be an early indicator of motor or cognitive difficulties that may impede the child's learning progress the following year, or may simply be indicative of physical immaturity.

In other districts, this same type of readiness assessment is made by the kindergarten teachers themselves shortly after school begins. Based on assessment information and observations regarding children's classroom functioning, teachers can usually tell by mid-year which students would benefit from an extra year of maturation before beginning first grade. If parents have concerns about their kindergartener's progress, this is the time to compare notes with the teacher and, if warranted, seek remedial help for their child.

Whether a child's entry into kindergarten is delayed by a year or the child spends a year in an extended readiness program—sometimes referred to as "transitional" or "developmental" first grade—that extra time can greatly improve the child's ability to tackle academic work. First, her visual and auditory abilities—Looker and Listener skills, in other words—are given an extra year to develop before being taxed by school work. Second, parents can make a special effort to develop the child's lagging skills. With time and with specially chosen learning-style modification techniques, many children are able to "catch up" before entering first grade. At the very least, the majority enjoy significant gains in visual, motor, language, and social abilities.

Repeating a Grade

Occasionally, social immaturity or underdeveloped learning skills simply are not identified during a child's preschool or kindergarten years. When this is the case, a child may benefit from repeating the grade during which her problems surfaced. However, the social and emotional variables involved in grade repetition increase in proportion to a child's age, and this, in turn, makes it difficult to offer concrete guidelines regarding this alternative. A move such as this should be considered on a case-by-case basis, with the child's parents conferring with the teacher, the school psychologist or outside professional, and sometimes the child herself. Grade repetition is not the answer for every struggling learner, to be sure. When appropriate and when sensitively handled, however, it can make the difference between satisfactory mainstream school progress and a permanent place beneath the wing of the school's learning disabilities specialist.

Sometimes, a child may be too old for grade repetition to be an option. She may have begun school a year later than her peers or have spent a year in a developmental class. Or, she may be approaching adolescence with fragile self-esteem that cannot withstand any additional blows. When repeating a grade is not possible, there are still steps that can be taken to make your child's academic life easier. Here are a few suggestions.

- Provide as much support as possible in the form of Resource Lab or Learning Disabilities Lab assistance, after-school tutoring, and the use of multisensory materials that combine your child's inborn learning style with her less-favored ways of learning.

- Reduce expectations for your child's academic performance. She may not be able to do grade-level work in a particular subject even with support.

- Build self-esteem through nonacademic pursuits such as music lessons, horseback riding, or team sports.

- Pre-tutor your child by reading ahead in a problem subject to familiarize her with new vocabulary and concepts.

- Strongly recommend that your child's teacher make whatever classroom modifications are appropriate to your child's grade level: shortened assignments, permission to take tests without time restrictions, the assistance of a calculator or oral testing, preferential seating, and assignment of a peer tutor.

GENERAL GUIDELINES FOR SUPPORTING
AND WORKING WITH A CHALLENGED LEARNER

Whatever the cause of a child's learning problems, and regardless of the steps taken toward remediation, it's important to recognize that her classroom difficulties have emotional repercussions, and that she will require sensitive handling both at home and at school to prevent further damage to her self-image. Here are some suggestions that will help you provide your struggling learner with a supportive, low-stress environment.

- Focus on enjoying the time you and your child spend together. Be sure to include one-to-one time that is not related to school work.

- Make your child aware of her strengths, and provide opportunities for her to develop them. If she's a good runner, urge her to try soccer. If she loves animals, seek out farms or zoos to visit, consider riding lessons, or get a family pet.

- Boost your child's self-esteem by encouraging self-reliance. As early as possible, urge your child to select her own clothes, choose what she wants to eat, and express her own ideas. Ask her often, "What do you think?" and "How do you feel?"

- Be aware of negative influences at your child's school, like children who tease, a teacher who's overly critical, or homework expectations that are unrealistic. Also, act as your child's advocate regarding the scheduling of support services and her inclusion in activities to which she is entitled. If you become aware of a problem—say, that your child's speech therapy conflicts with her favorite music class—call for a conference with her teacher to explore the matter.

- Make your child aware of how she learns best, and stay nearby for support during homework sessions. Let your child occasionally take on the role of teacher while you play the student. For example, suggest that *she* dictate her spelling words to *you* and then correct your efforts.

- Keep your own emotions in check when you assume the role of teacher at home. Frustrated exclamations such as "Don't you listen when I explain things?" or "You're not even trying!" can be devastating to a child.

- Remember that patience is the key when working with struggling learners. Try to keep your expectations realistic, accept that your child will occasionally lose ground, focus on your child's accomplishments, and be generous with praise.

- Because children with learning problems already expend so much energy trying to keep up with their peers, they may find competition quite distressing. To prevent further erosion of your child's self-esteem, steer her away from highly competitive situations.

- Provide your child with plenty of multisensory materials—that is, toys and activities that stimulate both her favored sense and a weaker one. The earlier chapters of this book will guide you in identifying your child's learning style and picking those techniques and materials that will help her strengthen weak skills, further develop strong skills, and apply her strengths to the mastery of course work.

- Help your child to relax once school is out. Guard against tying up all of her free time with activities, appointments, and therapies, and allow plenty of opportunities for her to play by herself or with friends, as she chooses.

All parents want the very best for their children, but it really doesn't pay to agonize over your struggling learner's future. As we've discussed, the origin and nature of most learning problems are very much in question, and there's little point in worrying about your child's college or career possibilities until it's actually time to make those choices. As no one can predict the effects of time, maturation, and therapeutic services on a child's learning skills, it makes much more sense to stay in the present, providing support, acknowledging frustrations, and celebrating even the smallest successes together.

If you find it frustrating to work with your child, consider employing a professional tutor. Certainly, the tensions that can arise when a parent tries to assume the role of home teacher often spill over to other areas of the parent-child relationship. Now, as always, your child needs your unflagging support and reassurance much more than she needs another set of goals and expectations. Chances are, your struggling learner is surrounded by academic specialists much of the time. But, the all-important role of parent is yours alone!

sights and fine motor tasks that made Michael, in Chapter Two, so solemn and wide-eyed, and made Kim-Lee, in Chapter Eight, feel uncomfortable around members of the opposite sex. Paul's Mover orientation, described in Chapter Three, affected the emergence of his speech, while Beth's, in Chapter Seven, made her feel most at ease with younger playmates, who placed far fewer social demands than her fourth-grade peers.

The child with the strongest self-esteem is the child who is able to achieve academic success, social competence, *and* confidence in his athletic ability. Because children's perceptions and responses are dictated by learning style, however, very few can attain this sort of developmental balance on their own. That's where parents come in. Right from the start, you can help your child by providing a made-to-order combination of toys and sensory experiences. Ideally, a child's interactions and play will, first, enhance his preferred learning style—as in the case of a Listener toddler whose parents form a play group to provide the access to other children that so delights their sociable son. The other portion of a child's activities should combine his preferred sense with play experiences that help develop his weaker skills. The kindergarten Mover whose parents teach him hopscotch to help him with number recognition is a perfect example. Both kinds of experiences are beneficial. Affirming a child's preferred learning style gives him immense pleasure,while stimulating his less-preferred senses opens up options for later learning that, without intervention, simply would not exist!

It is best, of course, to start this kind of parental intervention in the preschool years. Yet, as the stories of eighth graders Kim-Lee, Mark, and Shawn illustrated, even adolescence is not too late to effect a change in a child's academic performance. For the younger set, a parent's aim should be achieving the type of developmental balance described above. But, the introduction of academic work in the primary grades signals the need for a change of focus, from improving less-developed learning skills to equipping a child for the mastery of reading, spelling, and math within the boundaries of his learning style. You see, as children get older, many begin to resist attempts to make them use weaker skills, although the age at which this happens varies according to the child's personality and the nature of the parent-child relationship. Additionally, because most youngsters become involved with play dates and after-school activities at about the same time that academic work begins to loom large, it pays for parents to be practical about time spent with their children. At this point, it's best to focus on improving work and study skills through learning strategies that call the child's inborn

sensory preference into play, and through multisensory materials—
items and activities that appeal to the both the preferred learning
channel and a less-favored sense. It's been my experience that multisensory materials are helpful even during the teen years.

Chapter Nine demonstrated that there are a host of physical and
learning-style-based conditions that can go unnoticed until they begin
to impede a child's academic performance—usually during first grade.
Many children, in fact, so strongly favor one style of learning over the
others that their learning problems can be reversed only with professional assistance. When a child becomes completely reliant on a single
mode of perception and response—for example, when a Mover spends
six years disregarding auditory signals in favor of motion—a learning
disability can result. Early identification of this type of disability, however, increases the degree to which it can be tempered. And here, again,
learning strategies and multisensory materials come in quite handy. In
fact, even when a disability is organic in origin, the materials and tactics
presented in this book can help to minimize the student's problem.

In the long run, a child's post-high school plans are often dictated by
learning style. The child who experiences nothing but success in the
classroom is certainly the most likely to consider college. Yet, even
among this group, social confidence, family relationships, and academic
strengths—all of which are offshoots of learning style—influence the
choices made in twelfth grade. Will a student thrill at the prospect of a
large university where lecture classes number in the hundreds, or be
drawn to the more personal atmosphere of a private, perhaps boys- or
girls-only institution? Once enrolled, will he become involved in inter-
collegiate sports, or find his niche in student government? Will he
declare a major as a second-semester freshman, or follow a liberal arts
curriculum throughout his four years?

And, what of the high school seniors who opt for vocational training,
or forgo higher education altogether? Among this group, as well, the
choices are many. The selection of physical labor over a desk job or of a
high-profile trade over a behind-the-scenes position is as much a function of learning style as is the choice of leisure-time activities.

Of course, it's easy to imagine an "unmodified" Looker studying in
his single room at a small college renowned for its fine arts programs.
And you can just as easily picture a Listener quickly achieving his goal
of membership in the leading fraternity of a sprawling school, or a
Mover delighting in a landscaping business that enables him to spend
workdays outdoors while allowing for rainy-day gym workouts and
racquetball games. In each case, the individual is making a choice based

on likes and dislikes, strengths and weaknesses that have become firmly entrenched over the years.

Certainly, parents should never lose sight of the unique individuals who are their children, loving them unconditionally through life's struggles and successes. But, this book has been all about *increasing* children's options for the future, and I hope I've convinced you that your child needn't be limited to "typical" Looker, Listener, or Mover career paths, simply because of the learning style with which he was born. With your help, for example, your Listener child can develop sufficient Looker skills to consider careers in medicine or the fashion industry—options that might not be open to him without timely learning-style-based intervention.

Can you really maximize your child's learning ability? Absolutely! And, in doing so, you'll be giving your child one of life's greatest gifts—a loving parent's attention and time. This book has achieved its purpose if you are now in closer touch with your child, and eager to have a hand in guiding his learning experiences. I wish you all the best.

Recommended Reading List

The following books, each related to personal learning styles in children or adults, can provide you with additional information about inborn sensory preference and its effect on learning ability. Although their professional perspectives and target populations may differ somewhat from mine, each of these authors has documented studies and personal experience that parallel my work with young Lookers, Listeners, and Movers.

Armstrong, Thomas. *In Their Own Way: Discovering and Encouraging Your Child's Personal Learning Style.* Los Angeles, CA: Jeremy P. Tarcher, 1987.
Provides practical advice for fostering a child's individuality at home and at school.

Bandler, Richard, and Grinder, John. *Frogs Into Princes: Neuro Linguistic Programming.* Moab, UT: Real People Press, 1979.
Offers the now-classic introduction to NLP.

Barbe, Walter, and Swassing, Raymond. *Teaching Through Modality Strengths: Concepts and Practices.* Columbus, OH: Zaner-Bloser, 1979.
Describes auditory, visual, and tactile learners.

Dunn, Rita, and Dunn, Kenneth. *Teaching Children Through Their Individual Learning Styles.* Reston, VA: Reston Publishing Co., 1978.
Identifies variables that affect student learning.

Gardner, Howard. *Frames of Mind*. New York: Basic Books, 1983.
Presents the author's theory of seven different types of intelligence.

Grinder, Michael. *Righting the Educational Conveyor Belt*. Portland, OR: Metamorphous Press, 1989.
Applies Neuro Linguistic Programming concepts to education.

Hart, Leslie. *Human Brain and Human Learning*. New York: Longman, 1983.
Applies the results of neurological research to education.

Irlen, Helen. *Reading By the Colors*. Garden City Park, NY: Avery Publishing Group, 1991.
Presents and discusses the Irlen Method as a solution to some reading disabilities.

Markova, Dawna. *The Art of the Possible: A Compassionate Approach to Understanding the Way People Think, Learn, and Communicate*. Berkeley, CA: Conari Press, 1991.
Discusses learning styles and communication in adults.

McGuiness, Diane. *When Children Don't Learn*. New York: Basic Books, 1985.
Explains male/female differences in learning and why boys are more often labeled "learning disabled."

Resources

A few of the playthings and educational materials suggested in this book are available only through mail-order catalogue. In each of these cases, the company from which the item may be purchased has been noted in the text, and the address and phone number of that company have been listed below. Remember that the catalogues available from the following sources offer far more than the items I have recommended. No doubt, you'll find within their pages many other exciting ideas for your learner!

Aristoplay, Ltd.
P.O. Box 7529
Ann Arbor, MI 48107
(800) 634–7738

Aristoplay offers a catalogue of fascinating games that teach. Most items allow for multi-level play, providing a continuing challenge for growing children, and allowing players of different ages to enjoy the games together.

Childcraft, Inc.
P.O. Box 29149
Mission, KS 66201
(800) 631–5657

This colorful catalogue is filled with high-quality play materials, each geared for a specific age group.

Cuisenaire Company of America, Inc.
12 Church Street, Box D
New Rochelle, NY 10802
(800) 237–3142

This specialty catalogue offers hands-on materials that teach math and science. While designed primarily for teachers, these materials come with complete instructions that enable most to be used successfully at home.

Dale Seymour Publications
P.O. Box 10888
Palo Alto, CA 94303
(800) 872–1100

Dale Seymour publishes four catalogues featuring unusual, high-quality supplementary educational materi-

als for every level from early childhood through high school.

The Heritage Key
6102 E. Mescal
Scottsdale, AZ 85254
(602) 483–3313

This "international children's catalog"
offers books, dolls, toys, and other cul-
tural-enrichment materials designed
to educate children about the customs
and languages of people around the
world.

Kaplan School Supply Corporation
1310 Lewisville-Clemmons Road
P.O. Box 609
Lewisville, NC 27023
(800) 334–2014

This catalogue is loaded with hands-
on materials for early childhood programs and the teaching of beginning
reading, science, and math.

Lakeshore Learning Materials
2695 E. Dominguez Street
P.O. Box 6261
Carson, CA 90749
(800) 421–5354

Lakeshore offers colorful multisensory
materials designed to teach readiness
skills through play.

Mind's Eye
Box 1060
Petaluma, CA 94953
(800) 227–2020

This catalogue features a large collection of books on tape, many of which
are narrated by famous people.

The Right Start
Right Start Plaza
5334 Sterling Center Drive
Westlake Village, CA 91361
(800) 548–8531

Right Start specializes in high-quality,
reasonably priced products and gifts
for infants and toddlers.

Toys to Grow On
P.O. Box 17
Long Beach, CA 90801
(800) 542–8338

This catalogue offers toys and games
for infancy through the grade-school
years, including personalized items.

Troll Learn & Play
100 Corporate Drive
Mahwah, NJ 07430
(800) 247–6106

In this catalogue, you'll find games,
playthings, and crafts designed to
stimulate imagination and creativity.

Index

Teachable

for Elementary and
Middle School Classrooms

Selected and Compiled
by John Hulse

Phi Delta Kappa Educational Foundation
Bloomington, Indiana
U.S.A.

Book design by
Victoria Voelker

Phi Delta Kappa Educational Foundation
408 North Union Street
Post Office Box 789
Bloomington, Indiana 47402-0789
U.S.A.

Printed in the United States of America

Library of Congress Catalog Card Number 98-65437
ISBN 0-87367-804-4

TABLE OF CONTENTS

SPELLBOUND AND LEARNING:
An Introduction to Using Movies in the Classroom
by Donovan R. Walling

When I was an elementary school pupil in the 1950s, the best that my teachers could manage might be a few minutes of projected still photographs. These came in the form of film-strips, many still in black and white. But on weekends I often spent Saturday afternoons being spellbound at the movies, which for a youngster in those days usually meant a full course of cartoons, newsreels, an adventure serial, a short subject, and one or two feature films.

Certainly, many of my teachers back then must have dreamed about bringing the two worlds together: the movies and the classroom. But few were able to do so because of the technical constraints of the time. The invention of video-tape made the realization of that dream a possibility. And when the video form finally settled — after evolving through reel-to-reel and BETA — into the familiar shape of the VHS cassette, it became downright easy for teachers to integrate movies into their instructional repertoires.

Teaching with movies — feature films, made-for-television movies, and TV and theater shorts — is quite different from using movies as rewards. Using a movie as a reward for good behavior or goal accomplishment is simple: Pick a movie the students like and want to see and show it; serve popcorn if you don't mind cleaning up the mess or know a kindly cus-todian. *Teaching* with movies takes a bit more work — but it can be worth it. And it can make classroom instruction both optimally effective and, in many cases, as entertaining as showing movies as rewards.

Planning Ahead

Selecting and previewing teachable movies are the first steps. Begin by reviewing the instructional unit you plan to

teach. What are the "big ideas" that you want students to learn? Which movies might best convey those ideas or motivate students to think about the subject matter at hand?

Next, preview those movies. When you preview a movie, do so with a notepad in hand. Watch the entire movie, but keep the remote control for the VCR handy:

- Begin by setting the counter on the VCR at zero, and then note the position of important scenes in the movie. This will make showing the movie in class easier, because you can "pre-edit" to focus on key parts and fast-forward through unnecessary sections.
- Pause the action and make notes, such as important visual cues that you will want to point out to students, sections of dialogue that are important to the plot, or questions you want to be certain to ask.
- Locate the logical breaks in longer movies. You may want to show only a few minutes of the movie each day for several days, rather like chapter-a-day reading.

Once you have decided on a movie to use, also check to see if teaching resources may be available. Several years ago, for example, I developed a teaching packet — summary, vocabulary list, tests, and so on — for William Gibson's play, *The Miracle Worker*, which was made into the well-known film starring Anne Bancroft and Patty Duke (see p. 163). Similar packets and other resource materials are available from various publishers and can make it easier to integrate a movie into the instructional unit.

Incidentally, that *Miracle Worker* packet was published by Perfection Learning Corporation, which publishes a variety of similar supplementary instructional materials. Their address is 1000 North Second Avenue, Logan, Iowa 51546. Phone: 1-800-831-4190. They have a site on the World Wide Web at **http://www.plconline.com**. Another company that produces study guides, called "Novel Ties," is Learning Links,

Inc., 2300 Marcus Avenue, New Hyde Park, NY 11042. Phone: 1-800-724-2616. Their web site is at http://www. learninglinks.com.

Before Viewing

When you are ready to use a movie in the classroom, be certain to set the stage for the students. Discuss the basic plot, the main characters, and how the movie fits with the unit of study. If the movie is based on a book or story, have the students read that version first. What should they look for as they watch the movie? Do you want them to compare and contrast versions of the same information — for example, How is the movie version different from the book? This is a particularly useful process when the movie is used in connection with literature study. Many books and stories — and even poems — have been made into movies.

Other movies may relate to learning themes, such as "the world of work" or "the wonders of science." What information should the students be alert to? It may be helpful to provide a set of preview questions, so that students can look for specific answers as they watch the movie.

These activities are comparable to the "activating prior knowledge" strategy used in reading instruction. To get the most out of a movie, students need to know what to anticipate and how the movie will connect to their reading, writing, or research activities. Another way to accomplish this goal is to ask students to develop their own anticipation guides, based on class discussion or preliminary reading.

Breaking the longer movie into teachable segments is easy to do. Simply preview the movie as suggested previously, note the counter number at which each segment begins, and then use those notations to set up the video each day. Be certain to set the VCR's counter on zero when you start to preview the movie and when you begin showing the movie for the first time, but do not reset the counter between segments.

Finally, another strategy that is easy to employ because of the videotape format is editing by using the fast-forward feature. In previewing the movie, you may discover sections or subplots that add little to the instructional value of the movie. By noting the counter numbers of these unnecessary sections, you can fast-forward through them, thereby saving time and possibly preventing confusion.

During Viewing

Flexibility is a major advantage of using movies on videotape in the classroom. For example, it is not necessary to watch any movie in a single sitting, especially if it is a feature film. Breaking the movie into three to five sections can optimize its use as a teaching tool. When this strategy is used, of course, it also will be important to use bridging summaries: Ask students to discuss what happened in the previous segment, just as you might ask them to summarize the previous day's chapter before reading the current day's chapter of a read-aloud book. And at the end of the day's viewing, take time to ask students, What do you think will happen next? Both summary and anticipation are important for maintaining continuity over several days' viewing.

Another type of flexibility is the ability to replay important scenes. Often it is helpful to students' understanding to watch a scene, discuss it, and then watch it again to look for a new interpretation or missed information. Movies on video make it easy to employ this strategy. If students are comparing information in the movie to information in a book, they can do so on the spot and then replay that section of the movie to check for accuracy. For example, when second-grade students watch a GeoKids Series (p. 121) movie about chameleons, they can stop the videotape and compare what the movie says to what they have read in their science book — or what they have observed about the classroom chameleon.

For students of all ages, keeping a film diary or learning log can be an effective learning device. Ask students to write a summary of each day's viewing, answer the previous day's preview questions, and write down their anticipation questions. Can they predict what will happen next? Then check after the next day of viewing: Was the prediction accurate? Help the students use their learning logs to connect the movie content to the information they learn through reading, discussion, and research in the library or on the Internet.

After Viewing

After viewing the entire movie (or all of the selected segments), take time for a general discussion and summary. What were those "big ideas"? How does the movie connect to other information the students have learned?

After viewing also is a good time to suggest further reading and other movie connections. With so many movies available on video and easy to obtain in many local libraries or video rental stores, students can watch the selected movie again on their own or find related movies in just the same way that they might search for related books in the school library. In fact, many school libraries are doing what many public libraries now do: They are stocking videos that students can check out and view at home.

This flexibility also makes it easy for students to share what they are seeing and doing at school with their parents. Students and their parents might be encouraged to watch some movies together. And home-school projects can be designed to draw parents into their children's learning activities.

Questions About Copyright

Most videotaped movies that are rented from stores or checked out of libraries are labeled "For Home Use Only." This notice has caused concern in the education community.

However, it is generally accepted that the "fair use" rules of copyright allow for showing such videos in the classroom — provided that a few simple guidelines are followed. Commercially produced videotapes of movies may be used in the classroom *as a part of instruction*. Such movies may not be used for "public performances." As construed by the copyright rules, such public performances may include showings on school property (such as in the auditorium) that are open to the public and for the purpose of entertainment or for cultural purposes (Helm 1986, p. 36).

The public performance use is what the "For Home Use Only" label is designed to discourage.

> The rental of a videotape bearing the "For Home Use Only" warning and used for instructional purposes in a classroom would fall under the Section 110(1) performance exemption of the Copyright Act. (Botterbusch 1996, p. 22)

However, even in this notion of fair use there is some room for interpretation, particularly when the video is rented from a commercial firm. Technically, the rental store is not the copyright holder and so does not have authority to grant *any* performance rights. As a consequence of this openness to interpretation, some authorities advise education institutions to make their own policies with regard to using videotapes for instructional purposes. Therefore, teachers who plan to use movies in the classroom should check the school policy handbook to see if there are any restrictions against doing so.

What about videotaping movies off the television? Nine "Guidelines for Off-the-Air Recording of Broadcast Programming for Educational Purposes" were developed by a congressional subcommittee during the 1980s. While these are guidelines, not laws, they are important for schools to follow in the absence of a licensing agreement:

> 1. Videotaped recordings may be kept for no more than 45 calendar days after the recording date.

2. Videotaped recordings may be shown to students only within the first 10 school days of the 45-day retention period.

3. Off-air recordings must be made only at the request of an individual teacher for instructional purposes, not by school staff in anticipation of later requests by teachers.

4. The recordings are to be shown to students no more than two times during the 10-day period, and the second time only for necessary instructional reinforcement.

5. The taped recordings may be viewed after the 10-day period only by teachers to determine whether to include the program in the curriculum in the future.

6. If several teachers request the same program, duplicate copies are permitted to supply the requests, with all copies subject to the same restrictions that apply to the original recording.

7. The off-air recording may not be physically or electronically altered or be combined with others to form an anthology, though the recordings do not need to be shown in their entirety.

8. All copies of off-air recordings must include the copyright notice as recorded on the broadcast program.

9. These guidelines apply only to nonprofit education institutions, which also are "expected to establish control procedures to maintain the integrity of these guidelines." (Botterbusch 1996, pp. 23-24)

The guidelines also apply only to broadcast television — programs transmitted by television stations without charge to the public — not to cable, satellite, or distance education programs. Those forms fall under different guidelines that are more complicated than the guidelines above.

As communication technology changes, copyright laws and interpretations of fair use for educational purposes also change. As Michael Sullivan, executive director of the Agency for Instructional Technology, put it: "Simultaneous revolutions in education and technology are forcing a reexamination of the criteria for 'fair use,' embodied in the 1976 Copyright Revision Act" (Agency for Instructional Technology 1994, p. 4). Therefore, it will be important for teachers to check with school authorities regarding official policies on video use and to be alert to changes in the pertinent laws and their interpretations as reported in the professional media.

Spellbinding Instruction

Anyone who has been spellbound in the darkness of a movie theater knows that many movies are too good *not* to be used for instructional purposes. What other form could do a better job of bringing to life Carlo Collodi's wonderful tale of the puppet who wants to be a real boy than the classic Disney movie, *Pinocchio*? (See p. 59.) Yet beyond the songs and the drama and the sweetly drawn characters there lies an important question — What does it mean to be human? — a question worth considering in any classroom of growing children.

And for older students, what about *Amadeus*? (See p. 211.) No other form is quite as powerful and sweeping as film to capture the music and drama of this interpretation of the life of Mozart, taken from the stage play by Peter Shaffer. Few would disagree that this movie, a winner of numerous Academy Awards (including Best Picture), provides an effective vehicle for introducing students to the composer and his life and works in a way that is nothing less than — well — spellbinding.

Many movies are best used to address affective issues. Although many films can be useful in teaching cognitive skills, movies touch our emotions more often than our intellect. In so doing, they offer teachers ways of approaching hard-to-talk-about subjects, such as anger, disappointment, envy, and grief. Seeing the blind and deaf Helen Keller and her teacher, Anne Sullivan, struggling to communicate in *The Miracle Worker* cannot help but raise feelings of frustration in viewers. How do the characters deal with their frustration, and what might teachers and students learn from their struggles?

Movies, whether features or made-for-television efforts, make memories. Teachers who use movies as part of their teaching repertoire are choosing a powerful communication medium. Thus teaching with movies is an important responsibility that demands selecting movies with care, matching movies to the curriculum, and thoughtfully structuring the

integration of movie-viewing with reading, writing, research, and discussion. But when these steps are taken, the result is instruction that is not only effective but also memorable.

Notes

Agency for Instructional Technology. *What's Fair? A Report of the Proceedings of the National Conference on Educational Fair Access and the New Media*. Bloomington, Ind., 1994.

Botterbusch, Hope Roland. *Copyright in the Age of New Technology*. Fastback 405. Bloomington, Ind.: Phi Delta Kappa Educational Foundation, 1996.

Helm, Virginia. *What Educators Should Know About Copyright*. Fastback 233. Boomington, Ind.: Phi Delta Kappa Educational Foundation, 1986.

Donovan R. Walling directs the book publishing division of Phi Delta Kappa International. Previously, he was a classroom teacher and education administrator for more than two decades in the public schools.

HOW TO USE THIS BOOK

This book includes more than 100 movies. It is designed to be both a useful guide and a working notebook for the busy teacher who wants to have fingertip access to information about films and made-for-television movies that offer excellent instructional possibilities.

The movies listed in this compendium are arranged *alphabetically by title* and grouped under six subject headings:

- Classic Stories
- History and Culture
- Science and Nature
- Growing Up
- Around the World
- Music and Dance

The subjects and titles are listed in the table of contents. However, keep in mind that many movies might fall into more than one category. *To Kill a Mockingbird*, for example, is listed in Classic Stories, but it would be equally appropriate to place it in History.

Each movie is described on a single page, and on the facing page is space to write teaching notes. This simple design makes the symbol system in the righthand corner of each description "thumb-able." By thumbing the pages, the reader can see at a glance several important pieces of information about every movie.

Here is what the symbols mean:

 The first television set contains the suggested audience. The audiences are shown as follows:
P - Primary (preschool through grade 3)
I - Intermediate (grades 4 through 6)
M - Middle school (grades 7 through 9)
The word **ALL** designates movies suitable across grades preschool through 9.

The second television set tells whether the movie is in color (**C**) or black and white (**B&W**) or is animated (**A**), which may be assumed to be color animation.

The third television set shows the **running time** of the movie in minutes.

This award symbol is used when the movie has earned one or more distinguished awards.

Each movie description begins with the title of the movie at the top of the page. Below the title is the year in which the movie was produced or first released, though all of the movies included in this compendium have been rereleased one or more times.

The movie's suitability rating is listed next. Most of the movies in this book are rated either **G** (general audience) or **PG** (parental guidance suggested). The exceptions are those movies labeled **Not Rated**. A movie may be unrated because it was made before the rating system was instituted or because it was made for television or directly for video. Some of the movies that were made before the rating system was instituted have been given a rating on their rerelease, either in theaters or on video. No movies rated PG-13 or R have been included.

The rating information is followed by the director and then the featured actors. In the case of animated movies a "voices of" listing is provided. However, for some movies — documentaries and some short films, for example — this information may not be supplied.

The next piece of information is the distributor of the movie. Most of the movies in this compendium can be found in public library collections or local video rental stores. But in cases where a movie is not available at the local library or video store,

it normally can be obtained by contacting the distributor directly. A directory of distributors is provided at the end of this book.

Any awards (look for the symbol) are listed next. Only major awards are included; no effort has been made to track all of the awards that a movie may have garnered.

The remainder of each entry consists of two or three paragraphs of description. The movie descriptions are purposefully brief and are intended to provide only a sense of the story and a few other useful pieces of information. Points of departure for teaching also are suggested. But no attempt has been made to provide actual lesson plans, as all of the movies in this compendium are rich in potential teachable moments. Class themes, instructional objectives, and students' interests and abilities will be the most effective determining factors for how these many fine movies can be best used in elementary and middle school classrooms.

Finally, facing each movie description page is space for notes about the movie. This is a good place to jot down points to remember about the plot or characters; questions to ask students before, during, and after viewing; counter numbers for starting and stopping the videotape; and so on, as you preview the listed movie. The purpose for including the notes page is to make this compendium a working document and so that teachers can develop a succinct record of movies they have found valuable to use for instructional purposes.

CLASSIC STORIES

NOTES

THE ADVENTURES OF HUCKLEBERRY FINN

1985

Not Rated

Director: Peter Hunt

Features Sada Thompson, Samm-Art Williams, Lillian Gish, Richard Kiley, Jim Dale, Butterfly McQueen, Patrick Day, Geraldine Page, Barnard Hughes, and Frederic Forrest.

Distributor: MCA/Universal Home Video

This version of the Mark Twain classic was made for PBS television and may well be the best adaptation yet. I recommend it for older students, perhaps grade 4 and up, because of the frank depiction of slavery and some violence. I picked this version over many others because I believe this to be the best cast and, at 240 minutes, there is a much greater development of the characters and plot.

This is a good teaching film for several reasons, not least of which is its interpretation of the novel. Students might connect the two by reading aloud passages from the novel that correspond to scenes in the movie. They might compare and contrast how each medium conveys the same story. Screenwriting and storyboard activities can be used to extend students' understanding both of the novel and of the film form itself.

The movie also provides a valuable glimpse of 1800s America, which can connect it to social studies as well as American literature.

NOTES

ALICE IN WONDERLAND

1951

Not Rated

Directors: Clyde Geronimi, Hamilton Luske, and Wilfred Jackson

Voices of Kathryn Beaumont, Ed Wynn, Sterling Holloway, and Jerry Colonna.

Distributor: Walt Disney Home Video

Many versions of this incredible tale exist, but the Disney animated movie is a classic. (To be honest, I also picked this one because of Ed Wynn, a star of radio, television, and film. The great ones always should be remembered.)

Like most Disney films, this one takes some liberties with the novel. But that also gives students a chance to read the Lewis Carroll book and to discuss how Carroll's vivid images were translated into the film's animated drawings. An interesting previewing strategy might be to ask students to draw their own images, based on reading passages of the novel before watching the movie. Another creative connection might be to ask students to describe their own "wonderland."

NOTES

ANIMAL FARM

1955

Not Rated

Directors: John Halas and Joy Batchelor

Voices of Maurice Denham and Gordon Heath.

Distributor: Video Yesteryear

Animal Farm has seen several film treatments. This one is a British animated cartoon based on the George Orwell novel. The story is an allegory on communism, which may mean that it will be over the heads of younger children (though they may be entertained by it).

There is a good history lesson here, as the film can readily be connected to a study of the Western political climate from the start of World War II to the Cold War and beyond. The class might learn about the rise and fall of the Berlin Wall, and even about the nature of communism itself.

The different personality types in the film make for interesting discussion. Why do we make the decisions we make? Older students also might tackle the author's life and motivation. What was George Orwell's inspiration? Did the book fit his personality?

NOTES

BABE

1995

Rated G

Director: Chris Noonan

Features James Cromwell and Magda Szubanski.
Voices of Christine Cavanaugh, Miriam Margolyes,
Danny Mann, and Hugo Weaving.

Distributor: MCA/Universal Home Video

Awards: 1995 National Society of Film Critics Award
for Best Film; Academy Award for Visual Effects;
1996 Golden Globe for Best Film (Musical/Comedy)

Nominated for several Academy Awards, including Best Picture, this warm-hearted and engaging fable tells the story of a super-intelligent pig named Babe, whose unusual talent for sheep-herding is recognized and encouraged by Babe's farmer/owner (Cromwell). The film comes from Australia and is based on Dick King-Smith's book, *The Sheep-Pig*.

This film paves the way for discussions about nonconformity, trusting your instincts, and believing in yourself. Students can be encouraged to examine the outlook of the farmer and his wife, the contest judges, and the neighbors and to discuss the obstacles the farmer faces because of his unconventional pig. Why does he stand up for what he believes?

Students also might consider how the different types of animals "cooperate" with each other and the results of their efforts.

NOTES

BAMBI

1942

Rated G

Director: David Hand

Voices of Bobby Stewart, Stan Alexander, Cammie King, Peter Behn, Donnie Dunagan, Sterling Holloway, Ann Gillis, Tim Davis, and Sam Edwards.

Distributor: Walt Disney Home Video

Loosely based on a book by Felix Salten, this Disney classic deals with some of the harsh realities that animals face growing up in the forest. But most of the movie is light-weight fare and good even for very young children, with the possible exception of the scene in which Bambi's mother is killed. But even that can offer a way of talking about grief and loss.

For younger viewers, the opportunity to engage in music activities based on the movie will be important. Songs include "Little April Shower," "Love Is a Song," "The Thumper Song," and "Let's Sing a Gay Little Spring Song" — all of which are catchy and singable.

This is an excellent film to examine the use of music to create moods, such as heightening the dramatic content of the visuals. For older students, the movie also might serve as a way to enter discussion about endangered species and other environmental issues.

NOTES

THE CANTERVILLE GHOST

1996

Rated PG

Director: Syd Macartney

Features Patrick Stewart, Neve Campbell, Ed Wiley, Raymond Pickard, Cherie Lunghi, Donald Sinden, Joan Sims, Leslie Phillips, and Ciaran Fitzgerald.

Distributor: Hallmark Home Entertainment

Like most classics, this one has seen several movie versions. The original story was written by Oscar Wilde. This recent film is distinguished by an excellent cast, including Patrick Stewart as the cursed Elizabethan spirit, Sir Simon de Canterville.

Sir Simon is doomed to haunt the family mansion until a prophecy is fulfilled. Much to the chagrin of Sir Simon, an American family moves into the old home. But then Sir Simon meets Virginia, the little girl in the family, and realizes that she may have the answer to help release his spirit.

There are a few scary scenes — ghosts and flying objects, but nothing too extreme — that make this a better film for 4th grade and up. But even the scary moments can be useful, as they offer a good opportunity to talk with students about what scares them and how they deal with the things they fear. This and related topics make for good writing starters, too.

NOTES

DAVID COPPERFIELD

I, M

B&W

130 min

1935

Not Rated

Director: George Cukor

Features W.C. Fields, Lionel Barrymore, Maureen O'Sullivan, Freddie Bartholomew, Basil Rathbone, Lewis Stone, Elsa Lanchester, Madge Evans, Arthur Treacher, Una O'Connor, Frank Lawton, and Roland Young.

Distributor: MGM/UA Home Entertainment

Awards: One of the 10 Best Films of 1935 from the National Board of Review Awards; also nominated for several Academy Awards, including Best Picture and Best Film Editing.

An all-time favorite movie, this outstanding film version of Charles Dickens' novel stars 1930s child actor Freddie Bartholomew, who gives a fantastic performance as David. As the film progresses, viewers watch the Copperfield character grow from orphaned child to young man in Victorian England.

While the treatment of the novel is light and whimsical (note comedian W.C. Fields in the role of Mr. Macawber), the film offers an excellent opportunity for students to learn about Victorian England and Charles Dickens. Teachers should not hesitate to play selected scenes more than once and to involve students in role playing. Many students will learn from discussions about the main characters and what seems to motivate them to act in certain ways.

For older students this film also offers a way to begin learning about social issues, such as poverty, homelessness, and child custody.

NOTES

HANNA-BARBERA STORYBOOK CLASSICS: VARIOUS TITLES

1973

Not Rated

Distributor: Turner Home Entertainment

The Hanna-Barbera company that gave us Yogi Bear also produced a series of short animated features adapted from great works of literature. The "performers" in these cartoons are the Hanna-Barbera cartoon characters.

Subjects include: Black Beauty, The Count of Monte Cristo, Cyrano de Bergerac, Daniel Boone, Davy Crockett, Gulliver, Heidi, Jack and the Beanstalk, and Oliver and the Artful Dodger. There also are versions of *Last of the Mohicans, The Three Musketeers,* and *20,000 Leagues Under the Sea.*

For younger students, these light-hearted treatments offer a fine introduction to several great books. Many of the films deal with very strong heroic characters. A good point of discussion would be, What makes a hero?

NOTES

HEIDI

1993

Rated G

Director: Michael Rhodes

Features Noley Thornton, Jason Robards Jr.,
Jane Seymour, Lexi Randall, Sian Phillips, Patricia Neal,
Benjamin Brazier, and Michael Simkins.

Distributor: Walt Disney Home Video

This is the made-for-television version of the Johanna
Spyri classic. Filmed on location in Austria, the movie features Noley Thornton, who is effective in the title role as an orphan taken away from her grandfather in the mountains to live with her rich but unhappy aunt in the city.

A good follow-up discussion with students might include comparing how male heroes and female heroes resolve their problems in different ways. How might the story have been different if the main character was a boy, instead of a girl?

NOTES

THE INDIAN IN THE CUPBOARD

1995

Rated PG

Director: Frank Oz

Features Hal Scardino, Litefoot, Lindsay Crouse, Richard Jenkins, Rishi Bhat.

Distributor: Columbia Tristar Home Video

Based on the best-selling children's book by Lynne Reid Banks, this movie tells the story of a nine-year-old boy named Omri (Hal Scardino), who receives a toy Indian as a birthday present. When Omri places the toy in a cupboard, the toy Indian magically comes to life without growing any larger. The Indian, named Little Bear, has been transported in time from the year 1761 and desperately wants to return to his own place and era.

The themes of responsibility and growing up are compelling discussion points that can be drawn from this movie, which is particularly well-suited to boys' needs and interests in grades 2 through 6.

The movie also offers starting points to talk about friendship. What qualities make a great friend?

NOTES

IN SEARCH OF DR. SEUSS

1994

Not Rated

Director: Vincent Patterson

Features Kathy Najimy, Matt Frewer, Christopher Lloyd, Patrick Stewart, Eileen Brennan, and Robin Williams, and the voices of Billy Crystal and Howie Mandel.

Distributor: Turner Home Entertainment

Kathy Najimy is a reporter who is guided through Seussland with the help of the Cat in the Hat (Matt Frewer) and other characters. This tribute to children's author and illustrator Theodore Geisel (1904-91) includes songs, readings from some of his best-loved stories, and animated clips from some of the well-known Dr. Seuss films.

This is a great film to learn about a children's story writer, but it also provides a glimpse into how journalists work. Students might do some of their own journalistic research and interviewing with classmates or other teachers, their parents, neighbors, and so on.

NOTES

JAMES AND THE GIANT PEACH

1996

Rated PG

Director: Henry Selick

Voices of Richard Dreyfuss, Susan Sarandon, David Thewlis, Simon Callow, Jane Leeves.

Distributor: Walt Disney Home Video

Director Selick, who also made *The Nightmare Before Christmas*, is an expert stop-action animator. He brings Roald Dahl's 1961 children's novel to the screen with a number of delightful touches.

The film begins with live actors before moving into animation. James is an orphan whose parents were eaten by a rhino, and so he lives with two mean aunts. A tree in their yard produces a peach that grows to enormous proportions. When James decides to crawl inside the peach, he meets an assortment of friendly insects: a centipede (Richard Dreyfuss), a spider (Susan Sarandon), and a ladybug (Jane Leeves). Randy Newman's spritely musical score adds to the enjoyment.

This film offers an excellent opportunity to study modern animation, as well as the movie's themes of friendship and trust. Like most of Roald Dahl's books, this one is rather different in print from the movie adaptation. Thus another topic of discovery might be comparing the two versions of the story, Dahl's original and the movie.

NOTES

LASSIE, COME HOME

1943

Rated G

Director: Fred M. Wilcox

Features Roddy McDowall, Elizabeth Taylor, Donald Crisp, Edmund Gwenn, May Whitty, Nigel Bruce, Elsa Lanchester, and J. Pat O'Malley.

Distributor: MGM/UA Home Entertainment

Award: Voted one of the 10 Best Films of the Year by the National Board of Review Awards in 1943.

Based on the novel by Eric Knight, this is the first of the Lassie feature films. In this movie Lassie is sold to a rich businessman from the city. But the dog wants desperately to get back to his farm home and so begins a long, difficult journey. The story is good, but it is the cast of well-known actors that makes this version a truly memorable film.

An obvious avenue of discussion would be to ask students to describe pets they have had or wanted to have. What were the special characteristics that made them love their pets? Students also might be engaged in discussions about loyalty and responsibility. The "going home" theme also could be explored in various contexts.

NOTES

A LITTLE PRINCESS

1995

Rated G

Director: Alfonso Cuaron

Features Liesel Matthews, Eleanor Bron, Liam Cunningham, Rusty Schwimmer, Arthur Malet, Vanessa Lee Chester, Errol Sitahal, Heather DeLoach, and Taylor Fry.

Distributor: Warner Home Video

This film is a wonderful fantasy based on the children's book by Frances Hodgson Burnett. Set in the World War I period, a young English girl whose father is away at the war is sent to a boarding school in New York City. The school is run by a rigid headmistress. The girl, Sara, is played by Liesel Matthews. When her father is reported killed, the head-mistress (Eleanor Bron) makes Sara work as a servant to pay her tuition.

This is a first-rate production and makes a good vehicle for discussing adversity and how students can respond to hardship. For more mature students the movie also can stimulate discussion about class systems and racial differences arising from the British domination of India.

NOTES

MARY POPPINS

1964

Not Rated

Director: Robert Stevenson

Features Julie Andrews, Dick Van Dyke,
Ed Wynn, Hermione Baddeley, David Tomlinson,
and Glynis Johns.

Distributor: Walt Disney Home Video

Awards: Academy Awards for Best Actress (Julie Andrews),
Best Film Editing, Best Song ("Chim Chim Cher-ee"),
Best Visual Effects, and Best Score; 1965 Golden Globe
Award for Best Actress in a Musical/Comedy (Julie Andrews).

Based on the books by P.L. Travers, this film classic from Disney is still delightful after more than 30 years. A magical English nanny sails into a conservative London household and succeeds in reconnecting a distant father with his children. Along the way the film explores British class differences.

This is an ideal teaching vehicle for exploring drama and music. Students can learn more about musical theater and movies by staging their own version of this or another story. The film's use of coordinated animation and live action is especially intriguing — and entertaining.

NOTES

MATILDA

1996

Rated G

Director: Danny DeVito

Features Rhea Perlman, Danny DeVito, Embeth Davidtz, Mara Wilson, and Pam Ferris.

Distributor: Columbia Tristar Home Video

Based on the children's book by Roald Dahl, this film tells the story of Matilda, a young girl whose life is made miserable by her monstrous parents and a horrible school principal whose idea of fun is to grab a girl by her pigtails and throw her out the window. But Matilda's first-grade teacher, Miss Honey, encourages her; and soon Matilda discovers that she has magical powers. Thus Matilda is able to take a measure of revenge on those who have oppressed her.

Like most of Dahl's fiction, this story is full of fantasy; and the live action film has cartoon-like elements and some amazing special effects. In fact, it is a good film starter for talking about special effects. But it also is effective as a vehicle for encouraging discussion about home and school frustrations and how to handle them.

NOTES

NATIONAL VELVET

1944

Not Rated

Director: Clarence Brown

Features Elizabeth Taylor, Mickey Rooney, Arthur Treacher, Donald Crisp, Anne Revere, Angela Lansbury, Reginald Owen, and Norma Varden.

Distributor: MGM/UA Home Entertainment

Awards: Academy Award winner for Best Film Editing and Best Supporting Actress (Anne Revere).

Based on the novel by Enid Bagnold, this well-known film stars a 12-year-old Elizabeth Taylor as Velvet Brown. She wins a horse named Pie in a drawing and is determined to enter it in the Grand National Steeplechase. An excellent cast highlights this story of a determined young girl and her desire to become a champion.

This film might lead to a discussion about the goals that students set for themselves and the process of goal-setting itself. What do they want to accomplish in the next few years? And how can they go about making their dreams come true.

NOTES

OLD YELLER

1957

Rated G

Director: Robert Stevenson

Features Fess Parker, Dorothy McGuire, Tommy Kirk, Jeff York, Kevin Corcoran, Chuck Connors, and Beverly Washburn.

Distributor: Walt Disney Home Video

Bason on the novel by Fred Gipson, this is the story that Disney made into its first "boy and his dog" adventure. Travis (Tommy Kirk) is a 14-year-old boy who is left in charge of his father's farm while Dad is away. His younger brother (Kevin Corcoran) brings home a stray dog, Old Yeller, who ends up saving the young boy's life but contracts rabies in the process. The sad ending, when Yeller must be destroyed, may be too emotional for the youngest viewers.

This is a good movie to connect to pet care. A classroom visit by a veterinarian would make another good connection to the story. The theme of loss and grief is another powerful connection.

NOTES

101 DALMATIONS

1961

Rated G

Directors: Wolfgang Reitherman, Hamilton Luske, and Clyde Geronimi.

Voices of Rod Taylor, Betty Lou Gerson, Lisa Davis, Ben Wright, Frederick Warlock, and J. Pat O'Malley.

Distributor: Walt Disney Home Video

Adapted from the children's book by Dodie Smith and one of the biggest money-making animated films of all time, this Disney classic tells the story of Roger and Anita and their dalmations, Pongo and Perdita. The dogs have puppies, which are kidnapped by Cruella de Vil, who lusts after their skins to make a spotted coat. The dogs rescue their puppies from Cruella's clutches — along with 84 more dalmation puppies — and embark on an adventurous journey home.

Younger viewers in particular will find this movie a good starting point to talk about selfishness and responsibility. Older readers can compare the book to the movie adaptation — and to the more recent, live-action Disney version of the same story.

NOTES

PETER PAN

1960

Not Rated

Director: Vincent J. Donehue

Features Mary Martin, Cyril Ritchard, Sondra Lee, Heather Halliday, and Luke Halpin.

Distributor: Goodtimes Entertainment

This live-action version of J.M. Barrie's play may not be as well-known as the Disney movie, but it has some real advantages over the animated film. This version was filmed for television from a 1954 Broadway performance of the musical play. The story is about a boy (Peter Pan, played by Mary Martin) who never grows up. He returns to real-world London in search of his lost shadow and ends up taking the Darling children back to Never-Never Land with him. There, they battle the evil Captain Hook.

This is an excellent film for a student's first look at musical theater and can lead to a lively discussion of differences among performance media. As a starter for imaginative play-acting and creative writing, few works are more engaging than *Peter Pan*.

NOTES

THE PIED PIPER OF HAMELIN

1984

Not Rated

Director: Nicholas Meyer

Features Eric Idle

Distributor: CBS/Fox Video

This **made-for-television** version of the Robert Browning poem is an excellent example of the shows created for Shelley Duvall's "Faerie Tale Theatre" in the 1980s. All tend to be somewhat tongue-in-cheek versions of popular tales. (See *Rip Van Winkle* and *The Snow Queen* in this section.)

In this story a man with a magic flute (Monty Python's Eric Idle) charms all of the rats out of the village of Hamelin. But when the town officials refuse to pay his fee, he takes revenge by luring all of the children out of the town as well.

Because this story was first cast as a poem, the film makes for a good introduction to reading poetry in general. And the serious themes of ethical behavior, promises kept and broken, and revenge also can be used for discussion and writing by students.

NOTES

PINOCCHIO

1940

Rated G

Directors: Ben Sharpsteen, Hamilton Luske.

Voices of Dickie Jones, Cliff Edwards, Evelyn Venable, Walter Catlett, Frankie Darro, Charles Judels, and Don Brodie.

Distributor: Walt Disney Home Video

Based on the stories by Carlo Collodi, this Disney classic was the company's second major animated feature (after *Snow White*). Many critics consider it Disney's finest effort. Pinocchio is a little wooden puppet made by Geppetto, the woodcarver, and then brought to life by a good fairy. But Pinocchio wants to be more than a puppet; he wants to be a real boy. Famous songs include: "When You Wish Upon a Star," "Hi-Diddle-Dee-Dee (An Actor's Life for Me)," and "Give a Little Whistle."

Seeing this film is a great way to start a unit on puppet-making. And, of course, the songs are fun for music classes at any grade. Students also might be encouraged to think about what makes people human, connecting Pinocchio's aspirations to real life.

NOTES

THE PRINCESS BRIDE

I, M

C

98 min

1987

Rated PG

Director: Rob Reiner

Features Cary Elwes, Mandy Patinkin, Robin Wright, Wallace Shawn, Peter Falk, Andre the Giant, Chris Sarandon, Christopher Guest, Billy Crystal, Carol Kane, Fred Savage, Peter Cook, and Mel Smith.

Distributor: Columbia Tristar Home Video

Based on the novel by William Golding (author of *Lord of the Flies*), this movie tells the story of a young maiden (Robin Wright) who is taken to the kingdom of Florin to marry a prince. But the prince, who is interested only in money and power, plans to do away with her right after the ceremony. Her only hope is to be rescued by her one true love (Cary Elwes).

This charming bedtime story has satire for adults and older students as well as swashbuckling action that will please all ages. The movie might encourage a number of writing and literature exercises, for example, an examination of how traditional folktales form the basis for new tales.

NOTES

RABBIT EARS STORYBOOK CLASSICS: VARIOUS TITLES

1988

Not Rated

Distributor: Columbia Tristar Home Video

This acclaimed video series includes many favorite fairytales that are read by popular celebrities. The visuals include some beautiful illustrations (some are animated) that help bring the stories to life. Among the titles are "How the Leopard Got His Spots," "The Legend of Sleepy Hollow," "Red Riding Hood," "The Tale of Peter Rabbit," "Goldilocks," "The Three Little Pigs," and many more. Audio versions also are available and have been broadcast over public radio stations as "Rabbit Ears Radio."

These short movies offer starters for students who want to flex their artisitic muscles by drawing or painting to illustrate their own favorite tales. More advanced students will be eager to try their hand at writing their own folktales or presenting stories in the manner of the videos.

NOTES

RIP VAN WINKLE

I, M

C

60 min

1985

Not Rated

Director: Francis Ford Coppola

Features Harry Dean Stanton and Talia Shire.

Distributor: Knowledge Unlimited

Like "The Pied Piper of Hamelin," this version of the famous Washington Irving story is from Shelley Duvall's "Faerie Tale Theatre" series. Rip Van Winkle wanders into the Catskill Mountains, where he drinks himself to sleep — a nap that lasts for 20 years. When Rip awakens he finds the world much changed.

Although this film, with Harry Dean Stanton as Rip, has some scenes that might be too scary for younger viewers, older youngsters will find the story captivating. An effective follow-up will be comparing the original story to the Shelley Duvall adaptation. This story also makes a good discussion starter about the nature of time and history. What might students find if they fell asleep and woke up 20 years later? Creative writing opportunities are abundant with this rich material.

NOTES

THE ROBERT MCCLOSKEY LIBRARY

1990

Not Rated

Distributor: Children's Circle Westwoods Studios

This video features several wonderful stories by writer and illustrator Robert McCloskey. The stories include: "Time of Wonder," "Make Way for Ducklings," "Lentil," and "Blueberries for Sal." At the end of the video is an interview with the author that was conducted in 1964.

This video offers an oppourtunity to discuss the process of writing, especially based on the interview section of the film. Students might be encouraged to write their own stories based on themes from McCloskey's work.

NOTES

SARAH, PLAIN AND TALL

1991

Rated G

Director: Glenn Jordan

Features Glenn Close, Christopher Walken, Lexi Randall, Margaret Sophie Stein, Jon DeVries, and Christopher Bell.

Distributor: Republic Pictures Home Video

Adapted for television from Patricia MacLachlan's novel and nominated for nine Emmy Awards, this film tells the story of Sarah, a New England school teacher who journeys to Kansas in the early 1900s. Sarah is supposed to care for a recently widowed farmer and his children with the "arrangement" to become his wife. The "arrangement" eventually turns into true love.

While the love story aspect may seem to make this a poor choice for the classroom, the film is a worthwhile drama that offers a thoughtful glimpse into daily life and social customs in the fading years of the Old West. For that historical aspect alone, it is worth viewing. But it also is a fine interpretation of an excellent novel.

NOTES

THE SECRET GARDEN

1993

Rated G

Director: Agnieszka Holland

Features Kate Maberly, Maggie Smith, Heydon Prowse, Andrew Knott, and John Lynch.

Distributor: Warner Home Video

Based on the story by Frances Hodgson Burnett, this movie portrays the story of Mary Lennox, an orphan who brings a long-neglected garden back to life and, with it, the tomb-like Yorkshire mansion where she has been sent to live. The transformation eventually affects all of the characters in the story. This is a well-constructed adaptation of a classic and a beautiful-looking film with many warm moments.

As a follow-up, students might discuss places, either in their home or some place they have visited, that made them feel special. The subject of friendship also could be discussed: how differences between people need not lead to disharmony and how lasting friendships are formed. This also is a good beginning-of-the-year film for talking about friendship and cooperation at school.

NOTES

THE SECRET OF NIMH

P, I

A

82 min

1982

Rated G

Director: Don Bluth

Voices of John Carradine, Dom DeLuise, Elizabeth Hartman, Aldo Ray, Derek Jacobi, Edie McClurg, Wil Wheaton, and Peter Strauss.

Distributor: MGM/UA Home Entertainment

This film is great for younger viewers. The animated feature was adapted from Robert C. O'Brien's *Mrs. Frisby and the Rats of N.I.M.H.* Director Don Bluth was a Disney artist and, along with other Disney notables, put together this superb film.

In the story Mrs. Frisby, a recently widowed mouse, discovers a top-secret group of ultra-intelligent rats, who have escaped from a laboratory at the National Institute of Mental Health and who go to great lengths to protect her and her family.

This film makes a good starting point for discussions about the cooperation and self-sacrifice it takes to protect those who cannot protect themselves. Students also might discuss how the families manage to stay together despite terrible adversity.

NOTES

SKEEZER

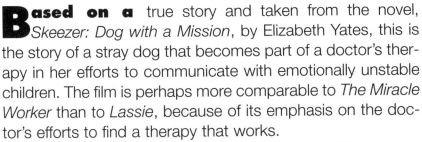

1982

Not Rated

Director: Peter Hunt

Features Dee Wallace Stone, Karen Valentine, Justine Lord, Leighton Greer, and Tom Atkins.

Distributor: Live Entertainment

Based on a true story and taken from the novel, *Skeezer: Dog with a Mission*, by Elizabeth Yates, this is the story of a stray dog that becomes part of a doctor's therapy in her efforts to communicate with emotionally unstable children. The film is perhaps more comparable to *The Miracle Worker* than to *Lassie*, because of its emphasis on the doctor's efforts to find a therapy that works.

This film is an excellent vehicle for talking with students about how scientists go about solving problems. The students also might consider the problems associated with mental illnesses and emotional disabilities.

NOTES

THE SNOW QUEEN

P, I

C

60 min

1983

Not Rated

Director: Peter Medak

Features Lauren Hutton, Linda Manz, David Hemmings, Melissa Gilbert, Lee Remick, and Lance Kerwin.

Distributor: CBS/Fox Video

This is an excellent story of true friendship and courage from the "Faerie Tale Theatre." The original version is a Hans Christian Andersen story. Shelley Duvall narrates the film version about a girl and boy who grow up together until the boy is captured by the Snow Queen (Lee Remick) and held hostage in her ice palace. The girl then begins the difficult journey to come to his rescue.

This film will give students an opportunity to discuss elements of friendship, trust, and courage. Students also could discuss how the young girl in the story handles adversity and compare her adventure with heroines and heroes in other stories.

NOTES

SNOW WHITE AND THE SEVEN DWARFS

1937

Not Rated

Director: Ben Sharpsteen

Voices of Adrianna Caselotti, Harry Stockwell, Billy Gilbert, Jim Macdonald, Pinto Colvig, Lucille LaVerne, and Stuart Buchanan.

Distributor: Walt Disney Home Video

This was the first major animation film from Walt Disney and still is a major hit with young people. The story was adapted from a Grimm Brothers' fairy tale. It features memorable characters, beautiful animation, and a score full of singable songs, such as "Whistle While You Work," "Some Day My Prince Will Come," and "Heigh Ho."

For children interested in art, seeing this film could lead to studying different types of drawing, from this 1930s style of illustration (also seen in Disney's *Fantasia*; see p. 215) to the breezy, open styles of later Disney efforts, such as *Aladdin* (see p. 209), or independents, such as *The Point* (see p. 171).

Students also can examine differences among story types, such as myths, folktales, and fairytales. The seven dwarfs also offer an opportunity to talk about personalities and personality types.

NOTES

SO DEAR TO MY HEART

1949

Not Rated

Director: Harold Schuster

Features Burl Ives, Bobby Driscoll, Harry Carey, Beulah Bondi, and Luana Patten.

Distributor: Walt Disney Home Video

Based on *Midnight and Jeremiah*, by Sterling North, this charming and often overlooked Disney film tells the story of a boy who tries his best to earn enough money to enter his black sheep at the county fair. Several scenes in the film use animation and live action together. And there are some remarkable songs, including "Lavender Blue," "Billy Boy," "County Fair," and "Sourwood Mountain."

Students could discuss filmmaking techniques by studying the use of live action and animation together. And this is a good movie to connect to a folk music unit. Other topics for discussion might be responsibility, setting goals, and accepting challenges.

NOTES

TO KILL A MOCKINGBIRD

1962

Not Rated

Director: Robert Mulligan

Features Gregory Peck, Brock Peters, Phillip Alford, Mary Badham, Robert Duvall, Rosemary Murphy, William Windom, and Alice Ghostley.

Distributor: Knowledge Unlimited

Awards: 1962 Academy Award for Best Actor (Gregory Peck), Best Adapted Screenplay, Best Art Direction/Set Direction (B&W); 1963 Golden Globe Awards for Best Actor-Drama (Peck) and Best Score.

Adapted from the Pulitzer Prize-winning novel by Harper Lee, this well-known film won numerous Academy Awards. Gregory Peck delivers a stellar performance as Atticus Finch, an Alabama lawyer trying to defend an African-American client in the 1930s. Harper Lee based her character of "Dill" on her childhood friend, Truman Capote.

This film provides a powerful platform to discuss racial prejudice and race issues in general, including the civil rights movement of the 1960s, which provides the cultural backdrop against which the 1930s story was filmed.

NOTES

WILLY WONKA AND THE CHOCOLATE FACTORY

1971

Rated G

Director: Mel Stuart

Features Gene Wilder, Jack Albertson, Denise Nickerson, Peter Ostrum, Roy Kinnear, Aubrey Woods, Michael Bollner, Ursula Reit, and Leonard Stone.

Distributor: Warner Home Video

Adapted from *Charlie and the Chocolate Factory* by Roald Dahl, *Willy Wonka* is the story of a young boy named Charlie who wins a trip to the most wonderful — and the most bizarre — candy factory in the world. The factory is run by the magical and mysterious Willy Wonka (Gene Wilder). Inside, Wonka leads Charlie and four other young winners on an amazing tour of the factory, but danger awaits for any child who misbehaves. A musical score by Anthony Newly and Leslie Bricusse adds to the strangeness.

The story takes place in a candy factory, so the students could discuss places that they would like to visit. How candy is made and what ingredients go into its creation, or the health facts behind some of our favorite treats are other potential topics.

NOTES

WISHBONE SERIES: VARIOUS TITLES

1996

Not Rated

Distributor: Polygram Video

This series of short films features Wishbone, a brave, loveable, Jack Russell terrier, whose adventures connect to a variety of stories by authors ranging from Homer to Mark Twain, Sir Arthur Conan Doyle, and Stephen Crane.

PBS actor/producer Larry Brantley supplies the voice for Wishbone and, with his story-telling gifts, encourages an appreciation of literature and fantasy as the terrier lives out many classic stories. Program titles include: "A Tail in Twain," "Homer Sweet Homer," "Salty Dog," "Terrified Terrier," "The Prince and the Pooch," "The Slobbery Hound," and "Twisted Tail."

NOTES

THE YEARLING

1946

Not Rated

Director: Clarence Brown

Features Gregory Peck, Jane Wyman, Claude Jarman Jr., Chill Wills, Henry Travers, Jeff York, Forrest Tucker, and June Lockhart.

Distributor: MGM/UA Home Entertainment

Awards: 1946 Academy Awards for Best Color Cinematography and Best Interior Decoration; 1947 Golden Globe Award for Best Actor-Drama (Gregory Peck).

Adapted from the Marjorie Kinnan Rawlings novel about a young boy's love for a yearling fawn, this movie is set in the period following the Civil War. Claude Jarman was awarded a special Oscar as Outstanding Child Actor for his portrayal of a boy who comes of age in this story of unqualified love.

This is a film for animal lovers that lends itself to discussions ranging from wilderness preservation to pet care and veterinary medicine. The Civil War setting also is interesting, and some connections to American history can be made.

HISTORY AND CULTURE

NOTES

AN AMERICAN TAIL

1986

Rated G

Director: Don Bluth

Voices of Dom DeLuise, Madeline Kahn, Phillip Glasser, Christopher Plummer, Nehemiah Persoff, and Will Ryan.

Distributor: MCA/Universal Home Video

This animated adventure, created under the hand of Stephen Spielberg, tells the story of the immigrant Mousekewitz family and offers some pretty good lessons about the challenges and hardships of immigrants and about diversity of cultures.

A sequel, *An American Tail: Fievel Goes West*, is aimed at adults as well as children and features genre takeoffs that will be over most students' heads. This second movie (1991, rated G, 74 min.) showcases the vocal talents of John Cleese, Dom DeLuise, Phillip Glasser, Nehemiah Persoff, Amy Irving, Jon Lovitz, and James Stewart. It was directed by Phil Nibbelink and Simon Wells. MCA/Universal is the distributor.

NOTES

ANNE FRANK REMEMBERED

1995

Not Rated

Director: John Blair

Features narration by Kenneth Branagh and Glenn Close.

Distributor: Columbia Tristar Home Video

Award: 1995 Academy Award for Best Documentary Feature.

Actor/director Kenneth Branagh provides the main narration, with Glenn Close reading diary excerpts, in this Academy Award-winning documentary that tells the story of the Frank family during World War II. Based on Anne Frank's journals, this film also includes the only known footage of Anne, as she watches a wedding from her window.

Students might be led in discussions about aspects of the documentary as a film form, possibly comparing the documentary to other types of historical films. Other discussion and research topics include life during times of war, the Jewish struggle for survival during World War II, and related topics.

NOTES

GRANDPA WORKED ON THE RAILROAD

1994

Not Rated

Features Bruce Phillips.

Distributor: Fast Forward

Folksinger Bruce Phillips plays grandpa and teaches the children about the history of steam locomotives and the railroad. The youngsters are encouraged to make up rhymes about what they have learned.

Students might follow the lead of the film and create different rhymes about locomotives and the railroad. This film also might fit nicely into a unit on different modes of transportation or a unit about the opening of the West.

NOTES

POCAHONTAS

1995

Rated G

Directors: Mike Gabriel and Eric Goldberg

Voices of Irene Bedard, Judy Kuhn, Mel Gibson, Joe Baker, Christian Bale, Billy Connolly, Linda Hunt, David Ogden Stires, Russell Means, and James Apaumut Fall.

Distributor: Walt Disney Home Video

Awards: 1995 Academy Awards for Best Song ("Colors of the Wind") and Best Score; 1996 Golden Globe Award winner for Best Song ("Colors of the Wind").

Disney came in for some well-earned criticism for historical inaccuracy in this fantasy version of the Pocahontas story. However, the film does offer a strong tale about how different cultures react when they come into contact. And so the movie can offer some starting points for discussing racial prejudice and cultural stereotypes.

Older students may be interested in reading about the real Pocahontas and then discussing the differences between reality and movie portrayals of historical figures. Discussion also might lead to learning more about Native Americans.

NOTES

1776

1972

Rated G

Director: Peter Hunt

Features Ken Howard, Blythe Danner, William Daniels, Howard da Silva, Ronald Holgate, Donald Madden, Ralston Hill, Virginia Vestoff, and Stephen Nathan.

Distributor: Columbia Tristar Home Video

Award: One of the 10 Best Films of the Year from the National Board of Review.

This film version was adapted from the Broadway musical about America's first Continental Congress. In the film the congressional delegates sing and dance as they establish the rule of law in Colonial America and write the Declaration of Independence.

This movie offers an above-average history lesson with many points of departure for dicussions about the birth of our nation. Older students may be asked to read and discuss the Declaration of Independence.

NOTES

SOUNDER

1972

Rated G

Director: Martin Ritt

Features Cicely Tyson, Paul Winfield, Kevin Hooks, Taj Mahal, Carmen Mathews, and James Best.

Distributor: Knowledge Unlimited

Awards: One of the 10 Best Films of the Year from the National Board of Review; National Society of Film Critics Award for Best Actress (Cicely Tyson)

This **award**-winning movie was based on a novel by William Armstrong and tells the story of an African-American family's struggles as sharecroppers in Louisiana during the Great Depression. The story is told from the point of view of a boy named David (Kevin Hooks), whose father is put in prison for stealing to help feed his family. That action forces the family to work even harder just to survive. But David studies hard during his father's absence and discovers that education is his way out of poverty.

This is a great film for students to learn about life during the Depression and the experiences of many black Americans during that period. The movie also offers starting points for discussions of racial prejudice, poverty, and the value of education. Family issues are at the center of the movie, and those issues also might be included in related reading, writing, and research.

NOTES

STORIES FROM THE BLACK TRADITION

1992

Not Rated

Distributor: Children's Circle Westwoods Studios

Award: The stories are Caldecott Award winners.

This video features readings of five Caldecott Award-winning children's books from the "Children's Circle." The books are *The Village of Round and Square Houses*, by Ann Grifalconi; *Goggles!* by Ezra Jack Keats; *A Story — A Story*, by Gail E. Haley; *Mufaro's Beautiful Daughters*, by John Steptoe; and *Why Mosquitoes Buzz in People's Ears*, retold by Verna Aardema.

Each story offers opportunities to talk about a variety of subjects, from fitting in to overcoming obstacles. Older students also might take up a study of how such stories could be turned into plays and try their hand at adaptation with an eye to acting out the stories themselves.

SCIENCE AND NATURE

NOTES

ANIMALS ARE BEAUTIFUL PEOPLE

1984

Not Rated

Director: Jamie Uys

Distributor: Warner Home Video

This is a funny, rather sentimental film about the wildlife in South Africa. It was first released in South Africa and then rereleased after the success of director Jamie Uys' hilarious movie, *The Gods Must Be Crazy*.

This movie might be used to make some interesting connections in students' minds about wildlife in general and about species of animals that are specific to certain geographic regions.

NOTES

ARIEL'S UNDERSEA ADVENTURE SERIES: VARIOUS TITLES

1992-93

Not Rated

Voices of Jodi Benson and Sam Wright.

Distributor: Walt Disney Home Video

These short films from Disney feature Ariel (the mermaid) and Sebastian (the crab) from Disney's feature film, *The Little Mermaid*, in a series of animated tales:

Volume 1: Whale of a Tale

Volume 2: Stormy the Wild Seahorse

Volume 3: Double Bubble

Volume 4: In Harmony

Volume 5: Ariel

Young students might discuss ocean life, and documentary videos can be found to add real-life aspects of oceanography to complement these stories.

NOTES

ASTRONOMY 101: A BEGINNER'S GUIDE TO THE NIGHT SKY

1994

Not Rated

Distributor: Mazon Productions

Children who are interested in astronomy will be delighted by this video. The story centers on a young girl and her mother who take watching the stars seriously.

The movie is a good starting point for showing students how to use a telescope to view the planets and stars and discussing aspects of modern and ancient astronomy.

NOTES

DIGGING DINOSAURS

1994

Not Rated

Distributor: Quality Video

This two-part documentary and instructional program offers an amazing tour of the history of dinosaurs. The videos include computer animation and live-action footage of trips to museums, paleontology labs, and dinosaur excavation sites. Each video is about 75 minutes long.

These videos offer an excellent opportunity for students to discuss the evolution of life on the planet and to investigate the various theories about how dinosaurs came to be extinct. Such discussion also might lead to seeking out information about other endangered species and what environmentalists and animal conservationists are trying to do to save them.

NOTES

FERNGULLY: THE LAST RAINFOREST

1992

Rated G

Director: Bill Kroyer

Voices of Samantha Mathis, Christian Slater, Robin Williams, Tim Curry, Jonathan Ward, Grace Zabriskie, Richard "Cheech" Marin, Thomas Chong, Tone Loc, and Jim Cox.

Distributor: CBS/Fox Video

This animated big-screen release about saving the rain forest features the vocal antics of Robin Williams as a bat with a zany sense of humor. The youngest viewers will enjoy the animated animals, and there is plenty of action to captivate the older students. (Interesting voices, including Cheech and Chong, should amuse the adults in the room, too.)

Beyond the fun, however, this film makes some important points about the value of rain forests and can provide starters for discussion, research, and writing about environmental issues.

NOTES

50 SIMPLE THINGS KIDS CAN DO TO SAVE THE PLANET EARTH, PARTS 1 AND 2

1992

Not Rated

Distributor: Churchill Media

David Jana's book of the same title is the source of this two-volume set of videos. Part One is "Water and Resources," which tells the story of how students helped clean up Pigeon Creek. Part Two, "Greenlife, Wildlife, Energy, and Air," answers students' questions about a variety of related environmental subjects.

The book is a good starting point for this set of videos. And the videos themselves offer a number of opportunities to discuss environmental issues, such as recycling and global warming. These movies may be especially helpful when starting a study unit on local environmental issues or beginning a local project, such as a neighborhood clean-up.

NOTES

GEOKIDS SERIES: VARIOUS TITLES

1995

Not Rated

Distributor: Columbia Tristar Home Video

This series of short films from National Geographic is superb. Puppets Sunny Honeypossum and Bobby Bushbaby take young viewers on journeys through the animal kingdom. Three titles in this GeoKids Series are: "Camouflage, Cuttlefish, and Chameleons Changing Color," "Chomping on Bugs, Swimming Sea Slugs, and Stuff that Makes Animals Special," and "Tadpoles, Dragonflies, and the Caterpillar's Big Change."

These short films provide younger students with excellent introductions to interesting animals and nature-study topics, such as the food chain and natural selection.

NOTES

THE LAND BEFORE TIME

1988

Rated G

Director: Don Bluth

Voices of Pat Hingle, Helen Shaver, Gabriel Damon, Candace Hutson, Burke Barnes, Judith Barsi, and Will Ryan.

Distributor: MCA/Universal Home Video

Stephen Spielberg made this feature film about five orphan dinosaurs near the end of the Age of Reptiles. The dinosaurs bond together to try to find a place called the Green Valley, a place where they believe that they can survive when most dinosaurs are facing extinction. This is a film filled with good humor but some heartbreaking moments, such as when a baby brontosaurus sees his mother die. (He sees her again in dinosaur heaven.)

This is an entertaining movie but also can be used to good advantage to launch a unit on dinosaurs or to talk about endangered species. For older students this movie also offers starting points to talk about theories of how the Earth came to be and why the dinosaurs are extinct.

NOTES

MAGIC SCHOOL BUS SERIES: VARIOUS TITLES

1995

Not Rated ·

Voice of Lily Tomlin.

Distributor: Kid Vision

Lily Tomlin is the voice of Ms. Frizzle, the science teacher. Each *Magic School Bus* movie is really a science lesson cleverly disguised as a cartoon in which a class of bright kids and their teacher go on some pretty amazing field trips. One minute the bus can be visiting a farm, and the next it can be exploring the galaxy. Or the bus can become so small that the students can examine a flower from the inside!

Every episode showcases the humor and vocal talents of comedienne Lily Tomlin. The series includes:

The Magic School Bus for Lunch
The Magic School Bus Gets Eaten
The Magic School Bus Gets Lost in Space
The Magic School Bus Goes to Seed
The Magic School Bus Hops Home
The Magic School Bus Inside Ralphie
The Magic School Bus Inside the Earth
The Magic School Bus Kicks Up a Storm
The Magic School Bus Plays Ball

NOTES

SAMSON AND SALLY: THE SONG OF THE WHALES

1984

Not Rated

Distributor: Celebrity Home Entertainment

Based on the book, *Song of the Whales*, by Brent Haller, this film was produced in Norway. It centers on two orphaned whales, Samson and Sally, who search for Moby Dick, believing that the great whale will save all the whales from the "iron beasts."

This environmentally concerned, animated film stands out when compared to other eco-friendly cartoons because of its superior underwater drawings and strong writing. Students might discuss environmental issues, organizations such as Greenpeace, the history of whaling, and related topics.

NOTES

SHAMU AND YOU: EXPLORING THE WORLD OF BIRDS

1992

Not Rated

Distributor: Video Treasures

This little film features everything from songs and stories to animation and actual wildlife footage. With a guide, Shamu, students get to meet and examine a number of winged creatures, including parrots, flamingos, owls, hummingbirds, vultures, and eagles.

There are several other "Shamu and You" films, including "Exploring the World of Mammals," "Exploring the World of Reptiles," and "Exploring the World of Fish." All of these are great introductions to animals of various types.

Using the bird film, students might discuss the various species of birds shown in the movie and then move to such topics as life expectancy of different types of birds, migration patterns, and mating rituals.

GROWING UP

NOTES

ALAN AND NAOMI

1992

Rated PG

Director: Sterling VanWagenen

Features Vanessa Zaoui, Lukas Haas, Michael Gross, Kevin Connolly, and Amy Acquino.

Distributor: Columbia Tristar Home Video

Based on a novel by Myron Levoy, this film probably is most suitable for mature students. The story takes place in Brooklyn in 1944 and deals with a young girl's memory of her parents' death at the hands of the Nazis. Older students likely will find this to be a beautiful film about two young people coming of age under difficult circumstances.

Clearly, there are historical connections to any study of World War II that can be made using this film. Students also might discuss the individual characteristics of the two children. How do they handle adversity in different ways, and what role does their "new family" play as they learn how to live without their parents?

NOTES

BACH AND BROCCOLI

1987

Not Rated

Director: Andre Melancon

Distributor: Family Home Entertainment

This film actually is the third in Canadian producer Rock Demer's "Tales for All" series of films for the family. The story centers on a young girl and her pet skunk, Broccoli, as they try to convince her musician uncle to adopt her instead of letting her go to a foster home. The story also earns kudos for its honest development of its characters.

This is a great film to discuss different aspects of a character's personality and how scenes are written for a film. A class discussion might begin by watching individual scenes and then talking about the emotions that are being played out.

If handled with sensitivity, a discussion of foster homes also might be undertaken, particularly if some children are living in foster homes and feel comfortable about discussing their experiences.

NOTES

BASIL HEARS A NOISE

1993
Not Rated
Distributor: Republic Pictures Home Video

Basil is a bear puppet who explores an enchanted forest to discover who has been playing tricks on his friends. Along the way the shy Basil develops courage and self-reliance. This sweetly charming story also features many upbeat Muppet songs.

This is a good movie for young children, which teachers can use to start discussions about shyness, self-confidence, and self-reliance.

NOTES

BE MY VALENTINE, CHARLIE BROWN/IS THIS GOODBYE, CHARLIE BROWN?

1983

Not Rated

Directors: Phil Roman (for *Be My Valentine*) and Bill Melendez (for *Is This Goodbye*).

Written by Charles Schultz.

Distributor: Snoopy's Home Video Library

This video contains two Peanuts television specials. In "Be My Valentine, Charlie Brown," Charlie Brown wants desperately to receive a Valentine's Day card. "Is This Goodbye, Charlie Brown?" revolves around Lucy and Linus, who must deal with the possibility that they may be moving to another town because their father may be transferred.

The first film is a good vehicle for talking about Valentine's Day and the etiquette of (and expectations about) giving and receiving greeting cards. This is a good seasonal topic and also might be tied to an art activity in which students make cards for one another or their parents.

The second film touches on a more serious topic: moving and feelings of dislocation. About 20% of children in the United States move during any given school year, and so this is a pertinent topic for discussion, particularly in schools with high levels of transience.

NOTES

BEETHOVEN LIVES UPSTAIRS

1992

Not Rated

Director: David Devine

Features Neil Munro, Illya Woloshyn, Fiona Reid, Paul Soles, Albert Schultz, and Sheila McCarthy.

Distributor: BMG

Set in Vienna (though actually filmed in Prague), this movie is the fictional story of a 10-year-old boy named Christoph and his friendship with composer Ludwig van Beethoven. Their friendship takes time to grow because of Beethoven's eccentricities, but Christoph eventually discovers much about the hard work and inspiration behind Beethoven's music.

Beethoven's deafness makes this a good film to use as a discussion starter about how people cope with disabilities. Language-related topics also are plentiful, such as how we develop language, the nature of sign language, and so on. Many students will enjoy learning how to spell their names using the manual alphabet and can gain an appreciation of language by learning a little conversational signing.

Naturally, any film about Beethoven also opens a door to studying classical music, including compositions by Beethoven's contemporaries.

NOTES

CANDLESHOE

ALL

C

101 min

1978

Rated G

Director: Norman Tokar

Features Jodie Foster, Helen Hayes, David Niven, Vivian Pickles, and Leo McKern.

Distributor: Walt Disney Home Video

Based on the book, *Christmas at Candleshoe,* by Michael Innes, this story centers on a fortune that is hidden somewhere on an estate called Candleshoe Manor and on a con man's (Leo McKern) plan to find and steal it. Jodie Foster plays a young California girl who happens to look exactly like the missing heiress of Candleshoe Manor. David Niven is wonderful doubling as the butler and an aristrocrat trying to entertain the lady of the manor (Helen Hayes).

This entertaining film has many well-written parts that offer opportunities to discuss character development. But the story also is about a young girl growing up in unusual circumstances, which might provide opportunities for students to talk about their own growing-up issues.

NOTES

DUMBO

1941

Not Rated

Director: Ben Sharpsteen

Voices of Sterling Holloway, Edward Brophy, Verna Felton, Herman Bing, and Cliff Edwards.

Distributor: Walt Disney Home Video

Awards: 1941 Academy Award for Best Score; 1941 National Board of Review Awards 10 Best Films of the Year.

This classic from Disney is a growing-up story about a baby elephant. Dumbo grows up in the circus, where everyone teases him about his enormous ears — until he learns that he can fly. Then he not only becomes a big star in the circus but also finds confidence in himself and performs heroic deeds.

Brilliantly animated (including an amazing dancing pink elephants sequence), Dumbo also features songs written by Ned Washington, Frank Churchill, and Oliver Wallace, including "I See an Elephant Fly," "Pink Elephants on Parade," and "Baby Mine."

This is a wonderful film for discussing the emotions of insecurity and the desire to fit in and to belong to a group. Students also might discuss individualism, the strength it takes to be unique, and how to make what appears to be a "negative" into something positive.

NOTES

THE ELECTRIC GRANDMOTHER

P, I

C

49 min

1981

Not Rated

Director: Noel Black

Features Maureen Stapleton and Edward Herrmann.

Distributor: Baker and Taylor Video

This made-for-television movie is a marvelous story from Ray Bradbury. A widower (Herrmann) and his three children acquire an ultra-sophisticated robot grandmother (Stapleton), who teaches the children about enduring love and trust.

The Electric Grandmother is an excellent vehicle for discussing the sources for what students learn. Where do we get our information as we are growing up? And how likely are we to believe something if it is presented by an unfamiliar source?

This film also develops its characters well. Students might study the behavior of the children in the movie and discuss the changes they notice in their own behavior (or the behavior of their brother or sister) as they are growing up.

NOTES

FAT ALBERT AND THE COSBY KIDS, VOLUME 1

1973

Not Rated

Voice of Bill Cosby.

Distributor: Barr Films

The Cosby Kids emphasize communication skills in this feature from the made-for-television Fat Albert cartoon series. Two of the kids have to have their tonsils removed in this episode, which uses comedy to demonstrate such communication skills as listening, talking, and sharing. Additional episodes are available.

Like many of the episodes in this popular series, this story provides a way of beginning to talk about issues and problems that are typical of childhood. The cartoon approach and Cosby's well-crafted humor make serious topics highly approachable.

NOTES

THE FLINTSTONE KIDS: "JUST SAY NO"

1989

Not Rated

Distributor: Turner Home Entertainment

The Flintstone Kids is a spinoff from the popular Flintstones cartoons. This particular film focuses on the dangers of using drugs.

For younger students this is a good movie for introducing drug awareness. Older students might find the movie useful as a way of studying how the "say no to drugs" message can be communicated to younger students.

NOTES

FOR THE LOVE OF BENJI

1977

Rated G

Director: Joe Camp

Features Benji (a dog), Patsy Garrett, Cynthia Smith, Allen Fiuzat, and Ed Nelson.

Distributor: Facets Multimedia

For the Love of Benji is one of several movies featuring the shaggy little dog, Benji. In this one Benji and his young owners travel to Greece. Much of the film is shot from the dog's point of view. A noteworthy feature is that the audience gets to see how Benji reacts to people; and his reactions are keyed not to what people say, but to what they do.

Clearly, the film offers an opportunity to introduce Greece and Greek culture and history to elementary students. But it also is a good film to use as a discussion starter to talk about perception and how one person's perception, or understanding, of a situation may differ from another's. Students might be encouraged to explore aspects of "body language": What is communicated by the way a person stands, sits, or gestures?

NOTES

THE GIRL WHO SPELLED FREEDOM

1986

Rated G

Director: Simon Wincer

Features Jade Chinn, Wayne Rogers, Mary Kay Place, Kieu Chinh, and Kathleen Sisk.

Distributor: Walt Disney Home Video

This **inspirational** Disney made-for-television movie is about a Cambodian girl who is a war refugee. The movie tells the story of the girl's tremendous struggles to adapt to her new home in Tennessee and ends when she triumphs in her effort to become a national spelling bee champion.

This uplifting film can provide an opportunity for students to talk about their own struggles to overcome the obstacles to success in their lives. The movie also is a useful film to show to students in multicultural settings and should encourage discussion about the challenges faced by people who come to the United States as immigrants and refugees.

NOTES

GRYPHON

1988

Not Rated

Director: Mark Cullingham

Features Amanda Plummer, Sully Diaz, and Alexis Cruz.

Distributor: Public Media Video

*G**ryphon originally** aired as part of the PBS *Wonder-Works* television series. The story, set in an inner-city school, revolves around a new substitute teacher who incorporates a healthy dose of magic into her lessons. The lessons themselves are examples of imagination, beauty, and creativity.

This film should help students to stretch their creative muscles. Students might tackle a variety of assignments — painting, drawing, writing, or performing — to challenge their imagination and creative instincts.

Another aspect of this film that is worth exploring, particularly with older students, is the inner-city setting. Students might consider how such a setting is similar to or different from their own environment and what challenges such a setting might pose for teachers and students.

NOTES

HOMEWARD BOUND: THE INCREDIBLE JOURNEY

1993

Rated G

Director: DuWayne Dunham

Features Robert Hays, Kim Greist, Jean Smart, Veronica Lauren, and Benj Thall. Voices of Don Ameche, Michael J. Fox, and Sally Field.

Distributor: Walt Disney Home Video

In this recent remake of the 1963 Disney film, a brave trio of animals form a strong bond of love and trust through several difficult adventures. The animals' voices are performed by Don Ameche, Michael J. Fox, and Sally Field.

Growing up, loving, and trusting are themes worth exploring after students view this emotional but thought-provoking movie. The film also makes a good starting point for talking about personality and character development, as students can examine the three animal protagonists, whose thoughts are given voice by the actors behind the scenes.

NOTES

MIRACLE ON 34TH STREET

1947

Not Rated

Director: George Seaton

Features Maureen O'Hara, John Payne, Edmund Gwenn, Natalie Wood, and William Frawley.

Distributor: Critics' Choice Video

Awards: 1947 Academy Awards for Best Story, Best Screenplay, and Best Supporting Actor (Gwenn).

Far better than the remake, this 1947, black-and-white version is a Hollywood classic about a little girl (Natalie Wood) who refuses to believe in Santa Claus. When Kris Kringle (Edmund Gwenn) goes on trial, he must prove himself not only to the court but also to the little girl. It has as beautiful an ending as has ever been filmed. (This movie also is available in a colorized version, but I prefer the black-and-white one.)

This film is better saved for older students, as some younger students may not be ready to have their belief in Santa Claus challenged. But for older students, the movie makes a good discussion starter for talking about childhood beliefs and what it means to grow up.

The movie also provides a starting point for studying holiday folklore and traditions, which need not be limited to Christmas. What are the American traditions surrounding Halloween or Valentine's Day? Do other countries have similar or different traditions for these holidays?

NOTES

THE MIRACLE WORKER

1962

Not Rated

Director: Arthur Penn

Features Patty Duke, Anne Bancroft, Victor Jory, Inga Swenson, Andrew Prine, and Beah Richards.

Distributor: MGM/UA Home Entertainment

Award: 1962 Academy Awards for Best Actress (Anne Bancroft) and Best Supporting Actress (Patty Duke); 1962 National Board of Review 10 Best Films of the Year and Best Actress (Bancroft).

*T**he Miracle Worker*** is an intense, emotional film about Helen Keller, a blind, deaf, and mute girl, and Anne Sullivan, the teacher who cracks open Helen's shell of darkness and silence. The film was adapted for the screen by William Gibson, based on his successful stage play.

Certainly a poignant growing-up film, this movie also offers an excellent opportunity to teach students about handicapping conditions and how people deal with them. The communication theme in the movie is a powerful motivator for students interested in learning more about how the blind and deaf communicate.

NOTES

THE MUPPET MOVIE

ALL

C

94 min

1979

Rated G

Director: James Frawley

Features Jim Henson's Muppets and Charles Durning, with cameo appearances by Edgar Bergen, Milton Berle, Mel Brooks, Madeline Kahn, Steve Martin, Carol Kane, Paul Williams, Bob Hope, James Coburn, Dom DeLuise, Elliot Gould, Cloris Leachman, Telly Savalas, and Orson Welles.

Distributor: Jim Henson Productions

Kermit the frog leaves the swamp and ventures off to Hollywood to try and become a star. On the way he is joined by Fozzie Bear, Miss Piggy, and the rest of the Muppets. But Kermit had better watch out because he is being chased by Doc Hopper (Charles Durning), a restaurant owner who specializes in frog legs!

A charming musical score by Paul Williams includes "I'm Going Back There Someday," "Movin' Right Along," and "The Rainbow Connection."

This is a good growing-up film that can start students discussing their own hopes and dreams for the future. The classic question is, What do you want to be when you grow up?

NOTES

PAST THE BLEACHERS

I, P

C

120 min

1995

Rated PG

Director: Michael Switzer

Features Richard Dean Anderson, Barnard Hughes, Grayson Fricke, Glynnis O'Connor, and Ken Jenkins.

Distributor: Hallmark Home Entertainment

This Hallmark made-for-television movie is based on a novel by Christopher A. Bohjalian. The film is a sentimental story about a father (Richard Dean Anderson) grieving about the death of his son. In spite of his grief, he agrees to coach his late son's Little League baseball team and, in the process, forms a friendship with an old man (Barnard Hughes) and the team's star player, which helps him work through his sorrow.

This film is a good aid for students interested in discussing feelings of loss and times in their lives when they have felt sad. Students also might discuss the process of recovery and the steps necessary to begin the healing process.

NOTES

PLAY-ALONG VIDEO SERIES: VARIOUS TITLES

1989

Not Rated

Features Jim Henson's Muppets.

Distributor: Orion Home Video

These short films are designed to help younger children express themselves. Young viewers learn how to use their imagination, how to tell jokes and funny stories, how to sing along with the characters, and even how to draw the Muppets.

Titles in the series include: "Hey, You're as Funny as Fozzie Bear," "Mother Goose Stories," "Sing-Along, Dance-Along, Do-Along," and "Wow, You're a Cartoonist!"

NOTES

THE POINT

1971

Not Rated

Director: Fred Wolf

Original broadcast narrated by
Dustin Hoffman. Video version narrated by Ringo Starr.

Distributor: Family Home Entertainment

This animated fable (made for television) is a real find.
It starts out with a father reading his son the story of
"Oblio," a child with an unusually round head who is ostra-
cized by his community simply because, in his community,
everyone's head is pointed. Oblio and his dog, Arrow, are
exiled to the Pointless Forest, where self-discovery awaits.
Harry Nilsson wrote and performed the outstanding music for
this timeless classic.

This charming film makes an ideal vehicle for discussing
individuality and how individual differences sometimes cause
hardships. Older students, in particular, can extend this discussion to the themes of prejudice, stereotyping, and tolerance. Students might ask themselves, How do I react to people who seem different from me?

NOTES

THE RESCUERS

1977

Rated G

Directors: Wolfgang Reitherman, John Lounsbery, Art Stevens.

Voices of Bob Newhart, Eva Gabor, Geraldine Page, Jim Jordan, Joe Flynn, Jeanette Nolan, and Pat Buttram.

Distributor: Walt Disney Home Video

The premise of this movie for younger viewers is that a parallel "United Nations" exists in the animal world and is run by a bunch of mice in the basement of the real United Nations. The mice also operate the Rescue Aid Society, and the story begins when they receive a plea for help from a girl named Penny. The delegate from Hungary (Eva Gabor) and a mouse janitor (Bob Newhart) set out to find Penny, and the adventure begins.

This surprisingly good film is a great vehicle for launching students on research about the real United Nations and its goals and accomplishments. This film also would be useful to discuss different charitable organizations throughout the world.

NOTES

SESAME STREET KIDS' GUIDE TO LIFE: LEARNING TO SHARE

1995

Not Rated

Features Jim Henson's Muppets and Katie Couric.

Distributor: Random House Home Video

This is a film for young viewers in which Elmo (one of the Muppets) gets help from television news personality Katie Couric and Sesame Street friends to learn about sharing and taking turns. Songs include: "Sharing," "Cooperation Station," "This Is My Train," "What Is a Friend?" and "Two Heads Are Better Than One."

Teachers of young children will find this video valuable for teaching children how to share and cooperate. The segment featuring the song, "What Is a Friend?" also offers a way of beginning to discuss the characteristics of friendship.

NOTES

SESAME STREET PRESENTS FOLLOW THAT BIRD

1985

Rated G

Director: Ken Kwapis

Features Jim Henson's Muppets, Carroll Spinney, Chevy Chase, John Candy, Sandra Bernhard, Dave Thomas, Joe Flaherty, and Waylon Jennings.

Distributor: Warner Home Video

Sesame Street's Big Bird leaves the gang behind after suffering an identity crisis and tries to join a family of real birds. But soon Big Bird becomes homesick. During a dangerous journey home, he discovers that home is truly where the heart is. The story is excellent and well-matched with music by jazz great Lennie Niehaus and Van Dyke Parks.

Follow that Bird presents a fine opportunity for students to talk about what "home" means to them and feelings of homesickness. And Niehaus' music can provide a good opening to talk about jazz and to get students interested in music.

NOTES

SESAME STREET PRESENTS PUT DOWN THE DUCKIE

1994

Not Rated

Features Jim Henson's Muppets, John Candy, Jane Curtin, Paul Reubens, Paul Simon, Gladys Knight, Alistair Cooke, Phil Donahue, Andrea Martin, Danny DeVito, Rhea Perlman, Martina Navratilova, Itzhak Perlman, Pete Seeger, Jeremy Irons.

Distributor: Random House Home Video

It may be stretching the "Growing Up" category, but this video includes some of the best sketches from the long-running PBS series. Dozens of celebrity cameos and musical numbers make this a real treat. Particularly noteworthy are the spoofs of Alfred Hitchcock, TV news, and Masterpiece Theater, which is transformed into "Monsterpiece Theater" and hosted by Alistair Cookie (Cookie Monster).

Various topics are raised in this compilation, and some wonderful musical numbers will provide starters for discussion and creative play.

NOTES

THE SWAN PRINCESS

1994

Rated G

Director: Richard Rich

Voices of Jack Palance, Michelle Nicastro, Howard McGillin, Liz Callaway, John Cleese, Steven Wright, Steve Vinovich, and Sandy Duncan.

Distributor: Turner Home Entertainment

Based loosely on the same story that inspired Tchaikovsky's ballet, *The Swan Princess* tells the story of Prince Derek, who falls in love with the beautiful Princess Odette. But an evil sorcerer named Rothbart (Jack Palance) also loves Odette and covets her kingdom. And so Rothbart kidnaps Odette and turns her into a swan. Derek attempts a rescue, but Odette has already planned her own escape with the help of a puffin (Steve Vinovich), a slow-talking turtle (Steven Wright), and a very funny frog (John Cleese). Lex de Azevedo provides excellent music for the film.

This is a good movie to introduce students to ballet. They might see a short segment from a film of the Tchaikovsky ballet and compare it to this version of the story, for example. This movie also lends itself to discussions about heroes and self-reliance.

NOTES

THE TALE OF THE FROG PRINCE

1983

Not Rated

Director: Eric Idle

Features Robin Williams and Teri Garr.

Distributor: CBS/Fox Video

Written and directed by Eric Idle of Monty Python fame and brought to television by Shelley Duvall's "Faerie Tale Theatre," this hilarious version of the fairy tale stars Robin Williams as the victim of an angry fairy's spell (turning him into a frog) and Teri Garr as the self-possessed princess who saves him with a kiss.

Beyond the humor, this video offers good starting points for discussing anger and how students deal with adversity. It also makes a good launcher for a unit on fairy tales, folktales, and myths.

NOTES

TOY STORY

1995

Rated G

Director: John Lasseter

Voices of Tom Hanks, Tim Allen, Annie Potts, John Ratzenberger, Wallace Shawn, Jim Varney, Don Rickles, R. Lee Ermey, and Laurie Metcalf.

Distributor: Buena Vista Home Video

Awards: 1996 Golden Globe Award for Best Film Musical/Comedy, and Best Story; 1995 MTV Movie Award for Best On-Screen Duo (Hanks and Allen). It also won seven Annie Awards (given by ASISA, an animators' association), including Best Animated Feature and Best Director.

This is Disney's first entirely computer-generated animated feature. The toys in the story belong to a boy named Andy. Whenever Andy is out of the room, the toys come to life, led by a cowboy doll named Woody (Tom Hanks). When Andy gets a new spaceman Buzz Lightyear toy (Tim Allen), Woody feels as though his "favorite toy" status may be in jeopardy. Danger and comedy ensue as Woody and Buzz "negotiate" a truce.

NOTES

WHAT DO YOU WANT TO BE WHEN YOU GROW UP? VAROUS TITLES

1994-95

Not Rated

Distributor: Tapeworm Video Distributors

In one film, *Railroaders*, students can spend some video time with railroad workers and learn what it is like to work around locomotives and many types of trains.

Another film, *Zoo Crew*, takes young viewers to the Fort Worth (Texas), Cincinnati (Ohio), and San Antonio (Texas) zoos, where they learn about the care and feeding of various animals.

Both of these short documentary films are excellent for helping young children explore the world of work.

AROUND THE WORLD

NOTES

ALLEGRO NON TROPPO

1976

Rated PG

Director: Bruno Bozzetto

Voices of Maurizio Nichetti and Maurizio Micheli.

Distributor: BMG

In this Italian film, live action is mixed with animation and set to classical music. Perhaps its closest American counterpart is Disney's *Fantasia*, because this film also features a series of wildly entertaining skits. A particular highlight is the "evolution of life" sequence set to Ravel's "Bolero."

This is a good film to use as a starter for creative writing or artwork. Students also might examine the music in terms of the emotions being evoked in the various sequences.

NOTES

AWAY WE GO: ALL ABOUT TRANSPORTATION

1996

Not Rated

Director: Jonathan Larson

Distributor: Rainbow Educational Video

Newt the Newt is a salamander puppet. He and two young friends make their way through New York to catch a flight home. This live-action mini-musical features songs about all the methods of transportation they use during their journey. The music was created by Bob Golden and the late Jonathan Larson (who wrote the music for *Rent*).

This film provides an opportunity for students to discuss methods of transportation and to write poems or stories about them. Students also might discuss the pros and cons of each method of transportation and which ones they have experienced.

NOTES

DARBY O'GILL AND THE LITTLE PEOPLE

1959

Not Rated

Director: Robert Stevenson

Features Albert Sharpe, Sean Connery, Janet Munro, and Estelle Winwood.

Distributor: Walt Disney Home Video

Set against an idealized Ireland, this Disney movie tells the story of Darby O'Gill (Albert Sharpe), who falls into a well where he is captured by his old friend, the King of the Leprechauns, and is granted three wishes. The Banshee and the Death Coach provide some scary moments, but the film also has some great writing and special effects.

This film provides students with a good starting point for a discussion of fantasy, as well as some of the figures in Irish legends. Older students might be interested in comparing and contrasting light and dark themes in folklore. Darby's three wishes might lead to a writing assignment: If you were granted three wishes, what would you wish for and why?

NOTES

JIMBO AND THE JET SET, VOLUMES 1 AND 2

1994

Not Rated

Distributor: Video Collectibles

Jimbo Jet (not to be confused with a jumbo jet) is a small airplane that takes younger viewers on animated adventures to far-off places. Each volume offers about a dozen short adventure stories.

These are good beginning stories to discuss travel, geography, and history. Students also learn about various occupations in the course of the adventures.

NOTES

OPEN A DOOR: 3-PART SERIES

1994

Not Rated

Distributor: Beacon Films

This film series follows a child through many adventures as he travels around the world. Countries visited include New Zealand, Sweden, Canada, Tanzania, Holland, England, Cyprus, the Philippines, and Poland. Each film is about 32 minutes long.

This series provides opportunities for the students to discuss and compare the different cultures and traditions of the countries visited in the film. Students might be quizzed about which landmarks belong to which country, and they might even learn a few words of a new language.

NOTES

PRINCE BRAT AND THE WHIPPING BOY

I, M

C

97 min

1994

Rated G

Director: Syd Macartney

Features Truan Munro, Nic Knight, Karen Salt, George C. Scott, Kevin Conway, Vincent Schiavelli, Andrew Bicknell, and Jean Anderson.

Distributor: Columbia Tristar Home Video

Adapted from a novella by Sid Fleischman, *Prince Brat and the Whipping Boy* tells the story of Jemmy (Truan Munro), an orphan living on the streets of Brattenburg in Germany with his younger sister, Annyrose (Karen Salt). The pampered Prince Horace (Nic Knight) has been playing jokes around the castle, but the king's guards catch Jemmy instead. Jemmy makes his escape to find his sister, but the Prince decides to tag along.

Filmed on locations in North Rhine-Westphalia and Burgundy, this film offers a historic look at German culture and also provides a way to begin discussing class differences and what they have meant in German and other societies, both in the past and today.

NOTES

SHAKESPEARE: THE ANIMATED TALES

1993

Not Rated

Distributor: Random House Home Video

Originally televised on HBO, this series of videos features animated versions of some of Shakespeare's most accessible plays. Author Leon Garfield made the abridgments as an introduction to Shakespeare for young people. The fascinating animation was done in Armenia and Russia.

Works in the series include *A Midsummer Night's Dream*, *Hamlet*, *Macbeth*, *Romeo and Juliet*, *The Tempest*, and *Twelfth Night*.

The youngest students will find the stories interesting, while older students can begin to compare the animated tales to excerpts from Shakespeare's plays. Several film versions of Shakespeare also might be shown to high-achieving middle school students, using these animated versions as introductions.

NOTES

WE ALL HAVE TALES: VARIOUS TITLES

1991
Not Rated
Distributor: Society for Visual Education

This is another series of films from the Rabbit Ears company (see p. 63). The stories are introduced by celebrity narrators who also provide the voice-over for the animation. The stories are drawn from around the world. Included are William Hurt telling "The Boy Who Drew Cats," from Japan; Whoopi Goldberg telling "Koi and the Kola Nuts," from Africa; Raul Julia telling "The Monkey People," from South America; Robin Williams telling "The Fool and the Flying Ship," from Russia; Denzel Washington telling "Anansi," from Jamaica; Ben Kingsley telling "The Tiger and the Brahmin," from India; Michael Caine telling "King Midas," from Ancient Greece; and many others.

These films offer excellent opportunities for students to learn about the folklore of other countries. Many students will be able to compare and contrast the stories after they have seen several of the videos.

MUSIC AND DANCE

NOTES

ALADDIN

1992

Rated PG

Directors: John Musker and Ron Clements

Voices of Robin Williams, Linda Larkin, Jonathan Freeman, Scott Weinger, and Gilbert Gottfried.

Distributor: Walt Disney Home Video

Awards: 1992 Academy Awards for Best Song ("A Whole New World") and Best Original Score; 1993 Golden Globe Awards for Best Song ("A Whole New World") and Best Score; 1993 MTV Movie Award for Best Comedic Performance (Robin Williams).

One of the most successful animated cartoons of all time, this madcap version of Aladdin tells the story of a street urchin who does battle with an evil sorcerer and his wise-cracking parrot in order to win the heart of a princess. Robin Williams' lightning-fast jokes carry this film a long way, giving the adults something to smile about as the youngsters are swept up in the adventure.

A good class exercise would be to ask students to compare the characters and story from this film with other animated adventures, such as *The Lion King*, *Hercules*, *Pocahontas*, and *Beauty and the Beast*. The Disney company is known for taking liberties with the original stories, and so comparing the literature or history with the film version can give students a solid research experience.

NOTES

AMADEUS

1984

Rated PG

Director: Milos Forman

Features F. Murray Abraham, Tom Hulce, Simon Callow, Roy Dotrice, Elizabeth Berridge, Jeffrey Jones, Christine Ebersole, and Kenny L. Baker.

Distributor: Republic Pictures Home Video

Awards: 1984 Academy Awards for Best Picture, Best Director, Best Actor (F. Murray Abraham), Best Adapted Screenplay, Best Art and Set Direction, Best Costume Design, Best Make Up, and Best Sound.

Playwright Peter Shaffer adapted his own play about the intense and possibly deadly rivalry between 18th century composers Wolfgang Amadeus Mozart and Antonio Salieri for this panoramic screen version. The movie was shot in Prague, convincingly cast as old Vienna.

This is a dark film in many ways and so is best suited for older students. In addition to providing an excellent glimpse into the life of Mozart — and life in the 18th century in general — the movie also offers a range of dynamic classical music. Students might extend their music study by listening to other works by Mozart and Salieri.

NOTES

B AUTY AND THE BEAST

1991

Rated G

Directors: Kirk Wise and Gary Trousdale

Voices of Paige O'Hara, Robby Benson, Rex Everhart, Richard White, Jerry Orbach, David Ogden Stiers, Angela Lansbury, Jesse Corti, and Jo Anne Worley.

Distributor: Walt Disney Home Video

Awards: 1991 Academy Awards for Best Song ("Beauty and the Beast") and Best Score; 1991 Golden Globe Award for Best Film (Musical/Comedy).

his movie is the first animated feature ever to be nominated for the Best Picture Academy Award. The Disney version of the story features a strong voice cast, innovative animation, and Oscar-winning songs by Alan Menken and Howard Ashman. The deluxe video version also features a rough cut of the film, a soundtrack CD, lithographs, and an illustrated book.

This film provides an excellent opportunity to ask the students to compare these characters with others in assorted animated adventures. Older students also might watch the early black-and-white version of this story as filmed by Jean Cocteau and look for echoes of that film in the Disney version.

NOTES

FANTASIA

1940

Not Rated

Directors: Various segments by James Algar, Samuel Armstrong, Ford Beebe, Norman Ferguson, Jim Handley, Wilfred Jackson, Hamilton Luske, and Bill Roberts.

Voices of Leopold Stokowski, Deems Taylor, Walt Disney, and Hugh Douglas.

Distributor: Walt Disney Home Video

This **1940** classic features a series of vignettes that combine cartoon animation and classical music. The video release was restored to match the original theater release. Highlights include Mickey Mouse as a sorcerer's apprentice, the life cycle of dinosaurs set to Stravinsky, and a stunning rendition of "A Night on Bald Mountain."

This movie is particularly appropriate for a creative exercise combining art and music. For example, teachers might follow a viewing of the film by playing other classical compositions and asking students to draw pictures based on the images that the music conjures up for them. This type of creative expression also could be extended to writing.

NOTES

I CAN DANCE

1989

Not Rated

Distributor: Music for Little People

29
min

This documentary film shows a ballet class of five girls and one boy, whose teacher instructs them in the basic ballet positions.

This video would make a good introduction to movement exercises for younger students, but it also offers some good technical basics for older students who might be interested in studying other types of dance.

See also, *I Want to Be a Ballerina*, page 219.

NOTES

I WANT TO BE A BALLERINA

1993

Not Rated

Distributor: Music for Little People

The San Jose Dance Theater performs highlights from Tchaikovsky's "Nutcracker Suite." Dancers from 4 to 17 years of age give little girls tips and show them what it takes to become a ballerina. We are shown various aspects of the ballerinas' lives, from classes to backstage make-up and costuming.

This video is ideal for girls, but boys also may find aspects of it interesting.

See also, *I Can Dance*, page 217.

NOTES

THE KING AND I

1956

Not Rated

Director: Walter Lang

Features Yul Brynner, Deborah Kerr, Rita Moreno, Martin Benson, Terry Saunders, Rex Thompson, Alan Mowbray, and Carlos Rivas.

Distributor: CBS/Fox Video

Awards: 1956 Academy Awards for Best Actor (Yul Brynner), Best Art Direction/Set Decoration (Color), Best Costume Design, Best Sound, and Best Score; 1957 Golden Globe Awards for Best Actress in Musical/Comedy (Deborah Kerr) and Best Film Musical/Comedy.

This film features wonderful performances and one of Rogers and Hammerstein's most popular scores. Based on the novel, *Anna and the King of Siam*, by Margaret Landon, the stage production on Broadway ran for more than 4,000 performances with Yul Brynner, who revived it in later years on tour. Deborah Kerr's singing was dubbed by Marni Nixon, who also worked in *West Side Story* and *My Fair Lady*.

This classic film provides an opportunity for students to discuss the culture conflicts of the English governess as she tries to bring the values of the West to the Asian king and his children. Younger children may be bored by the love story but will find the king's children engaging. Older students might want to read *Uncle Tom's Cabin*, which is transformed into a play within the play and picks up the theme of race relations.

NOTES

SCHOOLHOUSE ROCK: VARIOUS TITLES

1974

Not Rated

Voice of Jack Sheldon

Distributor: Knowledge Unlimited

This is a popular, acclaimed educational series from ABC television. Whether teachers want scientific concepts, history lessons using catchy songs and animation, or grammar basics, these short videos are entertaining and well-produced. Some of the songs used in the history series, for example, include, "Sufferin' Through Suffrage," "I'm Just a Bill," and "Shot Heard 'Round the World."

Because they are designed to be educational, the videos can be readily integrated into the curricula for history, science, or grammar.

NOTES

SINGIN' IN THE RAIN

1952

Not Rated

Directors: Gene Kelly and Stanley Donen

Features Gene Kelly, Debbie Reynolds, Donald O'Connor, Jean Hagen, Cyd Charisse, Millard Mitchell, Douglas Fowley, Madge Blake, and Rita Moreno.

Distributor: MGM/UA Home Entertainment

Awards: 1953 Gloden Globe for Best Actor in a Musical/Comedy (Donald O'Connor); 1952 National Board of Review Award as one of 10 Best Films of the Year.

Simply put, one of the best movie musicals of all time. This is an excellent film to discuss the history of movies and how the entire industry was thrown into turmoil in the 1920s by the advent of sound on film.

The lyrics and music are by Arthur Freed and Nacio Herb Brown. The songs include "All I Do Is Dream of You," "Should I?" "Singin' in the Rain," "Wedding of the Painted Doll," "Broadway Melody," "You Are My Lucky Star," and the classic show-stopper sung by Donald O'Connor, "Make 'Em Laugh."

The Kathy Seldon character, played by Debbie Reynolds, could be used as an example of someone who sets a goal, such as breaking into movies, and then must work hard to get a break.

NOTES

THE SOUND OF MUSIC

1965

Not Rated

Director: Robert Wise

Features Julie Andrews, Christopher Plummer, Eleanor Parker, Peggy Wood, Anna Lee, Norma Varden, Portia Nelson, Marni Nixon, and Charmian Carr.

Distributor: CBS/Fox Video

Awards: 1965 Academy Awards for Best Adapted Score, Best Director, Best Film Editing, Best Picture, Best Sound; 1965 Director's Guild of America Award for Best Director; 1965 Golden Globe Awards for Best Actress in a Musical/Comedy (Julie Andrews) and Best Film Musical/Comedy; 1965 National Board of Review Award as one of the 10 Best Films of the year.

This outstanding film version of the Rogers and Hammerstein musical is based on the true story of the von Trapp family of Austria and their escape from the Nazis during World War II. Julie Andrews plays a novice who leaves the church to become a governess for Captain von Trapp's seven children and later marries the captain.

Classroom connections to history and music are obvious. But *The Sound of Music* also is a growing-up film about children of various ages.

NOTES

THE WIZARD OF OZ

1939

Not Rated

Director: Victor Fleming

Features Judy Garland, Margaret Hamilton, Ray Bolger, Jack Haley, Bert Lahr, Frank Morgan, and Billie Burke.

Distributor: MGM/UA Home Entertainment

Awards: 1939 Academy Awards for Best Song ("Somewhere Over the Rainbow") and Best Original Score. Judy Garland received an Individual Award for outstanding performance as a screen juvenile.

This movie was loosely adapted from the L. Frank Baum tale, which was a metaphor for the sociopolitical and economic conditions at the turn of the century. MGM went straight for the entertainment value and produced one of the most beloved films of all time. The story revolves around a young farm girl named Dorothy who gets caught up in a tornado and wakes up in Oz, a place filled with flying monkeys, munchkins, a talking scarecrow, a tin man, and a cowardly lion. In order to return to her Kansas home, she must appease the Great Wizard and defeat the Wicked Witch of the West.

The 50th anniversary video edition contains rare footage of Ray Bolger's "Scarecrow Dance" and a "Jitterbug" sequence and clips of Buddy Ebsen as the Tin Man before he left the film because of an allergic reaction to his make-up. Two books that come highly recommended are Virginia Glasgow Koste and L. Frank Baum's *The Wonderful Wizard of Oz* (New York: Dramatic, 1990) for grades 4 and up and Aljean Harmetz's *The Making of The Wizard of Oz* (New York: Knopf, 1977/1984) for grades 6 and up.

NOTES

YELLOW SUBMARINE

1968

Rated G

Directors: George Dunning and Dick Emory.

Voices of John Clive, Geoffrey Hughes, Peter Batten, Paul Angelis, and Lance Percival.

Distributor: MGM/UA Home Entertainment

This first full-length animated British feature in 14 years was wildly acclaimed on its release and is still considered a classic example of op-art animation. The Beatles fight the terrible, music-hating Blue Meanies to try and save Pepperland, Strawberry Fields, and Sgt. Pepper. The live pop group appears in a short scene at the end of the film. Songs include "All You Need is Love," "When I'm Sixty Four," "A Day in the Life," "Lucy in the Sky with Diamonds," "Yellow Submarine," and "Nowhere Man."

This film provides students with an extraordinary example of imagination in narrative. Students might be encouraged to write stories on their own based on popular music or to discuss the storyline of the film to explore the imagination behind its creation.

DISTRIBUTORS

Many of the movies on videotape in this compendium are available for sale or rent in local stores. However, when a movie cannot be obtained locally, it usually can be purchased directly from a distributor. Following is contact information for all of the distributors listed in the individual movie descriptions in this book.

Baker and Taylor Video
501 South Gladiolus Street
Momence, IL 60954
800-775-2300

Barr Films
12801 Schabarum Avenue
Irwindale, CA 91706
800-234-7878

Beacon Films
1560 Sherman Avenue, Suite 100
Evanston, IL 60201
800-323-9084

BMG
1540 Broadway
New York, NY 10036
212-930-4940

Buena Vista Home Video
350 South Buena Vista Street
Burbank, CA 91521-7145
818-562-3568

CBS/Fox Video
P.O. Box 900
Beverly Hills, CA 90213
800-800-2369

Celebrity Home Entertainment
22025 Ventura Boulevard, Suite 200
Woodland Hills, CA 91365
818-595-0666

Children's Circle Westwoods Studios
389 Newtown Turnpike
Weston, CT 06883
800-KIDS-VID (800-543-7843)

Churchill Media
6917 Valjean Avenue
Van Nuys, CA 91406-4716
800-334-7830

Columbia Tristar Home Video
Sony Pictures Plaza
10202 West Washington Boulevard
Culver City, CA 90232
310-280-8000

Critics' Choice Video
P.O. Box 749
Itasca, IL 60143
800-367-7765

Facets Multimedia
1517 West Fullerton Avenue
Chicago, IL 60614
800-331-6197

Family Home Entertainment
15400 Sherman Way
Van Nuys, CA 91410
800-677-0789

Fast Forward
3420 Ocean Park Boulevard, Suite 3075
Santa Monica, CA 90405
310-396-4434

Goodtimes Entertainment
16 East 40th Street, 8th Floor
New York, NY 10016
212-951-3000

Hallmark Home Entertainment
6100 Wilshire Boulevard, Suite 1400
Los Angeles, CA 90048
213-549-3790

Jim Henson Productions
5358 Melrose Avenue, Suite 300W
Los Angeles, CA 90038
818-953-3030

Kid Vision
75 Rockefeller Plaza
New York, NY 10019
800-3KID-VID (800-354-3843)

Knowledge Unlimited
P.O. Box 52
Madison, WI 53701
800-356-2303

Live Entertainment
15400 Sherman Way
P.O. Box 10124
Van Nuys, CA 91410
818-988-5060

Mazon Productions
P.O. Box 2427
Northbrook, IL 60065
708-272-2824

MCA/Universal Home Video
100 Universal City Plaza
Universal City, CA 91608-9955
818-777-1000

MGM/UA Home Entertainment
2500 Broadway
Santa Monica, CA 90404
310-449-3000

Music for Little People
P.O. Box 1460
Redway, CA 95560
800-346-4445

Orion Home Video
1888 Century Park East
Los Angeles, CA 90067
310-282-0550

Polygram Video
825 8th Avenue
New York, NY 10019
800-825-7781

Public Media Video
5547 North Ravenswood Avenue
Chicago, IL 60640
800-826-3456

Quality Video
7399 Bush Lake Road
Minneapolis, MN 55439
612-893-0903

Rainbow Educational Video
170 Keyland Court
Bohemia, NY 11716
800-331-4047

Random House Home Video
201 East 50th Street
New York, NY 10022
800-733-3000

Republic Pictures Home Video
5700 Wilshire Boulevard, Suite 525
Los Angeles, CA 90036
213-965-6900

Society for Visual Education
6677 North NW Highway
Chicago, IL 60631
800-829-1900

Snoopy's Home Video Library
Media Home Entertainment
510 West 6th Street, Suite 1032
Los Angeles, CA 90014
213-236-1336

Tapeworm Video Distributors
27833 Hopkins Avenue, Unit 6
Valencia, CA 91355
805-257-4904

Turner Home Entertainment
P.O. Box 105366
Atlanta, GA 35366
800-523-0823

Video Collectibles
1500 Clinton Street
Buffalo, NY 14206
800-268-3891

Video Treasures
500 Kirts Boulevard
Troy, MI 48084
800-786-8777

Video Yesteryear
Box C
Sandy Hook, CT 06482
800-243-0987

Walt Disney Home Video
500 South Buena Vista Street
Burbank, CA 91521
818-562-3560

Warner Home Video
4000 Warner Boulevard
Burbank, CA 91522
818-954-6000

FILM RESOURCE BOOKS

Bergan, Ronald, and Karney, Robyn. *Foreign Film Guide*. London: Bloomsbury Publishing, 1992.

Green, Diana Huss. *Parent's Choice Magazine Guide to Videocassettes for Children*. Mount Vernon, N.Y.: Consumer Reports Books, 1989.

Kohn, Martin F. *VideoHound's Family Video Guide*. Detroit: Visible Ink, 1995.

Maltin, Leonard. *The Whole Film Sourcebook*. New York: New American Library, 1983.

Maltin, Leonard. *Leonard Maltin's 1998 Movie and Video Guide*. New York: Signet, 1997.

Mast, Gerald. *A Short History of the Movies*. New York: Macmillan, 1992.

Parkinson, David. *History of Film*. New York: Thames and Hudson, 1995.

ABOUT THE AUTHOR

John Hulse has been a freelance writer for 15 years. His short stories, essays, and poetry have appeared in more than 200 magazines, including *Cinemagazine* (Japan), *Global Tapestry*, *Crescent Moon* (England), *Beneath the Surface* (Canada), *Deep*, *Chaminade Literary Review*, *Rant*, *The New Press*, *True Romance*, *Touchstone*, *Libido*, *Catharsis*, *Catalyst*, and *Phase and Cycle*.

He has published three volumes of poetry and received awards from the Bay Area Poets Association and the Southern Writer's Association. His work also has been included in more than 25 anthologies and has been translated into three languages.

Hulse received a bachelor of science degree in radio, television, and motion pictures from Ball State University in 1985 and a master of arts degree in cinema studies from New York University in 1988.

MORE NOTES